SOUTH
PUGET SOUND
AFOOT & AFLOAT

THIRD EDITION

D0973128

SOUTH
PUGET SOUND

THIRD EDITION

Marge & Ted Mueller

THE
MOUNTAINEERS

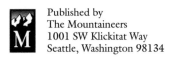

Published by
The Mountaineers
1001 SW Klickitat Way
Seattle, Washington 98134

0 9 8 7 6
5 4 3 2 1

Published simultaneously in Canada by Douglas & McIntyre, Ltd., 1615 Venables Street, Vancouver, B.C. V5L 2H1

Published simultaneously in Great Britain by Cordee, 3a DeMontfort Street, Leicester, England, LE1 7HD

Manufactured in the United States of America

Edited by Dana Lee Fos
Maps by Marge and Ted Mueller
All photographs by Marge and Ted Mueller
Cover design by Watson Graphics
Typography by Gray Mouse Graphics
Book design and layout by Gray Mouse Graphics

Cover photograph: Point Robinson lighthouse on Maury Island: insets: The Narrows bridge in Tacoma; Thea Foss Waterway and downtown Tacoma; walking the beach at Ed Munro Seahurst County Park.
Frontispiece: Boating on the Thea Foss Waterway in the heart of Tacoma
page 8: A sandy beach at Blake Island Marine State Park

Library of Congress Cataloging-in-Publication Data
Mueller, Marge.
    South Puget Sound, afoot & afloat / Marge & Ted Mueller. — 3rd ed.
        p.   cm.
    Includes bibliographical references and index.
    ISBN 0-89886-465-8
    1. Outdoor recreation—Washington (State)—Puget Sound.   2. Outdoor recreation—Washington (State)—Puget Sound—Directories.   3. Puget Sound (Wash.)—Guidebooks.   4. Marinas—Washington (State)—Puget Sound—Guidebooks.   I. Mueller, Ted.   II. Mountaineers (Society)   III. Title.
    GV191.42.W2M84   1996
    796.5'025'16432—dc20   95-46945
                                                                                          CIP

CONTENTS

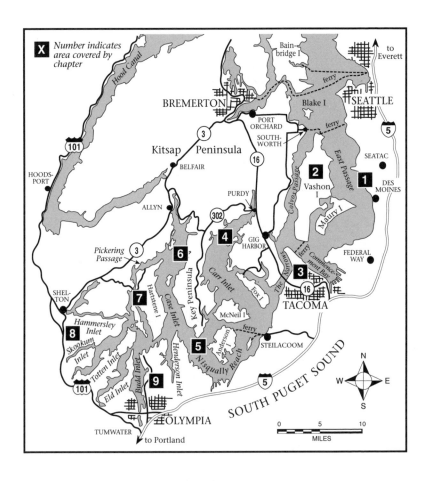

X *Number indicates area covered by chapter*

to Everett

Bain-bridge I

BREMERTON

ferry

Blake I

SEATTLE

PORT ORCHARD

SOUTH-WORTH

ferry

Hood Canal

101

3

Kitsap   Peninsula

BELFAIR

HOODS-PORT

16

SEATAC

East Passage

2

Vashon I

1

DES MOINES

PURDY

ALLYN

302

FEDERAL WAY

3

Pickering Passage

4

GIG HARBOR

Maury I

Colvos Passage

SHELTON

6

7

Hartstene I

Case Inlet

Key Peninsula

Carr Inlet

Fox I

The Narrows

ferry

Commencement Bay

16

3

TACOMA

McNeil I

Hammersley Inlet

8

Skookum Inlet

Totten Inlet

Budd Inlet

Henderson Inlet

Eld Inlet

5

Anderson I

ferry

STEILACOOM

Nisqually Reach

9

101

SOUTH PUGET SOUND

5

N
W   E
S

OLYMPIA

TUMWATER   to Portland

0   5   10
MILES

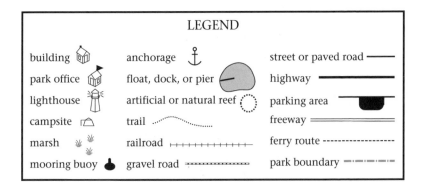

LEGEND

building

park office

lighthouse

campsite

marsh

mooring buoy

anchorage

float, dock, or pier

artificial or natural reef

trail

railroad

gravel road

street or paved road

highway

parking area

freeway

ferry route

park boundary

PREFACE

Because recreation and relaxation are generally considered synonymous with getting away from cities and concentrations of people, the heavily populated region of South Puget Sound may seem an odd recommendation for recreation seekers. Yet, for all its density of population, these lower fingers of the inland sea receive remarkably little use, even during prime vacation time. Perhaps all of the outdoor enthusiasts head north to crowd the fabled paradises of the San Juan Islands, Canadian Gulf Islands, and Desolation Sound, or perhaps—just perhaps—the recreation seekers do not know about all the boating, camping, biking, walking, birdwatching, fishing, scuba diving, and countless other fascinating adventures that are possible in the southern reaches of the sound.

Hence, this book—an attempt to describe all the major recreational sites, as well as the nooks and crannies, that are found on South Puget Sound. In doing so, we hope to lure residents into exploring their own treasure-filled backyard and acquaint visitors with the gems to be found.

Contrary to the appearance of many shorelines, real estate developers have not sealed off access to South Puget Sound to all but the lucky owners of a couple hundred feet of waterfront. In fact, the region covered by this book boasts over a hundred saltwater facilities found in city, county, and state parks, tidelands, and sites where boats can be launched for water-oriented recreation—a substantial public recreational capacity located among the private holdings.

This book, like the other volumes in our *Afoot and Afloat* series, is designed not as a guide for "how to do" the recreational possibilities of the area, but rather a "where to go" to do them. With the thought that exploration of any region is even more enjoyable if spiced with some background tidbits, information is included about the history and ecology, as well as other interesting facts about some of the areas.

The areas in this book were surveyed over a period of several years and rechecked just prior to publication of this third edition. Changes in facilities do occur, however. The authors and The Mountaineers would appreciate your letting us know of any changes to facilities so future editions can be updated. Please address comments to: The Mountaineers Books, 1001 SW Klickitat Way, Suite 201, Seattle, WA 98134.

Marge and Ted Mueller

Gnarled madrona branches frame a sailboat at Eagle Island State Park on South Puget Sound's Balch Passage.

INTRODUCTION

For people accustomed to the sprawling real estate developments that run along the east shore of the sound, much of South Puget Sound will come as a pleasant surprise. Many inlets are as natural as those found in the San Juans and Gulf Islands. Expanses of tree-cloaked hills stretch down to meet the water. Flotillas of waterfowl dabble in quiet, shallow coves. Seals, and even whales at times, inhabit the channels.

For the purposes of this book, we consider South Puget Sound as including everything south of an imaginary line drawn between Seattle's Alki Point on the east and the Kitsap Peninsula's Yukon Harbor on the west. Our area, then, encompasses all the waterways that were explored by Lieutenant Peter Puget and his crew in their expedition south from the mother ship, the *Discovery*, when it was anchored off the end of Bainbridge Island at Restoration Point.

A BRIEF HISTORY OF PUGET SOUND

Any understanding of the complex, multi-fingered waterways of Puget Sound must begin with the immense ice sheet that probed southward from what is now Canada and plowed across the then-flat lowlands of western Washington, gnawing deep channels through rock and soil. Between 25,000 and 15,000 years ago, up to 1,500 feet of ice covered the region. Each advance of the Puget lobe of the Cordillera Glacier sculpted the contours of today's sound, while recessions deposited the debris in the form of the glacial till that now makes up the cliffs adjoining the inlets.

With the retreat of the glaciers, the depressions left behind formed huge lakes of meltwater that finally drained to sea level when the Strait of Juan de Fuca melted free of ice. Today's inlets and islands were formed as this ocean linkage was completed.

While Western civilization blossomed in Europe and a new, democratic society was born on the eastern shores of the New World, the entire Northwest coast remained practically unknown to Euro-American explorers. The only residents were the coastal Indian tribes that inhabited scattered encampments and lived in relative peace on the abundance provided by the land. Food was to be had by merely gathering shellfish from the beaches, fish from the sea, and berries from the forests. Towering stands of cedar provided materials for shelter, clothing, and dugout canoes. With such plenitude, much time could be spent developing an elaborate religious and artistic culture.

Early Exploration

Although all of the West Coast of the continent was claimed for the British Crown by Sir Francis Drake when he sighted it in 1579, Drake himself is not believed to have explored any farther north than the southern coast of present-day Oregon. In 1592 a Spanish explorer, Apostolos Valerionos de Cephalonia, also known as Juan de Fuca, first discovered the strait that currently bears his name; he is not known to have ventured beyond the mouth of the strait, however. Further exploration from the north by the Russians and from the south by the Spanish established small outposts in Alaska and the Canadian coastal islands in the late 1700s, but the expanse of Puget Sound still remained undiscovered and unexplored.

The increasing importance of the fur trade, plus the hope of finding the rumored Northwest Passage across the top of North America, finally brought British explorers north to the area then claimed and tenuously held by the Spanish. Conflicts between Spanish and British fur traders led, in 1791, to the dispatch of British Captain George Vancouver with the 95-foot sloop of war *Discovery* and the 60-foot brig *Chatham*, and crews totaling 190 men. Vancouver was delegated to further explore the Northwest coast and to meet with Juan Francisco de la Bodega y Quadra, governor of Nootka (on what is now Vancouver Island), to negotiate the ownership of land along the coast.

In April 1792 Vancouver encountered an American explorer, Robert Gray, off the mouth of the Strait of Juan de Fuca. Gray told him of an Indian report that the waterway extended far inland. Vancouver decided to explore the reaches of this passage in order to pass time and portray to Quadra a casual indifference for the Spanish claims of sovereignty over the area.

While the Spanish governor cooled his heels in Nootka, Vancouver conducted a leisurely exploration of the southern shore of the strait. Landing at Protection Island at the head of Discovery Bay, he noted an archipelago of islands (the San Juans) to the north. He dispatched Lieutenant William Broughton in the *Chatham* to investigate them, while he took the *Discovery* around Point Wilson and south into the sound. The group made a small-boat exploration of Hood Canal as the mother ship anchored below a steep bluff. Encountering some of the region's characteristic weather, Vancouver named it Foulweather Bluff.

Continuing south to the vicinity of Restoration Point, off the south end of Bainbridge Island, the *Discovery* anchored. A small launch and cutter were prepared and, on May 20, 1792, Lieutenant Peter Puget and Joseph Whidbey, surveyor for the expedition and master of the *Discovery*, set off to investigate the network of waterways to the south—the area now known as South Puget Sound.

Puget and his crew rowed, sailed, and drifted with the tide, following the starboard shoreline down Colvos Passage, through the Tacoma Narrows, into Wollochet Bay, and on to the west end of Hale Passage. They camped here the first night and spent their second day exploring the shores of Carr Inlet, with an overnight stay on the western shore of Pitt Passage.

While the party attempted to circumnavigate Anderson Island, a storm forced them to seek refuge for the night in Oro Bay on the south side of

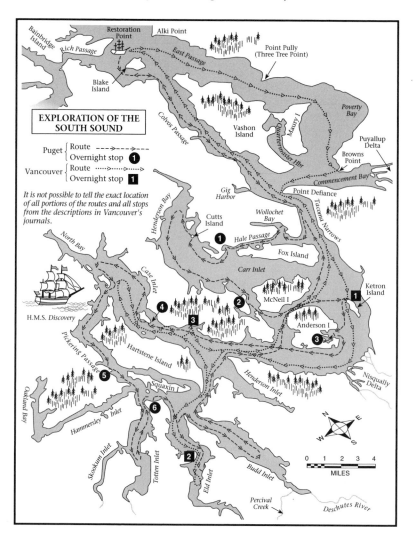

EXPLORATION OF THE SOUTH SOUND

Puget { Route - - ->- - -> - -
       { Overnight stop ①

Vancouver { Route ·····>···>···>
          { Overnight stop ■

It is not possible to tell the exact location of all portions of the routes and all stops from the descriptions in Vancouver's journals.

H.M.S. *Discovery*

the island. Fog and another storm delayed progress on the fourth day, but Puget was able to explore Case Inlet as far as Herron Island and set up camp there for the night. After determining the northern extent of Case Inlet, the party headed south through Pickering Passage, camping at Graham Point near the north end of Squaxin Island. On their sixth day the group left camp at dawn and explored the extent of Totten Inlet, with an overnight stay on the south shore of Squaxin Passage near Hope Island. Perhaps the typical early-morning fog obscured the entrance to Hammersley Inlet, for it was completely overlooked.

The final day of exploration encompassed Eld and Budd inlets, the southernmost reaches of the sound. Upon reaching Johnson Point on Case Inlet, Puget determined that all major channels of the waterway had been surveyed. Already overdue on his scheduled return, he took advantage of a favorable tide and a running breeze to travel through the night and all the following day. He reached the *Discovery* early in the morning on May 27, just a week from the time he had departed.

During Puget's absence, Vancouver led another group of men in the expedition's small yawl and cutter along the eastern shore of the sound. Making brief note of East Passage and Commencement Bay, but totally overlooking the mouth of the Puyallup River, Vancouver proceeded to Ketron Island, where he camped overnight. While anchored here he observed Lieutenant Puget's boats in the distance, returning north to the *Discovery*. After a brief examination of the waterways south into Eld Inlet and north into Case Inlet, Vancouver also headed north, reaching Restoration Point on May 29.

Peter Puget stopped overnight near this spot in Squaxin Passage, in the shadow of the Olympic Mountains.

Vancouver gave the name Puget Sound to all the waterways south of the Tacoma Narrows, but some unknown chartmaker later expanded it to include all of the area south of Admiralty Inlet. This is the generally accepted designation today, although there is a continuing argument that Puget Sound should also include waters to the north, up through the San Juan archipelago.

Having documented the extent of Puget Sound and made observations on the geography, natives, flora, and fauna of the virgin territory, Vancouver concluded that the region did not contain the route to the hoped-for Northwest Passage. Heading the boats north for their rendezvous with Quadra at Nootka, the party departed from Puget Sound. It was not visited again by Europeans or Euro-Americans for over thirty years.

Pioneer Settlement

Following the War of 1812, Great Britain and the United States concluded an agreement in 1818 that established the boundary between British Canada and the United States along the forty-ninth parallel between the Great Lakes and the Rocky Mountains. The little-known Oregon country west of the Rockies was left in an undetermined status, open to joint occupancy by both countries until one or the other could better establish a claim to sovereignty over the region.

Burgeoning fur trade along the Columbia River and the establishment of a major Hudson's Bay Company post on the river at Fort Vancouver finally led, in 1824, to tentative attempts to reach Puget Sound via river and overland access. The first European settlers, intent on establishing British sovereignty claims and agricultural trade with Russian settlements in Alaska, finally arrived in the area in 1833 and built Fort Nisqually on the shore north of the Nisqually Delta.

The United States government soon became convinced of the necessity of determining the economic value of the Oregon country, and expanding the American influence in the area. In 1838 Lieutenant Charles Wilkes was given command of the six vessels that comprised the United States Exploring Expedition, the country's first venture into "world class" scientific and territorial exploration. The expedition's four-year-long global cruise charted portions of the Antarctic coast, the Samoan Islands, the Fijis, and the Sandwich (Hawaiian) Islands before heading to North America.

Its mission on the Northwest coast was to explore and chart the region and, incidentally, to establish claims to the area for the United States government. The Wilkes Expedition arrived on Puget Sound in the spring of 1841. It spent five months meticulously charting the waters of the sound and conducting an overland survey of the Columbia River drainage; more than 250 geographic names in the region are the result of this mission. While many of the names honor members of the crew, Wilkes did not give his own name to a single landmark.

A major outcome of Wilkes's exploration was the recommendation that the valuable resources of the Pacific Northwest not be abdicated to the British and that American access and settlement be actively pursued.

In 1839 a Methodist mission was built near Fort Nisqually in an effort to bring Christianity to the Indians, and in 1845 the first American settlers reached the territory by traveling the Oregon Trail along the Columbia River to Fort Vancouver, then veering north along the Cowlitz River to Puget Sound. A year later the Treaty of 1846 officially established the Oregon Territory, with its northern boundary at the forty-ninth parallel. In following years the Puget Sound region was slowly populated by influxes of pioneers drawn by the prospect of Alaskan trade and the abundant timber, mineral, and marine resources.

The Indian War

The population growth and land acquisition by white settlers caused unrest among the Indians, who saw their tribal lands being overrun and their natural resources disappearing. In December 1854, on the delta of the Nisqually River along the banks of Medicine Creek (now known as McAlister Creek), Territorial Governor Isaac Stevens met with the chiefs of all the tribes living on the shores of South Puget Sound to negotiate a treaty for their land.

After three days of speeches, partying, and gift giving, and a reading (in English) of the lengthy treaty, the Indians agreed to relinquish their tribal lands for the sum of $32,500 and to move their people onto three meager reservations. All chiefs present signed the document, with the exception of Leschi, a chief of the Nisqually. Leschi objected to the inadequate reservation lands, and some say that his signature was forged on the final document. In spite of his protests, the Medicine Creek Treaty was ratified by Congress in March 1855.

In the following months the full impact of the treaty began to dawn on the other Indians. While many did move to the reservation lands, some, angered and disgruntled, joined Leschi in his efforts for a more equitable settlement. Others formed renegade bands, threatening the white settlers. Reports of bloody Indian wars in eastern Washington fueled the fears of Puget Sound settlers and they left their farms to gather in the protection of stockades.

On the west side of the Cascades, the war was primarily a series of small skirmishes. The military forces were unable to deal seriously with the guerrilla tactics of the Indians, and the Indians, small in number and unorganized, could not inflict significant damage on the white settlements.

The farmers, however, confined to the stockades, were unable to tend their crops and livestock, and the lumbermen could not fell trees for the mills. Pressure from citizens, as well as politicians who were critical of his

During the Indian War, stockades such as Fort Nisqually, seen here at Point Defiance Park, provided protection for settlers.

handling of the whole affair, forced Governor Stevens to renegotiate the terms of the Medicine Creek Treaty in the fall of 1856, giving the Indians more generous land allotments. A few months later, Leschi was captured, tried, and convicted for the murder of a settler—although he claimed he was innocent. On February 19, 1858, Leschi was hanged.

Industrial Growth

One of the most significant chapters in the history of the development of South Puget Sound was written by the railroads. By the 1870s some short rail lines already connected population centers on the sound, but the sought-after plum was a transcontinental line. Whichever city received the terminus of such a railroad would be assured an instant economic boom. With it would come goods and materials from the east for Pacific Northwest cities themselves and for shipment to Alaska and the Orient. On the return trip the trains would take the riches of the Northwest— lumber, coal, and marine and agricultural products—to eastern markets.

In 1873 the Northern Pacific Railroad made its announcement—the rail line heading west along the banks of the Columbia River and north along the Cowlitz River would bypass Olympia and Steilacoom and terminate on the shore of Commencement Bay in Tacoma. Although bankruptcy and subsequent reorganization of the company caused a ten-year delay in the actual arrival of the rail line, the fate of South Puget Sound was sealed. In the following ten years other transcontinental railroads built their tracks across Stevens Pass into Everett and across Stampede Pass into Tacoma; with the completion of the Milwaukee Railroad over Snoqualmie summit in 1909 the railroad boom ended. The economic role of South Puget Sound was limited to a relatively minor one as Washington State entered the twentieth century.

SOUTH PUGET SOUND TODAY

Slowly the far reaches of this vast waterway abandoned their aspirations to industrial importance and settled for the relatively slow-paced residential and single-industry communities that now predominate. That very lack of industrial growth makes South Puget Sound a prime recreational destination today.

The waters, of course, are open to all for boating, sports fishing, scuba diving, and other recreational pursuits. The shorelands, however, are another matter. Stretches of private holdings are interspersed with public parks and beaches, and the public areas may be difficult to find. This book is designed to guide the reader in finding and enjoying these public recreational areas of South Puget Sound.

Getting There

The waterways of the sound provide major avenues to South Puget Sound recreation for modern-day explorers from the north. Most of the lower reaches are within an easy day sail from the Seattle area. For people with trailerable boats, the region can be reached even more quickly from any of a multitude of private and public launch facilities in the area.

Highways make the farthest points of South Puget Sound but a half-day's journey from any of the northern population centers. The major north–south arterial, I-5, provides the quickest route to most of the land-accessible points. The Washington State ferry system provides a shortcut to the Kitsap and Key peninsulas and a more leisurely approach than the longer highway routes through Tacoma or Olympia.

Ferries or private boats provide the only access to several of the islands—Vashon and Maury, Anderson, McNeil, Ketron, and Herron. Most of the other islands, except for the very small ones, are reached by bridges.

Public Shorelines—Separating the Public from the Private

A major question of recreationists is: "Where can I go to find shoreline that is not private?" With the press of people moving to the area, beach-front property commands premium prices, and owners are becoming increasingly hostile to trespassers. Not that most violently object to an occasional wanderer along the water's edge of their property, but teeming hoards (attracted by guidebooks?) parading across one's beach tend to quickly dissipate civility. The boorish habits of a few visitors who engage in squatter's-rights picnics, discard debris like fall leaves, use beaches as bathrooms, and trench the shoreline in search of marine life, have certainly contributed to resident hostility.

Would that all visitors merely enjoyed scenery when passing and were considerate (as some are) of the rights and feelings of the beachfront residents. Would that the residents were equally considerate (as many are) of the casual beach walkers and did not greet them with a forest of "private property/no trespassing" signs and occasional snarling Dobermans. Unfortunately, reality and people being what they are, the question still remains: Where are beaches where the public is welcome?

Parks—State, County, and City

"Public" beaches imply ownership by some public agency—city, county, state, or federal. Most readily identifiable are the state parks, where beaches are generally associated with campgrounds, picnic areas, and other developed recreational uses. With the exception of those marine state parks accessible only by boat, the state parks on South Puget Sound generally provide a combination of tent and recreational vehicle (RV) campsites, with restrooms and showers.

County and city parks on South Puget Sound are for day use, offering picnic facilities and children's play areas. Although many have nice waterfront, most rely on access by car or bicycle; only a few offer floats or buoys. Fishing piers are a popular adjunct to several parks.

When state fiscal problems occur, they can mean cutbacks, affecting the availability of camping facilities and state park maintenance. Visitors may find restrooms locked off-season, and some parks may be closed down during the winter. Garbage pickup may be discontinued in some areas, so park cleanliness depends solely on the cooperation of its users. Financial burdens of counties and cities can lead to skimping on park maintenance. As a result, other than a few isolated showpieces, city and county facilities tend to show more wear from heavy use.

Several county parks remain undeveloped; in many cases these are

Blake Island is a marine state park in the South Sound.

primitive pieces of property deeded to the county for someone's tax purposes. Development dollars are even more difficult to come by than maintenance dollars, so these properties remain wild; most are inaccessible from land without difficult brush-beating or illegal passage through adjacent private lands. The beaches of such parks are relatively easy to reach from small boats that can be beached. Because these shorelands are usually untrammeled, they are good sites for beachcombing and exploring.

DNR Beaches

The original Washington State Constitution adopted in 1889 followed British common law history and held that all navigable waters and shorelands up to high tide line were property of the state. However, the 1889–90 legislature quickly abandoned this provision and approved sale of tidelands to private parties. Between then and 1971, when these sales were discontinued, more than half of the state's tidelands, including most of those on Puget Sound, were sold to private individuals at ridiculously low prices.

The state Department of Natural Resources (DNR) manages all of the remaining state shoreline, and has reacquired title over the years to a number of additional segments of tideland. Generally, these beaches are public below mean high tide, but most have no land access because the uplands above the high tide level are privately owned.

At one time boundaries between most DNR beaches and private property were marked with white posts topped with black and set in concrete; however, destruction of these markings (by natural forces or vandals) led the DNR to abandon any attempt to maintain public beach boundary markers. In recent years similar black-and-white posts have been used to mark the boundaries of offshore geoduck leases, so such posts should not be relied upon to delineate "your" beach from "their" beach. A booklet that describes public shellfish sites throughout the sound is available from the DNR at the address listed in appendix A.

City and County Road Ends

In some locations where a platted public road dead-ends into a beach, the road legally extends across the tidelands and is open to public access. Some of these road ends offer an easy place to launch hand-carried boats. However, the public beach is only as wide as the platted road, as no trespassing signs on either side usually remind.

If a road is private, or if it has not been platted across the beach, the tidelands are not public. Therefore it cannot be assumed that all road ends offer beach access. The road ends described in this book were checked by the authors and were legally open to public access at the time of publication.

Launching and Mooring Facilities

South Puget Sound is especially popular with owners of small boats, both because of its compact nature and because of the excellent fishing in many areas. Most of the public beaches on South Sound can be reached by small boats that can be beached. Therefore, getting boat to water becomes extremely important, and boat-launch locations are key to the enjoyment of the area.

Public launch facilities are generally supported by the state Department of Fish and Wildlife or local city and county governments. These facilities most often are surfaced ramps, extending outward to below low tide levels, where boat trailers can be backed down the ramp until their cargo floats free. Ramps are not always paved to extreme tide levels, however, so the surface should be explored before launching in order to avoid the exasperation of miring the tow vehicle or launching it along with the boat. Boaters using state Department of Fish and Wildlife launch ramps must have either a valid hunting or game fish license or must purchase a conservation license. The annual fee for the conservation license, as of 1995, is $10.

Sling launches, such as this one at Des Moines, are found at several marinas in South Puget Sound.

Many commercial launch facilities are also available—ramps, hoists, elevators, and whatever else economics and traffic will support. All commercial facilities charge launch fees, some one-way, some both in and out. Most provide parking for both trailers and tow vehicles.

Launch facilities change occasionally. Every effort has been made to keep locations mentioned in this book as current as possible, but over time public ramps are sold to private parties, leases expire, marinas go out of business, and facilities change.

Mooring for larger boats is available at floats and mooring buoys at several state parks. Marine state parks, which are accessible only by boat, all have mooring buoys, and a few have floats. A fee is usually charged for overnight mooring on state park floats and mooring buoys, but not for anchoring offshore. Numerous commercial marinas in or near metropolitan areas have guest moorage available.

Having Fun on the South Sound— Recreation and Facilities

Concentrated in this area at the beginning of Puget Sound is recreation as diverse as that to be found in highly touted vacation lands such as the San Juan and Gulf islands. Here you'll find boating to satisfy every taste from yachting to kayaking as well as scuba diving, bicycling, camping, picnicking, birdwatching, beachcombing, hiking, and swimming. A variety of nature preserves, historical sites, and scenic vistas make the South Sound a destination to please nearly every visitor.

Boating

Because this is a book centered around the saltwater highways of the sound, a good deal of it relates to enjoyment by boat. Many of the public beaches and four of the state parks described are accessible only by boat. Boating, as referred to here, runs the complete spectrum of conveyances that float, from kayaks and canoes to pleasure cruisers and sailboats.

South Puget Sound is very amenable to this generous definition, as its waterways are not the broad expanses of the Strait of Juan de Fuca and are therefore less foreboding to smaller craft. This does not imply throwing caution to the wind; more than seventy-five vessels, ranging from 10 tons to 200 tons, and an unknown number of smaller craft lie on the bottom of South Puget Sound. Cautions expressed for depth of water and speed of tidal flow reflect the authors' preference for sailboats but should be applied to other craft where appropriate.

Boating Safety. The relative proximity of land does not excuse the requirement for training in safe and sensible boating. Excellent boating-safety courses are available through both the U.S. Power Squadron and the U.S. Coast Guard Auxiliary. All boaters are strongly encouraged to take one of these courses before committing their own safety as well as that of a boatload of family or friends to the skipper's competence. Note that state law now requires that each occupant of a boat have available a wearable floatation device in case of emergency.

Be especially aware that these waters are frequently used by scuba divers. Use caution in the vicinity of known dive areas and be on the watch for the red flag with a white diagonal stripe that marks areas where scuba divers are working. When approaching bathing beaches, cut boat speed to a minimum and watch for swimmers in the water.

Weather. Because of the north–south orientation of most of the inlets, and the region's normal storm path from the southwest, severe winds can be generated in the passages during bad weather. The sunny afternoons of late summer and fall often exact their compensation in dense morning fog. The fact that the nearest shore is no more than a mile away is of little consolation when everything beyond 50 feet disappears into eerie, white nothingness.

Navigation. The southern portion of Puget Sound is rather shallow by comparison with its northern extremities. Many of the long finger inlets in the region are so shallow near their extreme ends that they become mudflats twice daily with the change of the tide. To avoid an embarrassing six hours or more stranded high and dry, boats of any draft are encouraged to make close use of nautical charts and tide tables, and even a depth sounder, if so equipped.

Good, current nautical charts covering the area should be carried by all boaters, along with an accurate compass and the knowledge of how to use both. A list of charts covering South Puget Sound appears in appendix B.

Tidal Current Considerations. "The tide" refers to change in the depth of water over the bottom. When the depth changes, the water must go somewhere, and when it does it generates tidal currents. Because the broad inlets of South Puget Sound are connected by relatively narrow channels, substantial tidal currents—up to 6 knots in the Tacoma Narrows—are generated in these passages. For a boat with a maximum speed of 6 knots or less, the tidal currents are obviously something to be reckoned with—cautiously and deliberately.

The various interconnecting waterways in the area give rise to some rather illogical tidal currents. For example, the current in Colvos Passage on the west side of Vashon Island always ebbs to the north, irrespective of the direction of flow on the opposite side of the island. Similarly, a tidal current eddy in the Tacoma Narrows tends to emphasize a flood tide on the north side of the channel and an ebb tide a few hundred yards away on the south side.

Small craft charts indicate position, direction, and average speed of the current at maximum flood or ebb tide at specific, measured points. A tidal current table (*not* a tide table) will provide the daily time for slack and maximum currents and speed variations associated with these measured points. Local anomalies in tidal currents are also noted in the tidal current tables.

Mooring. Public mooring buoys are set reasonably solidly, generally in 2 fathoms of water or more, with sufficient swing room to avoid midnight collisions with neighbors; however, they are not designed in either strength or placement to accommodate a rafted fleet of boats. The state Parks and Recreation Commission limits rafting on any single buoy to a maximum of four boats less than 24 feet in length, three boats between 25 and 36 feet in length, or two boats between 36 and 45 feet in length. Vessels over 45 feet are asked to avoid rafting on buoys; rafting is encouraged on floats where possible. When anchoring, be sure that your anchor is set solidly and placed far enough away from other boats to allow ample swing.

The Cascadia Marine Trail

Recent years have seen a renewal of interest in human-powered watercraft such as kayaks, canoes, and rowboats. These have the advantage of being able to navigate waters that are too shallow for other craft, and they provide an intimate water-level view of scenery, marine environment, seabirds, and aquatic mammals. However, they have the disadvantage of being more at the mercy of tidal currents, and they are limited in the distance that can be covered in a day-long paddle trip.

The Washington Water Trails Association is an organization of paddlers, formed in 1990, with an ambitious dream—the creation of a marine trail system with a chain of campsites that are a reasonable day's paddle apart. The Cascadia Marine Trail, as envisioned, would link 150 miles of inland waterways all the way from the southern reaches of Puget Sound to the Canadian border. Currently, the WWTA has successfully forged relationships with Washington State Parks, the DNR, and other city and county parks departments who have agreed to designate primitive shore-side campsites on their properties.

These campsites, which may be used only by persons in hand-powered boats, are all accessible from the water at points were craft can be easily beached and carried ashore. Sanitation facilities are available at or near the campsites, but other amenities are limited—often the site is just a spot level enough for a tent. Open fires either are not permitted or are strongly discouraged, and water is available only at those sites that are associated with other fully developed camping facilities.

An annual permit is required for use of Cascadia Marine Trail campsites, and a nominal overnight camping fee is also charged for use of campsites in state parks. As of 1996 there are seven Cascadia Marine

Trail sites within the region covered by this book, and additional sites are being negotiated. For more information contact the WWTA at the address listed in appendix A.

Walking and Hiking

Most of the areas covered in this book are relatively small, so footbound exercise must strain to be categorized as hiking. Several areas, however, have nature walks and short, easy, well-maintained trails that offer an abundance of treasures if traveled at a leisurely pace and with well-tuned observational skills. A number of parks have self-guided nature trails that are keyed to available brochures.

For long, wild walks, consult Harvey and Penny Mannings' *Walks and Hikes on the Beaches Around Puget Sound;* many of the walks connect the public beaches described here.

Bicycling

The nominal elevation of the South Puget Sound area invites travel by bicycle, although the allure may be deceptive, as the "flat" countryside is actually laced with stretches of small hills and valleys that wear a cyclist out with interminable 200- to 300-foot rises and falls as readily as any

A family prepares for an afternoon of bicycling at Tacoma's waterfront parks.

progressive 2,000-foot climb. However, cycling is a popular and energy-conserving method of exploring this rather compact region.

Many of the roads edging South Puget Sound are lightly traveled, yet are wide and paved. On a few routes bicyclists must compete with highway traffic, although several highways have designated bicycle paths alongside. Some of the state parks in the area have walk-in campsites especially suited to cyclists.

Erin and Bill Woods' book *Bicycling the Backroads Around Puget Sound* describes tours on Vashon Island; a companion volume, *Bicycling the Backroads of Southwest Washington*, also has trips to a number of the areas described here.

Picnicking and Camping

Nearly all of the developed state, county, and city parks in the South Puget Sound area have picnic facilities consisting of tables and either fire braziers, fireplaces, or fire rings. Most also have one or more picnic shelters that are available for reservation by groups. Contact the park or its information center at the phone number listed in appendix A for details about shelter reservations.

Most of the state parks offer camping, although in some cases it is of a limited nature. The State Parks Commission is considering a new centralized computer reservation system for all parks; if approved, the program will be implemented in 1996.

Most campgrounds are gated at dusk; picnic areas are open for day-use only; parking lots cannot be used for overflow camping. About half of these parks offer campsites. Several state parks in the area also have a few spots each designated as Cascadia Marine Trail campsites.

Facilities for the Disabled

In recent years there has been increased emphasis and funding to make park facilities accessible to the disabled, and several of the parks have restrooms, parking spots, and one or more picnic sites, shelters, or campsites that have been modified to eliminate access impediments. For more information, contact the individual park or its information center at the address listed in appendix A.

Beach Exploration

The populated and confined nature of South Puget Sound tends to eliminate the beach treasures found on the more open, less frequented beaches farther north. Its saltwater marshes, however, harbor interesting plant and marine life not readily seen elsewhere. Tolmie State Park provides one such view of a saltwater marsh.

Beachcombers can occasionally find historical treasures washed up on shore: debris from shipwrecks, some nearly a hundred years old, and pioneer artifacts that were imbedded in eroding underwater cliffs near areas of early settlement. The removal of historical artifacts is prohibited in some areas. Before taking anything away, be sure to check if it is legal.

All state parks and some city parks have regulations protecting non-food forms of marine life such as starfish and sand dollars. Even in areas that are unprotected by environmental regulations, beachcombers should not remove or destroy any of these animals. All play an important role in the food chain, and all add to the educational and aesthetic richness of the beaches. Tidelands at Lincoln Park and Saltwater State Park, as well as numerous other beaches on South Puget Sound, were once a tapestry of marine life but are now virtually barren owing to longtime abuse by beachcombers, coupled with the effects of pollution.

While beachcombers like to think that the tide twice daily brings in a fresh supply of driftwood and shells, even these are not a limitless resource, especially in the confines of South Puget Sound. Overzealous beachcombers are sometimes seen hauling off buckets of beach treasures, most of which will eventually be discarded. Seashells, small rocks, and driftwood often harbor tiny marine creatures. Handle beach treasures with care, enjoy them where you find them, and leave them for others to share.

Harvesting Seafood—Beach Foraging, Fishing, and Scuba Diving

One of the greatest excitements of the seashore is the prospect of gathering food fresh from the water for a seaside feast or a quick trip home to the dinner table. In many areas this is possible, but it is also closely regulated, and regulations change from time to time. It is the responsibility of the angler or seafood gatherer to be aware of all regulations.

The waters of Puget Sound are home to more than fifty varieties of sport fish, many of which make excellent eating. The central and deeper portions of most of the southern inlets are good areas for flatfish such as flounder, sole, and sand dab. Peale Passage, Pickering Passage, the north half of Case Inlet, and the waters off the south end of Fox Island are good for rockfish, cod, cabezon, and other bottomfish.

Salmon, the prize of Puget Sound sport fish, are frequently caught in areas where opposing tidal flows meet and form tide rips, concentrating food sources for the salmon. Typical of such areas are the waters just off Point Defiance, south of Fox Island, and off Johnson Point.

South Puget Sound is a favorite area for scuba diving, although many of the choice diving areas are subject to extreme tidal currents and thus are safe for divers only at slack tide. These diving grounds are noted for their populations of octopus and wolf eel, as well as sport fish.

Licenses and Limits. The Washington State Department of Fish and Wildlife requires one or more of the following licenses:

- *Personal Use Food Fish License* to fish for halibut, herring, lingcod, rockfish, perch, cod, pollock, hake, herring, anchovies, mackerels, sculpin, sea bass, skate, shad, tuna, shark, salmon, sturgeon, and related species. No license is required for smelt, carp, crayfish, or albacore tuna. Salmon and sturgeon also require a catch record card.
- *Personal Use Shellfish/Seaweed License* for harvesting crab, clams, oysters, shrimp, sea cucumbers, sea urchins, squid, scallops, barnacles, cockles, mussels, octopus, and seaweed.
- *Game Fish License* for freshwater game fish and steelhead from inland lakes and streams in the area.

Regulations. A pamphlet on fishing in Washington, published by the Department of Fish and Wildlife, is available in most sporting goods stores. It lists size and catch limits, seasons, and other restrictions for all types of shellfish as well as sport fish.

State parks generally permit the taking of those edible forms of marine life that are defined and regulated by the Department of Fish and Wildlife, but it may be prohibited in a few parks. In addition to fish, crabs, and mollusks, regulations cover animals such as sea cucumbers, squid, and shrimp. Before you fish, scuba dive, or beach harvest, check the regulations posted in the park. If none are posted, ask the park manager. In all state parks it is unlawful at any time to destroy or remove from the beaches any form of marine life, such as limpets, barnacles, and starfish, that is not regulated by the Department of Fish and Wildlife.

Digging Holes. State regulations dictate that holes dug in beaches in search of clams must always be filled. Do not rely on the incoming tide to do the job; it may take several turns of the tide for the displaced sand to be completely leveled. In the meantime, small marine animals exposed to the sun may die of dehydration. Recently the state Department of Fish and Wildlife, State Parks, and citizens' groups have undertaken a joint effort to enhance the geoduck population on several state park beaches. Clams were planted in plastic tubes to protect them during the first year of

Youngsters learn the fine art of fishing at Point Defiance Park.

their growth, and the planted areas are off-limits for the several years that it takes for this huge clam to grow to maturity. Please respect the harvest restrictions in the posted areas for future opportunities to harvest this giant clam.

Oyster Gathering. Removal of oyster shells from the beach is unlawful because large shells frequently hold several oyster larva that will die if the shells are discarded on land. Take a sharp knife and plastic containers to the beach and shuck oysters where they are found. Some gourmet beachcombers have been known to carry fresh lemons and a bottle of Tabasco sauce to the beach—and perhaps a chilled bottle of chablis—for a feast straight from the shell. Mollusks here are suffering from years of intense exploitation, coupled with pollution, and harvests tend to be more work for less reward than in more lightly visited regions. On some public beaches the DNR plants stock to help renew this dwindling resource. There are also several commercial oyster ventures in the western inlets, and sometimes oysters migrate from these to public beaches. Most public beaches do provide a chance to harvest shellfish at low tide.

Crabbing. Shallow water in South Puget Sound sometimes harbors crab, though mostly the red rock variety rather than the more popular Dungeness, which are found farther north. While red rock crabs are less meaty and a bit less succulent, in Washington State they are not subject to the size and sex restrictions applied to Dungeness.

Shrimping. Several varieties of shrimp are found in South Puget Sound. The best places to set mesh shrimp pots are in Carr Inlet between Cutts Island and Glen Cove and at the mouth of Budd Inlet. State regulations dictate the size of the mesh in shrimp pots.

Artificial Reefs. A number of artificial reefs, built in relatively shallow water, encourage the growth of marine life. While most of these are open for scuba diving, some are protected sanctuaries and taking living things with scuba gear may be prohibited. Check local regulations before diving.

Paralytic Shellfish Poisoning (Red Tide). When the state Department of Health periodically issues a "red tide warning" and closes particular beaches on the sound, the public usually reacts with confusion or skepticism. A clearer understanding of the phenomenon of red tide will lead to a greater respect for its dangers.

The name "red tide" itself contributes to some of the public's confusion, for it is not always visibly red, it has nothing at all to do with the tide, and not all red algae are harmful. Paralytic shellfish poisoning (PSP) is a serious, sometimes deadly, illness caused by *Gonyaulax catenella,* a toxic, single-celled, amber-colored alga that is present in small numbers at all times in the water. During the spring, summer, and fall, certain environmental conditions may combine to permit a rapid multiplication or accumulation of these microscopic organisms. Most shellfish toxicity occurs when the concentrations of *G. catenella* are too sparse to discolor the water; however, the free-floating plants sometimes become so numerous that the water appears to have a reddish cast—thus the name "red tide."

Bivalve shellfish such as clams, oysters, mussels, and scallops, which feed by filtering seawater, may ingest millions of the organisms and concentrate the toxin in their bodies. The poison is retained by most of these shellfish for several weeks after the occurrence of the red tide; butter clams can be poisonous for much longer.

When the concentration of the toxin in mollusks reaches a certain level, it becomes hazardous to humans who eat them. The toxins cannot be destroyed by cooking and cannot be reliably detected by any means other than laboratory analysis. Symptoms of PSP, beginning with the tingling of the lips and tongue, may occur within a half hour of ingestion. The illness attacks the nervous system, causing loss of control of arms and legs, difficulty in breathing, paralysis, and, in extreme cases, death.

Shellfish in all counties on Puget Sound are under regular surveillance by the state Department of Health. PSP (or red tide) warnings are issued and some beaches are posted when high levels of toxin are detected in tested mollusks. Warnings are usually publicized in the media; the state toll-free hotline, listed in appendix A, has current information as to which beaches are closed to shellfish harvesting. Crabs, abalone, shrimp, and fin fish are not included in closures because there have been no recorded cases of PSP in the Northwest caused by eating any of these animals.

These red rock crabs, caught at Joemma Beach State Park, will provide a tasty dinner. Crabs are not affected by red tide.

Pollution. A more insidious danger than PSP is pollution, both chemical and biological. With industry comes chemical waste; toxic wastes frequently find their way into the water, either directly or indirectly. Both the water and bottom mud of Commencement Bay have been found to have high levels of arsenic, copper, and cancer-causing PCBs.

Bottomfish, crab, and shrimp residing in the bay have excessive concentrations of these pollutants in their body tissues. While the ingestion of an occasional contaminated fish should not cause severe effects, a continuous diet of such animals can be a health hazard. Although industry along the sound is making some effort to "clean up its act," it will be many years before the concentrations of industrial pollutants reach an acceptable level.

Biological contamination occurs in areas where runoff from barnyards or sewage finds its way into the water or where large numbers of seals or sea lions congregate. In the far reaches of some of the inlets, where water movement is restricted, such pollution can be a hazard.

Swimming

Many beaches along the southern reaches of the sound are shallow and therefore warm enough for saltwater bathing in summer. Because of the close confines, wave action is nominal except in foul weather, and, with some notable exceptions such as the Tacoma Narrows, the current is weak near beaches and poses little hazard. However, none of the public beaches, including those in the state parks, have lifeguards; swimming is at the participant's risk and should not be done alone or unwatched.

Courtesy

Public facilities are acquired, developed, and maintained at the expense of all of us and for the enjoyment of all of us. This implies a mandatory respect for the rights of fellow recreationists so that all can enjoy their escape from daily routine. Unfortunately, there are a few who lack this respect and make a bad scene for the remainder of the population trying to use public facilities.

Recreationus horribilis, the worst of bad-mannered campers, makes a mockery of any first-come, first-served system by sending a vanguard to distribute camping equipment over several campsites and thereby establish a de facto reservation system. The practice is tacitly unfair and grossly insensitive to other campers. Where possible, report any such instances to resident park rangers.

The degree of escape that campers desire is certainly relative. Some choose to live closer to nature, with tents and campfires as their only amenities, while others prefer to enjoy the surroundings from the protection and comfort of an RV. Styles in camping are individual, and although another's taste may not coincide with your own, it can be accepted, providing it does not infringe on your enjoyment or preferred mode of camping.

An RV or a tent in the next campsite does not bother its neighbor by simply being there. This is not true, however, for the raucous snarl of motorized bikes permeating the entire campground or for a 200-watt amplifier blaring into unwilling ears. Equally offensive are animals who demonstrate their owner's complete disregard of campground leash regulations by romping through campsites with abandon and depositing their feces. In addition to keeping pets on a leash in all state parks, pet owners are required to clean up after them.

The amateur woodsman who hacks at the nearest tree, living or dead, leaves precious little for the next user of the campsite to appreciate. Campground enjoyment demands mutual respect for neighboring and succeeding campers. Camp in the form that you will, take satisfaction in the activities that you choose, but please do things in a way that will not destroy the camping experience of fellow recreationists.

The aquatic *Recreationus horribilis* is as abundant as the land variety. They can be found blocking large sections of floats by inappropriate boat placement, "reserving" buoys with dinghies, and rafting off moored boats without so much courtesy as to ask the permission of the owner. Again, consideration and respect for others dictates a true first-come, first-served attitude for facilities and respect for the property of other boaters.

Any pleasant anchorage can be an aquatic nightmare if continuously rocked by the wakes of nearby speeding boats. Again, consider the comfort of others and maintain a no-wake approach in the vicinity of anchorages and mooring areas.

The preceding comments regarding campground noise also apply to boaters. One person's music is another's noise. Do not force your preference on neighboring boaters.

Using This Book

Information summaries at the beginning of many of the site descriptions describe the facilities and recreation to be found at that site. If a location is very small, and the recreation is limited to a single activity such as boat launching or picnicking, the summaries are omitted.

A quick reference matrix at the back of the book provides an easy way to locate the best spot for a particular activity, such as camping, boat launching, or scuba diving.

The map sketches are drawn in perspective to give a general feel for the area. They may be adequate for general travel, although navigational charts are essential for water travel. A list of charts and more detailed maps is included in appendix B.

SAFETY CONSIDERATIONS

Boating and beach travel entail unavoidable risks that every traveler assumes and must be aware of and respect. The fact that an area is described in this book is not a representation that it will be safe for you. The areas described herein vary greatly in the amount and kind of preparation needed to enjoy them safely. Some may have changed since this book was written, or conditions may have deteriorated. Weather conditions can change daily or even hourly, and tide levels will vary considerably. An area that is safe in good weather at low or slack tide may be completely unsafe during inclement weather or at times of high tide or maximum tidal current. Exercise your own judgment and common sense. Be aware of your own limitations, those of your vessel, and of conditions when or where you are traveling. If conditions are dangerous, or if you are not prepared to deal with them safely, change your plans. Each year many people enjoy safe trips in the waters and on the beaches of South Puget Sound. With proper preparation and good judgment, you can too.

Emergency Assistance

The overall legal authority in all unincorporated areas of the state rests with the county sheriff. Emergencies and complaints should be referred to the local county sheriff's office at the number listed in appendix A.

Within state parks the park managers assume emergency assistance responsibilities; however, not all state parks have resident managers. Appendix A gives addresses and phone numbers for managers responsible for unmanned parks.

The Coast Guard has the primary responsibility for safety and law enforcement on the waters of Puget Sound. Marine VHF channel 16 is continuously monitored by the Coast Guard and should be the most reliable means of contact in case of emergencies on the water. The Coast Guard monitors Citizens Band channel 9 at some locations and times but has no commitment to a full-time radio watch on this channel. Several volunteer groups do an excellent job of monitoring the CB emergency frequency and will assist as best they can in relaying emergency requests to the proper authorities.

With the growing use of cellular telephones, the cellular providers in the Puget Sound area provide a quick-dial number, *CG, that immediately connects the caller to the Coast Guard Vessel Traffic Center in Seattle. This center coordinates all marine safety and rescue activities for the region.

The beach at Seattle's Lincoln Park provides a quiet respite from civilization's rat race.

CHAPTER ONE

EAST PASSAGE

The broad, busy channel of East Passage serves as the major entrance to South Puget Sound. It runs between the mainland and Vashon and Maury islands, beginning (loosely) at Seattle's Alki Point, flowing south past cities and subdivisions, and then ending at Browns Point, on the edge of Tacoma's Commencement Bay.

East Passage is the major water thoroughfare for commercial ocean traffic bound for Tacoma or Olympia. More than 3 miles wide throughout most of its length, the spacious waterway is free of any natural navigational hazards, and tidal currents are generally weak. Morning fog is common, especially during fall and winter, but it generally dissipates by noon. The winds that sweep up and down the length of Puget Sound accompanying storm fronts do, on occasion, kick up fairly sizable waves, especially when the wind direction opposes that of the tidal current.

Bays along the passage are for the most part broad and exposed, offering scant protection except at marinas, buoys, and private floats. The sand and gravel beaches extend only about 100 yards offshore before sinking below the 5-fathom level; beyond, the bottom drops more steeply to the 100-fathom depths of the center of the passage. Clams, crabs, and other sea life that would normally thrive on such beaches, however, have suffered from the overharvesting and pollution that come with dense population.

Steep underwater cliffs that support thick growths of marine life are marine pastures for a variety of fish; boat and pier fishing and scuba diving are popular pastimes here. Divers, and possibly even beachcombers, may also discover antique bottles and other historic treasures from the days of Indian villages and pioneer settlements.

SEATTLE SOUTH TO DES MOINES

Although heavily rimmed with homes, East Passage has over a dozen public access areas scattered along its east side. Here are viewpoints where bicyclists can pause for a scenic rest, beaches where frazzled families can

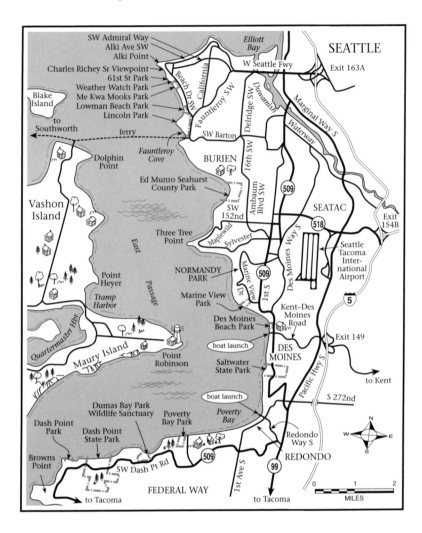

exhaust children's energy in sun and salt spray, and parks where city dwellers seeking respite from the lung and ear pollutants of civilization can escape to earth-scented forests and choirs of birds.

West Seattle Waterfront Parks (Seattle Parks)

Charles Richey Sr. Viewpoint. The first public access on the South Sound lies just south of Seattle's Alki Point. Here, a beachfront promenade along Beach Drive SW offers wide views across the sound to Vashon and Bainbridge islands. The concrete bulkhead that runs south for several blocks to 63rd Avenue SW is interrupted by ramps leading down to the rocky beach; benches are scattered along the grassy strip that edges the bulkhead. Midway along the viewpoint the narrow lawn widens to encompass a group of three sculpted boulders—the required public art on public property. A wide concrete shelf provides an excellent place to snooze or bask in the afternoon sun while watching boat traffic in East Passage. Some limited streetside parking is available.

Sixty-first Street Park. Two blocks south of the Charles Richey Sr. Viewpoint, at the intersection of Beach Drive SW and 61st SW, is a delightful little pocket beachfront park. It was begun in 1995 as a joint project by the Alki Community Council and the Seattle Parks and Recreation Department. The park, a 200-foot-wide wedge of grass and landscaping that tapers down to a sand and cobble beach, lies just north of a long condominium-topped pier that juts into East Passage. Views across the sound look into the throat of Rich Passage and beyond to peaks of the Olympic Mountains.

Weather Watch Park. In the early 1900s the steamer *Eagle* provided quick transportation between West Seattle and the Seattle waterfront. When better roads made the service obsolete, the 100-foot-wide section of street end from which the ferry ran laid fallow, the dock and steamer but memories. In 1990 West Seattle residents created a small park on the site, at the intersection of Beach Drive SW and SW Carroll Street—a perfect spot from which to watch changing weather over the sound.

A three-sided obelisk above the beach holds a tall pole that is topped by a flight of sheet metal ducks. Brass plates on the obelisk describe various cloud formations and tell historical vignettes of the region. A semicircular concrete bench offers a spot to sit and look across the sound to Blake and Vashon islands and Colvos Passage. Plantings at street level give way below to large chunks of driftwood that decorate a 100-foot-wide cobble beach.

Me Kwa Mooks Park and Emma Schmitz Memorial Viewpoint. A mile south of Alki Point, at the junction of Beach Drive SW and 58th Avenue SW, a pair of adjoining parks encompass a 6-block strip of beach and adjacent hillside. A grassy strip, progressively narrowing as it heads south, fills the 6-block-long area between the road and the beach bulkhead. Several park benches offer spots to relax and watch the ferries ply the sound. Below the northern half of the grassy strip is a terraced walkway with a 2-block-long concrete bench that invites leisurely afternoon sunning. Tidelands are rocky, with scattered boulders. The beach strip provides a pleasant stop on the bicycle route and jogging path that run along Harbor Avenue SW, Alki Avenue SW, and Beach Drive SW between Spokane Street and Lincoln Park.

Me Kwa Mooks was the name of a Nisqually Indian village in the area. The term, meaning "shaped like a bear's head," refers to the entire area, including Alki Point and Duwamish Head. The parks represent two of

Black brant geese play in the waves at Lowman Beach Park.

three parcels of land given to the city by Ferdinand and Emma Schmitz, a pioneer couple who arrived in Seattle in 1887 and settled on this property in 1907. The third area of their bequest, 50-acre Schmitz Park, is a few blocks inland.

East of Beach Drive SW, the upland section of 34-acre Me Kwa Mooks Park complements the beach strip with a picnic area and paths that lace dense woods that cover the adjacent hillside. This is the remains of the extensive grounds of the Schmitz estate, which at one time included elaborate flower gardens, an orchard, and a large, well-stocked trout pond.

Picnic tables dot a football-field-sized lawn. Short trails leave from both the north and south ends of the picnic area and duck through holly arches, raspberry thickets, and ivy patches as they meander across creeks and uphill through a woods of ivy-clad oak.

Lowman Beach Park. The Beach Drive bike route passes tiny Lowman Beach Park At 48th Avenue SW, 1½ miles south of Me Kwa Mooks Park. This urban meadow, scarcely 150 yards square, offers a bit of grass, a few trees, a tennis court, and a short strip of shorefront. The old battered bulkhead was recently replaced by a semicircular bowl that wraps around a miniature restoration of an undeveloped Puget Sound beach: beach grass bordering a sandy strip of shoreline that gives way to a gently sloping gravel beach at low tide. The new low bulkhead sports benches, an interpretive sign, and a barrier-free ramp leading to the beach.

One of the attractions of obscure little neighborhood parks such as this one is the chance for an unexpected discovery. On a windy February day, the authors spent an hour observing a squadron of migratory black brant geese playing in the waves quite near the park's shore.

Lincoln Park (Seattle Parks)

Park area: 130 acres
Access: Land, water (limited)
Facilities: Swimming pool (saltwater), baseball diamonds, football field, horseshoe pits, children's play equipment, wading pool, fitness trail, picnic shelters and tables, restrooms, concession stand
Attractions: Beachcombing, tidepools, swimming, picnicking, group sports, hiking, fishing, scuba diving

This gem of the Seattle city parks system covers 130 acres of choice waterfront property above the beaches of Point Williams and Fauntleroy Cove. Although Lincoln Park offers something for everyone, and attracts throngs of people annually, it still retains a bit of intimacy, with vegetation and steep hillsides separating many of the activities. Red-barked madronas and heavy brush cling to clay banks above the beaches. Across the sound rise the snow-draped Olympic Mountains, which have a surprising link to the park.

A survey officer of the Wilkes Expedition of 1838–42 named Fauntleroy Cove for his fiancée's family. He christened the most beautiful of the Olympic peaks seen from the shore for the young lady herself, Ellinor; Mount Constance and The Brothers were named for other members of her family. The romantic young officer, George Davidson, returned to the Midwest and married his sweetheart. Today the name Fauntleroy is widely used in West Seattle; however, the family probably never saw the land that bears their name.

The park property was originally a private summer resort, established in 1904. It was acquired piecemeal by the city between 1925 and 1930 to form the park. Bulkhead and beach improvements benefited from Works Progress Administration funding in the Depression years of the 1930s. Colman Pool at Point Williams, which was built in 1929, was improved to its present form in the 1940s.

To reach Lincoln Park from I-5, take Exit 163A if driving from the north, or Exit 163 if driving from the south; both are labeled to Spokane Street. Follow directional

Jogging on a Lincoln Park trail

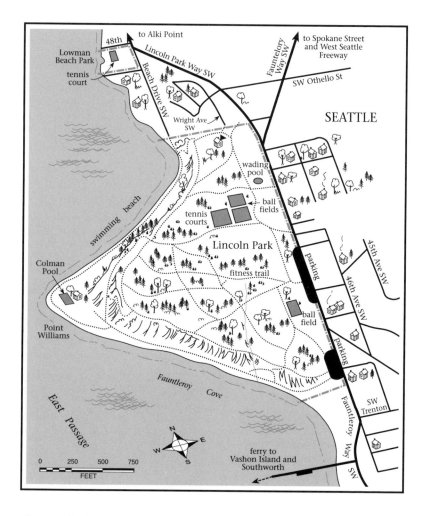

signs to the West Seattle Freeway. The freeway curves southwest to West
Seattle and finally becomes Fauntleroy Way SW. In 5½ miles Fauntleroy
Way SW forms the eastern boundary of Lincoln Park. Two large parking
lots at the south end and middle of the park are open from 6:00 A.M. to
11:00 P.M. daily.

A bicycle route begins at the east end of Harbor Avenue SW and follows the waterfront west around Alki Point and south to Lincoln Park via
Beach Drive SW.

Visitors arriving at the park in large boats should anchor well out and
dinghy ashore, but be aware that the beach slopes outward very gradually
and it may be necessary to wade a bit and drag the dinghy in. The rocky
tideflats of Fauntleroy Cove can be hard on bare feet and the bottom of an

Overhanging trees frame the beach and a picnic area at Lincoln Park.

inflatable. There are no public buoys; the several buoys south of the park near the Fauntleroy ferry terminal are private.

A launch ramp, indicated on some charts at Fauntleroy Cove, has been abandoned for some time. For land-to-water access, lightweight boats can be carried to the beach from the south parking lot.

The upland areas of the park consist of large, grassy fields shaded by huge, old-growth fir and divided into people-sized units by smaller trees and shrubs. You'll find enough picnic tables to host your entire family reunion and playfields to keep everyone busy. The greatest concentration of picnic facilities is at the south end, although picnic tables are scattered throughout the park, and a shelter is in the north end. Play areas rimming the east edge of the park, just a short walk from the parking areas, include two baseball diamonds, a football field, tennis courts, children's play equipment, and a wading pool. If that's not enough, there's ample space for Frisbee tossing or a quick game of catch.

Several miles of trails lace the forest. Heading north from the north parking lot, one path cuts west to a trail that angles down the bank to Colman Pool, while another path heads north past clusters of picnic tables scattered among the trees and arrives at play areas, the omnipresent picnic tables, and finally the park's maintenance shops as it continues north to the end of the park.

From the northeast corner of the park, one trail switchbacks down through trees and brush to the beach. A second trail, protected by a rustic log railing, follows the top of the bank, passing occasional viewpoints and picnic sites. Sweeping views extend northwest over Alki Point, Restoration

Point, Blake Island, ferries, and maritime traffic. The center of the park is woven with a joggers' fitness trail that starts and ends on the path 100 yards south from the north parking lot.

The beach below the north bluff can also be reached by bicycle or on foot from the dead end of Beach Drive SW. This section of beach consists of sand and driftwood, with gravel exposed at low tide. A fringe of kelp beds 50 yards offshore that often plays host to a variety of seabirds marks the inner safe limit of approach for deep-draft boats. Halfway between the north park boundary and Point Williams, a protective bulkhead separates the beach from the path. The wooded banks above the beach are occasionally scarred with scrambled trails—abandoned or unofficial, unsafe, and definitely not encouraged.

Point Williams is the site of Colman Pool, an outdoor, heated, saltwater swimming pool. Grassy picnic areas are north of the pool; a children's play lot is located to the south. The official trail to the north parking lot slants steeply up the bank north from the pool. To the south a wide, paved path passes picnic sites sequestered in madrona groves and two picnic shelters (which may be reserved by groups) before reaching the southern park boundary.

On this side of Point Williams the beach is rocky, scattered with boulders; kelp beds show it to be shallow some 200 yards out from shore. The Fauntleroy ferry adds action to the view with its regular departures from the terminal immediately south of the park.

Ed Munro Seahurst County Park (King County Parks)

Park area: 140 acres; 4,000 feet of shoreline
Access: Land, boat
Facilities: Picnic tables and shelter, beach fire rings, restrooms, outside showers, playground, fish ladder, marine laboratory, artificial reef, nature trail, disabled access
Attractions: Beachcombing, swimming, picnicking, scuba diving, fishing, hiking

First-time visitors to Ed Munro Seahurst County Park are usually quizzical about the huge metal "doughnut" mounted between a pair of posts near the beach. This abstract sculpture is a product of legislation that decreed mandatory art for public areas. To some the sculpture may seem redundant, because the most remarkable work of art is the park itself.

The facility was originally named simply Seahurst County Park, but the name of Ed Munro was added to honor the former county commissioner. This showpiece of King County saltwater parks is an outstanding example of how creative design can shape a beautiful natural setting to meet human needs. Earth mounds, landscaping, and a pair of parallel bulkheads divide the beach into intimate pockets, each just right for a family picnic or a private rendezvous with a beach blanket and a novel. The upper bulkhead is a prettily undulating concrete seawall. At the mid-tide level is a lower gabion bulkhead—a unique construction of riprap and wire mesh.

To drive to Seahurst Park from I-5, take Exit 154B (Burien, Sea-Tac Airport, Highway 518) west past the airport and over Highway 509, to where it becomes SW 148th Street at 1st Avenue SW. In 8 blocks turn north at Ambaum Boulevard SW, and in 4 blocks turn west on SW 144th Street. Park signs may be small and inconspicuous; in 1 mile watch closely for 13th Avenue SW and turn north, dropping downhill to the entrance in ½ mile. The park is open daily from 8:00 A.M. to 7:30 P.M.

From the park entrance gate, the steep road passes a large parking area halfway down the hill on the south side. The small parking area immediately above the beach is reserved on weekends and holidays for the elderly and handicapped, but it has a passenger drop-off and pickup loop for visitors who park in the lot above.

At the lower parking lot the beachfront divides both in function and in character. To the south the path crosses a bridge, then continues for 700 yards along the edge of a steep, wooded bank, past a picnic area just above the beach. The gabion bulkhead defines the upper beach; driftwood marks high water for the sand and tideflats. The steep bank above the picnic area is periodically cut by small creeks and covered with impenetrable brush.

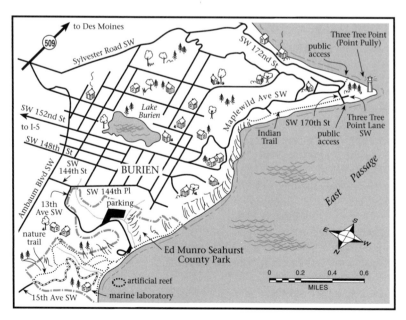

The beach at Ed Munro Seahurst County Park is wide and sandy below the bulkhead.

North from the lower parking area, the curves of the concrete bulkhead separate the large grassy plots from the beach. The grassy expanse offers benches, picnic areas, a playground, picnic shelters, and restrooms. A miniature fish ladder next to the caretaker's residence leads to an adjoining fish pond.

Enclosed pockets of sandy beach contain concrete fire rings and attractively arranged stumps and boulders. Outward from the lower gabion wall, the tide washes a sand and seaweed beach that grows rocky at its northern end.

At the far north end of the park is the two-story Marine Technology Occupational Skills Center, with a dry laboratory on the second floor and a wet laboratory on the first. Wooden beams, carved with stylized fish heads, extend outward between the two stories. The building is not open to the public; however, 20 viewing slots in an outside wall look into tanks containing local fish and marine life.

There are no mooring buoys, but shallow-draft boats can easily be beached on the gently sloping shore. Boaters approaching Seahurst Park should be watchful for skin divers who frequent a barge sunk just offshore. The sunken barge was placed there by the Parks Department for the benefit of scuba divers and local fish. It attracts a wide variety of sea life to an area that otherwise, because of the smoothness of the bottom, would be fairly barren.

A sign near the center of the park marks the start of a nature trail that wends uphill through the woodlands on the north end of the park. Most of the evergreens were logged from the area long ago, so the trees here are deciduous—mostly alder and maple. The trail heads north on a flat below the steep bluffs, then leads to a bridge crossing the main creek draining through the park. Paths lead downhill to the west alongside this drainage to emerge at the beach near the play area, and uphill to the east along the steep drainage wall to the park boundary. The main trail, which can be slick and muddy in spots, continues relentlessly uphill to the northeast, twice crossing the service road into the north end of the park, and finally reaches the top of the bluff at the gated service road entrance at the end of 15th Avenue SW.

Three Tree Point and Indian Trail

The name Three Tree Point was given to this area by early settlers who preferred that visually descriptive name over Point Pully, the one now shown on nautical charts. That name was given to the bluffy prominence in 1841 by the Wilkes Expedition in honor of Robert Pully, the ship's quartermaster for that expedition.

The prime recreational attractions of Three Tree Point are a historic ¾-mile bluff-top path called Indian Trail and a few public beach accesses sandwiched in among the dense residential development. A navigational light, which sits on private property at the end of the point, is not accessible to the public.

To reach Three Tree Point from I-5, take Exit 154B (Burien, Sea-Tac Airport, Highway 518) west to Ambaum Boulevard SW. Drive south 4 blocks to SW 152nd Street, then west 12 blocks to where the road changes names to Maplewild Avenue SW as it twists downhill. Where a cross-street sign marks SW 160th Street, the north end of Indian Trail emerges on the west side of the road; unfortunately, no parking is available in the vicinity. For parking, turn west from Maplewild onto SW 170th Place, just short of

Branches form an arch over Indian Trail.

the end of Three Tree Point. In 1 block, where 170th dead-ends, there is space for two or three cars west of the intersection of SW Three Tree Point Lane. The bit of public beach at the street end provides access for hand-carried boats; it is also a popular spot for scuba diving. All adjoining beaches are private.

North from the street end is Indian Trail, a narrow path that follows the water and power right-of-way between adjoining residences. This is what remains of a pre-pioneer route that traversed many miles of the shore. It is said the vestiges of the trail can also be found at other places along the banks of East Passage.

This section of Indian Trail is public, but the property on both sides, as well as intersecting access trails, is private. Enjoy views north across the sound and occasionally duck through dense shrubbery that grows over the path. Respect the privacy of the adjacent property owners—perhaps create some mutual respect (or at least detente)—so that residents can accept the continued existence of the trail.

The path ends at Maplewild Avenue SW. A return via the street is possible, but it rises and falls steeply between 160th and 170th. A two-way traverse of the reasonably level trail is less strenuous.

A second public beach access for hand-carried boats is at the bend of Maplewild Avenue SW just beyond 170th, where it turns south and becomes SW 172nd Street. Little to no parking is available, however. Use of all street-end accesses, including Indian Trail, is restricted to the hours between sunrise and sunset.

DES MOINES TO DASH POINT

Continuing south, the heavily residential shoreline gives way a bit to forested uplands. Two large state parks offer a bit of the backcountry among the suburbs. The city of Des Moines is a major nautical destination, with one of the best marinas to be found on the South Sound.

Land access is primarily from roads that branch from Highway 509 and twist down steep ravines to reach parks and communities tucked along the shore.

Marine View Park (Des Moines Recreation)

Access: Boat, land
Facilities: Sani-cans, trail
Attractions: Beachcombing

A number of years ago Normandy Park obtained, through a public bond issue, this chunk of bluff and beach property. The park sat dormant for some time, but in the late 1980s the community developed a fine trail to provide beach access.

The park can be reached by taking Exit 149 (Kent, Des Moines, Highway 516) from I-5. In 1¾ miles turn north onto Highway 509 (Marine View Drive). As Highway 509 bends uphill to the west, it becomes South 216th Place; it then returns to a northerly direction as 1st Avenue South. Here, at a poorly marked intersection, turn west onto SW 211th Street, which, in a half block, bends northwest and changes to Marine View Drive SW. A small incursion of private property edges the eastern boundary of the park along Marine View Drive for the next 200 yards. At the park's northern corner, just before the intersection of SW 208th Street, is the signed entrance gate, closed between dusk and dawn. The park can also be visited by boaters who can beach their craft.

A wooden staircase descends the final 50 feet to the beach at Marine View Park.

The trail to the beach—actually a paved service road—switchbacks very steeply downhill; several benches along the way provide a welcome respite during the climb back uphill. The path ends at the top of a 50-foot,

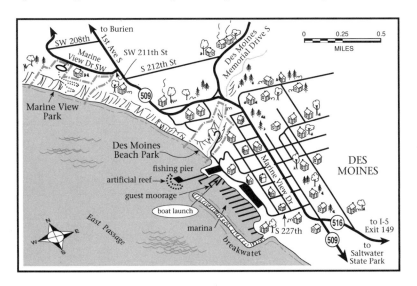

near-vertical clay bank. Here the challenge of the high bluff was over-come by construction of a three-story staircase and viewing platform. The upper level offers a panoramic view north to Three Tree Point, west across the sound to Vashon and Maury islands and the Point Robinson light-house, and south to Des Moines and Tacoma. The Olympic range frames the northwest horizon, and the frosted cone of Mount Rainier fills the skyline to the south.

The limits of the 1,000-foot-long rock and cobble beach are marked by pairs of poles in the beach at either end of the park. At a minus tide the cobble blends out into a pleasant sand beach.

Des Moines

Access: Land, boat
Facilities: Marina, boat launch (slings), fishing pier, artificial reef, fuel, marine supplies, guest moorage with power and water, groceries, restaurants, restrooms, boat rental, marine repair, disabled facilities
Attractions: Boating, fishing

The city of Des Moines may sound as if it were a transplant from the middle of Iowa, but its waterfront park dedicated to maritime pursuits makes it quite clear that its heart belongs to Puget Sound. The extensive city-operated marina and launch facilities are combined with a 670-foot-long public fishing pier. Come to fish or just to stroll the docks and enjoy the bustle of others fishing and boating.

The Des Moines marina offers some of the best moorage to be found on the South Puget Sound.

To reach the area, leave I-5 at Exit 149 (Kent, Des Moines, Highway 516). Drive 1¾ miles west to Highway 509, turn north, and in 1 block turn west on South 227th Street; follow it 2 blocks to the marina complex. Note that parking immediately adjacent to the fishing pier is reserved for cars with boat trailers; others may be ticketed and towed.

By boat, Des Moines is 15 nautical miles from Seattle's Elliott Bay and 9 nautical miles from Commencement Bay in Tacoma. A 2,200-foot rock breakwater forms a protected yacht harbor with space for 700 pleasure boats. Transient moorage for about 40 boats is available at floats in the north end of the basin near the breakwater entrance. Just inside the breakwater entrance a small "touch-and-go" float is provided for boats picking up or dropping off passengers.

Nearby a pair of sling lifts—capable of handling boats up to 36 feet—provide the first public launch facility south of Seattle. Don't plan on sleeping late in the guest moorage, as boat launching operations commence at 7:00 A.M. Launching continues to 7:30 P.M., when the gates to the launch and fishing pier parking area are locked.

A small store with marine supplies, bait, ice, and some groceries is near the launching lifts. The marina complex also includes a marine repair service and two restaurants. For those needing more in the way of ships' stores, a shopping center about 5 blocks from the visitors' floats provides a full line of groceries, liquor, and other necessary provisions.

At the entrance to the yacht basin, a 670-foot-long concrete fishing pier extending far out into the sound has fillet boards, rod holders, overhead lights for night fishing, and maps of reef locations. An artificial reef has been created below the outboard end of the pier, festooned with old nylon stockings fastened to the bottom and floated with Styrofoam balls in the toes to form a protective garden of ersatz kelp. The reef provides homes for various links in the food chain, culminating in such table fare as shrimp, crab, squid, cod, flounder, cabezon, rockfish, perch, and (rumors have it) an occasional salmon. Sunny weekends find the pier crowded with anglers of all ages, from Huck Finns to seasoned fishermen, who expertly land and fillet their evening meal. The reef is closed to all spear fishing; scuba diving is allowed only by special permit.

Des Moines Beach Park (Des Moines Recreation)

Park area: 19 acres
Access: Land, boat
Facilities: Picnic tables, restrooms, senior citizens center, disabled access
Attractions: Picnicking, beachcombing

Just north of the Des Moines marina, off the end of Cliff Avenue South, is tiny Des Moines Beach Park. The park is of special historical interest, as it was once a church camp. Although many of the original buildings have

Mallard ducks paddle in Des Moines Creek.

been removed or are no longer safe to enter, the remaining cabins are typical of those used in many such camps that were found along Puget Sound in the 1930s and '40s. A newer building addition is now an activity center for senior citizens and other community groups.

Des Moines Creek, which flows through the park, drains from Bow Lake. It runs for 3 miles along the edge of Sea-Tac Airport, through a golf course, and down a deep ravine before arriving at the park, and ultimately the sound. The ravine is held by King County Parks and Recreation Division as undeveloped property.

Over the years urbanization of the Des Moines Creek watershed has severely impacted the stream, surrounding vegetation, and native wildlife. A multi-agency task force has undertaken the job of improving the water quality of the creek in order to improve wildlife habitat and restore runs of salmon, cutthroat, and steelhead. Squirrels, raccoons, and mountain beaver live in the forested ravine, and towhees, jays, and robins nest there. Mallards, coots, and great blue herons feed in the stream and along the saltwater shore.

The beach strip at the entrance to the park has a lawn with picnic tables; views are south past the marina fishing pier to Vashon Island. North of a creek flowing through the gully, a shallow beach offers chances for some beachcombing, or at least the opportunity to play among a cacophonous horde of gulls.

Saltwater State Park

Park area: 88 acres; 1,445 feet of shoreline
Access: Land, boat
Facilities: Hiking trails, picnic shelters and tables, restrooms, artificial reef, 50 standard campsites, 2 primitive campsites, group camp, 4 group day-use areas, concession stand, food and beverage carts, 3 mooring buoys, trailer dump station, portions have disabled access
Attractions: Hiking, beachcombing, swimming, picnicking, camping, scuba diving, fishing

Right in the urban heart of metropolitan Puget Sound lies a marvelously green swale with beaches, hiking trails, and a forest-style campground. No carefully groomed lawns here—just rugged, utilitarian

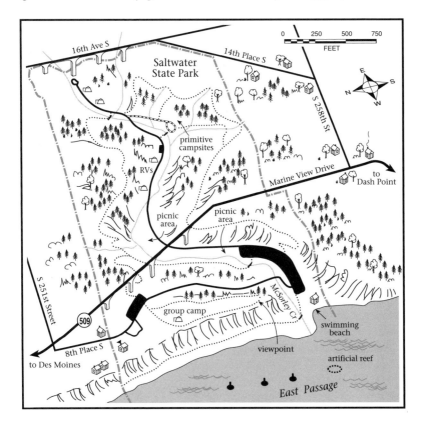

A rock bulkhead stabilizes the beach and walkway at Saltwater State Park.

facilities that annually attract (and withstand the use of) over 750,000 day users and some 17,000 campers. Here is the place for the office to hold its salmon bake, for the Cub Scouts to camp out, or for toddlers to squish sand between their toes and romp in the water on a hot summer day. Here is *not* the place for solitude, however. On a sunny Sunday you may have to wait in line in your car at the entrance, directed by a park attendant, waiting for someone to leave the park so there is room enough for you to enter. In winter, when the crowds are gone, the park still has charms for those who enjoy the invigorating sting of wind-driven salt spray and the woodsy smell of damp forest trails.

The park's urban location contributes to its popularity; it is less than a ½-hour drive from either Seattle or Tacoma and only minutes from the many bedroom communities in-between. The park can be reached from I-5 by taking Exit 149 (Kent, Des Moines, Highway 516), then turning south on Pacific Highway South. In ½ mile go west on South 240th Street, signed to Highline Community College and the park. In 1¼ miles intersect Marine View Drive (Highway 509) and head south for another ½ mile; turn west on South 251st Street for a half block to 8th Place South, which leads to the entrance.

Immediately inside the park is a large parking area adjoining a group camp area with a tree-shaded lawn, a picnic shelter, and a lovely old stone fireplace. The area, which is frequently used by scout and youth groups, is available for use only by advance arrangement with the park ranger.

The lawn ends at a bluff with viewpoints of the beach below and the southern reaches of East Passage.

The entrance road drops steeply downhill to two more parking lots, one near the beach and a larger one to the east along the ravine floor. The overnight camping area begins beyond the foot of the Marine View Drive bridge, which spans the park. Farther east, trailer sites give way to tent spots as the steep hills close in and the road ends.

Grassy plots with an abundance of picnic tables surround the two lower parking lots; two group shelters are adjacent to the creek northeast of the larger lot, one of which is disabled accessible. A children's play area and a concession stand with an adjoining picnic shelter are located above the beach southwest of the lower lot. The stand is open during the summer.

The waters of Puget Sound flow over the shallow, sandy tideflat at the south end of the beach and in summer warm to temperatures pleasant enough for wading and splashing. What sea life originally existed here has, sadly, long since been carted away from this heavily used beach. A boulder seawall defines a broad, man-made spit north of the beach and supports a wide pathway that heads north to the park boundary. More picnic tables, another picnic shelter, and stone fireplaces are found here, flanking the shore.

Three mooring buoys offshore are available for marine visitors. The protruding spit offers the best landing for dinghies and small boats; the beach to the south is so shallow that a wade ashore is usually necessary.

Scuba divers prepare to enter the water at Saltwater State Park.

White-blossomed trilliums are one of the many wildflowers found at Saltwater State Park.

A white can buoy with a diagonal red stripe about 150 yards offshore marks a reef created by tires and the remains of a sunken barge, placed there by the state in 1971 to provide a home for undersea life. The wreck, lying at the 50-foot depth, attracts scuba divers who come to observe the array of marine invertebrates, fish, and even octopus that find shelter here.

Saltwater State Park not only offers picnicking, camping, and a beach, but it also boasts nearly 2 miles of hiking trails with a seclusion unexpected for such an urban area. The main trail leaves the east parking lot near the restrooms and switchbacks to the top of the bluff through wildflowers, dense brush, and deciduous trees. Don't erode the trail by indulging in the obnoxious practice of cutting switchbacks. Once out of the ravine, the trail weaves through second-growth timber with side paths descending to the campground area. The path eventually drops to the drainage floor in the east part of the campground, crosses a bridge over McSorley Creek, then climbs to the bluff above the north side of the drainage. The trail heads west to a fork; one branch climbs beneath the bridge footings to the entrance parking lot, the other drops down to the creek bank, which it follows downstream to another bridge to the day-use area.

The path passes knotted old bigleaf maple trees, moss-covered logs, and spring blooms of trillium and skunk cabbage. Jays and crows call in the green canopy overhead, while wrens and sparrows rustle in trail-side shrubs. Here even slugs have their charms, as their slivery trails leave a delicate tracery on fallen leaves.

Saltwater State Park was acquired in 1929 through the cooperation of the Seattle/Tacoma Associated Young Men's Business Club and the *Seattle Star* and *Tacoma Times* newspapers. The Civilian Conservation Corps built facilities here in the 1930s, and the creek through the heart of the park was rerouted in the 1950s to extend the beach and enlarge the parking area. Additional parcels of land were acquired through 1974 to bring the park to its present size.

Redondo Waterfront Park (King County Parks)

Access: Land, boat
Facilities: Boat launch (ramp), fishing pier, restrooms, disabled access
Attractions: Fishing, boating, swimming, picnicking, scuba diving

A seaside hamlet often overlooked by motorists and boaters, Redondo has some salty elbow-to-elbow cottages along the shore drive and an outcrop of newer condominiums abutting a narrow road above the beach. The southern portion of the approximately ¾-mile beach is private.

For visitors, the major attractions of the Redondo waterfront are its fishing pier and boat launch. The long, T-shaped pier features a fish cleaning station, park benches, overhead lights for night fishing, and sections of railing lowered for the convenience of disabled and pint-sized anglers. The concrete launch ramp has an adjacent float for securing small craft when boarding and loading. A parking lot across the street has ample room for cars and boat trailers and is open from 7:00 A.M. to 8:30 P.M. Take along a picnic lunch to enjoy while soaking up the nautical atmosphere, or indulge in fish and chips from the nearby restaurant.

At the north end of the waterfront, a pleasant, sandy, 2-block-long beach is open to the public for swimming, sunbathing, or just plain lolling about. Scuba divers often use the beach as a start point for offshore dives.

To reach Redondo from I-5, take Exit 149 (Kent, Des Moines, Highway 516) and turn south on Pacific Highway South. In 2¾ miles turn west on South 272nd Street, which winds downhill to 10th Avenue South and then finally to South 281st Street, meeting the beach at Redondo.

In 1990 severe winter storms demolished sections of the bulkhead and roadway of Redondo Beach Drive South south from the launch ramp. The road is open, but there is no parking anywhere along the beach strip.

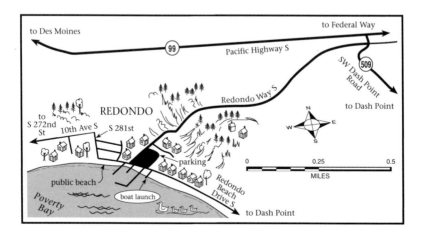

Poverty Bay Park (Federal Way Parks)

Park area: 47 acres
Access: Boat, limited land
Facilities: None
Attractions: Beachcombing, clamming, primitive hiking

This 47-acre parcel of brambled woods is unimproved county parkland awaiting possible development. To reach Poverty Bay Park, turn west from SW Dash Point Road onto SW 312th Street, which bends northwest into 21st Place SW, and then becomes 21st Avenue SW as it heads north in ¼ mile. In another ¼ mile turn west onto SW 304th Street and follow it as it bends north and becomes 24th Avenue SW. At a ᴛ-intersection, turn southwest onto SW 301st Place. In 1 block, at the intersection of 25th Avenue SW, you'll find enough parking space on the right for a couple of cars.

From the parking area, an unmaintained path leads into the woods and down a gully to the narrow beach. This primitive trail, with washed-out sections, downed trees, encroaching brambles, and muddy stretches, is easily seen at first, but becomes somewhat obscure as it drops down the last steep section to the beach.

The beach can also be reached via the water with boats that can be beached. A road end 1,000 feet east of the park boundary provides a narrow access point for hand-carried boats. To reach this access continue north on 21st Avenue SW. At a fork go right on 20th Place SW and follow it down a steep, wooded ravine to the road end, where there is parking space for two or three cars. Property and beach on either side of the road end are private.

Poverty Bay Park lies along the shore ¼ mile west of the road end. From the water the public beach has no clearly defined boundaries. The low bank is heavily overgrown above the narrow, cobble beach. Paddlers can continue on to Dumas Bay Park Wildlife Sanctuary, a short mile to the west.

Dumas Bay Park Wildlife Sanctuary (Federal Way Parks)

Park area: 19 acres
Access: Land, boat
Facilities: None
Attractions: Birdwatching, beach exploring

While some parks suffer from lack of public facilities, this one thrives on it—any elaborate development or heavy public use would surely destroy this delicate tideland environment. Fortunately, the Federal Way Parks Department plans to leave this nature refuge basically undisturbed.

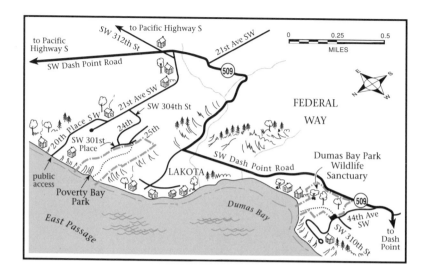

The park, fronting on tiny Dumas Bay, lies less than 1 mile west of Poverty Bay Park, just off SW Dash Point Road (Highway 509). To reach the park, turn off SW Dash Point Road at 44th Avenue SW. In ½ mile, just beyond SW 310th Street, is a paved parking lot at the park entrance. A wide, flat gravel trail leaves from here and wanders for 300 yards through woods and a small clearing before arriving at the beach. A few benches are provided for critter watching.

A creek threads through the maple and alder thicket, seeping into a cattail marsh and finally entering the bay. This environmental combination serves as a haven for a wide variety of land birds, waterfowl, and small wild animals. A quiet approach through the woods

Boxes are provided to encourage wood ducks to nest at Dumas Bay.

may be rewarded with sightings of wildlife. Watch, photograph, and enjoy, but do not litter or destroy.

Dumas Bay is quite shallow, drying well out into the sound at low tide. Even inflatables and flat-bottomed boats should use caution approaching the park from the water.

Dash Point State Park

Park area: 398 acres; 3,301 feet of shoreline
Access: Land, boat
Facilities: 110 standard campsites, 28 RV sites, group camp, restrooms, showers, picnic tables, picnic shelter, trailer dump station, concession stand, 7 miles of hiking trails, disabled facilities
Attractions: Hiking, beachcombing, swimming, picnicking, camping, kite flying, fishing, scuba diving

As does Saltwater State Park, Dash Point offers a forest campground, a beachfront, and hiking trails just a hop from the city. Although it is less heavily used than its northern counterpart, Dash Point has twice the shoreline and four times the land area that Saltwater does. This land, which

The wide, shallow beach at Dash Point State Park is ideal for sand play.

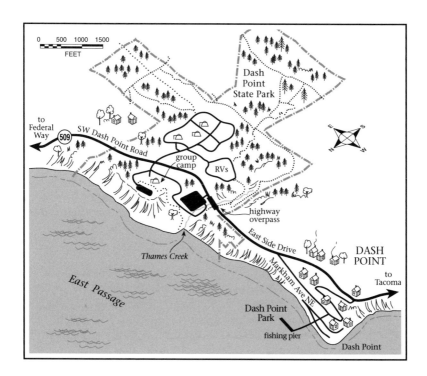

straddles the King County–Pierce County boundary, was acquired in four
separate parcels between 1958 and 1979 before reaching its present size
of nearly 400 acres. Some parts of the forested inland remain undeveloped except for hiking trails, which adds to the feeling of a wilderness in
the heart of the subdivisions.

To reach the park from the north, leave I-5 via Exit 143 (Federal Way,
South 320th Street). Take SW 320th Street west through Federal Way to
21st Avenue SW. Go north on 21st SW for 5 blocks to its junction with SW
Dash Point Road (Highway 509), then go west to Dash Point State Park.

From the south, take Exit 137 (Fife, Milton) and proceed north on 54th
Avenue East, which becomes Taylor Way in 1½ miles at the intersection
with Marine View Drive. Turn northeast on Marine View Drive, which
rounds the end of the Hylebos Waterway, then heads northwest. Marine
View Drive, which skirts the east side of Commencement Bay, becomes
East Side Drive as it climbs over Browns Point. At the western park boundary, it becomes SW Dash Point Road.

The road splits the park, with the day-use area lying to the north,
fronting on the water, and the overnight camping area to the south. Campsites on two loop roads, one for trailers and one for tenting, are tucked
away in timber and shrubbery.

More than 7 miles of trails wander through the forest of second-growth alder, fir, and maple. One leads through timber along the west side of the campground and down the ravine beneath the highway overpass to the lower level of the park and the beach. Other longer trails leave the camping area and skirt the south and east boundaries of the park.

The section of the park north of the highway is divided into three separate day-use areas. A picnic area is situated in a timbered flat atop the steep, 200-foot bluff rising from the beach. A ravine separates it from a large group campsite to the south. Trails wind down through the woods to connect both areas to the third day-use area, the beach.

Dash Point State Park is one of the few places in the sound where saltwater bathing can be enjoyable. The sandy slope is so gentle that the beach extends outward over 2,000 feet at a minus tide. The shallow tidelands give the summer sun an opportunity to influence the normally frigid water, which can run 10 to 15 degrees warmer here than in deeper water, making it ideal for swimming and wading. Caution: Lifeguards are not on duty—solo swimming can be dangerous.

The sandy expanse invites exploration and study of intertidal marine life, but pollution makes shellfish unsafe for consumption. There are picnic tables on the uplands above the sand and at a small, grassy plot between the beach and the large lower parking lot. The adjacent restroom has an outside shower for rinsing off swimmers and scuba equipment. A picnic shelter between the entry road and the parking lot has a bridge and an easy grade path for disabled access.

Dash Point Park (Tacoma Metropolitan Parks)

Access: Land, boat
Facilities: Picnic shelter, fishing pier, children's play area, restrooms, disabled access
Attractions: Fishing, picnicking, swimming, scuba diving

This city park in the town of Dash Point is quite different in character from nearby Dash Point State Park. The park's focal point is a 200-foot-long fishing pier that juts into East Passage. The pier is a favorite spot for throngs of fishermen, but even nonanglers can enjoy a stroll along the dock to admire the catch of others and to take in views downsound to Point Robinson and upsound to Dalco Passage and Point Defiance.

To reach Dash Point Park from the state park, drive west on Highway 509 (East Side Drive), and turn downhill on Markham Avenue NE. Markham turns north onto Soundview Drive NE, a block from the road end in a small parking lot at the park. Facilities are restricted to day use only. There are no docking or launching areas, but shallow-draft boats can land on the sloping beach.

Two shipwrecks, one just off Dash Point and the other about ¼ mile farther south, are popular exploration sites for scuba divers.

Anglers line the pier at Dash Point Park. This pier was replaced by a new one in 1995.

Onshore, a children's play area, picnic shelters, and park benches are interspersed on a narrow, grassy strip that separates the beachfront from the parking lot. Below the low concrete bulkhead, a block-long sandy beach that tapers gradually into the sound is ideal for swimming when the water warms enough to be tolerable.

CHAPTER TWO

Vashon and Maury Islands and Colvos Passage

Bounding the western edge of East Passage are a pair of large islands—Vashon and Maury. In reality they are physically one, joined at the community of Portage by a narrow isthmus that is crossed by a road. Colvos Passage, which is nearly a mile wide throughout most of its length, separates Vashon Island from the Kitsap Peninsula.

In May 1792 the members of the Vancouver Expedition became the first Europeans to sight Vashon Island and Colvos Passage. Captain Vancouver, still hoping to find the elusive Northwest Passage, cautiously anchored his expedition flagship, the *Discovery*, north of Blake Island and sent a launch and cutter commanded by Lieutenant Peter Puget to explore the waterways farther south. This small band of adventurers made their way up the sound via the passage and returned by the same route.

Vashon Island was named after one of Peter Puget's first commanding officers, James Vashon, but it was not until the Wilkes Expedition of 1838–42 that Maury Island and Colvos Passage received their names. The name Maury is for expedition member Lieutenant William Maury. As for Colvos Passage, perhaps Wilkes thought the name of his Greek midshipman, George Colvocoresses, was as long as the channel. He evidently gave up in his attempt to spell it, however, for he abbreviated it to Colvos on his charts and it has remained thus ever since. Be grateful.

Vashon and Maury Islands

Vashon and Maury islands serve as a bedroom community for the cities of Seattle, Tacoma, and Bremerton, and also as a semi-isolated sanctuary for a number of people who wish only to "do their own thing" —which includes not encouraging an onslaught of visitors from neighboring metropolitan areas. As a result, the public recreation facilities are not widely advertised, tend to be poorly marked, and (the residents hope) perhaps forgotten.

Large boats of the Washington state ferry system run between Seattle's

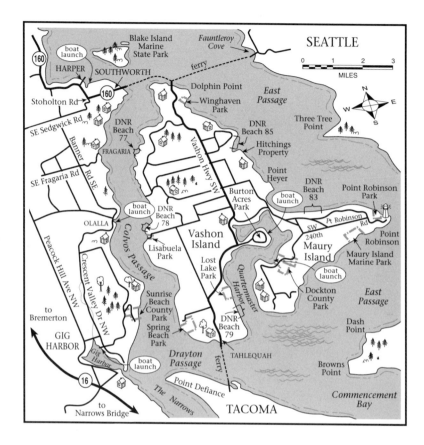

Fauntleroy landing to the north end of Vashon Island, and then continue on to Harper on the Kitsap Peninsula, while a small ferry operates between Tacoma and Tahlequah, on the south end of Vashon. The ferry ride from Seattle takes about 20 minutes, from Southworth about 10 minutes, and from Tahlequah 15 minutes.

The Fauntleroy ferry terminal is immediately south of Seattle's Lincoln Park. To reach it from I-5, take Exit 163A (Spokane Street) to the West Seattle Freeway. The freeway curves southwest to West Seattle and finally becomes Fauntleroy Way SW, which can be followed to the ferry landing.

To reach Southworth on the Kitsap Peninsula from Tacoma, drive across the Tacoma Narrows Bridge on Highway 16 and continue north. At the intersection with SE Sedgwick Road turn east and follow the road to Southworth. To reach it from Bremerton, drive south around Sinclair Inlet, then take Highway 16 south to the SE Sedgwick Road exit.

The terminal for the ferry to Tahlequah sits at the eastern edge of

Washington's state ferries, such as this one arriving at Vashon Island, are the successors to the Mosquito Fleet.

Tacoma's Point Defiance Park. To reach it, follow signs in Tacoma to the park; the landing is on Pearl Street, just inside the main entrance.

Most roads on the islands are inland, with a few high vistas of Colvos Passage, Quartermaster Harbor, and Point Defiance. The roads encircling Quartermaster Harbor frequently border the water, with several spots appropriate for picnicking. There are no overnight camping facilities, so unless lodging has been reserved at one of the few motels or bed-and-breakfast inns, visitors must leave by the evening ferry; however, all of the islands' 50-plus miles of highway are easily explored in a day.

Vashon and Maury are a bicycling delight; roads are lightly traveled, and the main road, Vashon Highway SW, has a wide shoulder.

North End Boat Ramp

Access: Land, boat
Facilities: None
Attractions: Fishing, paddling, scuba diving

The Washington state ferries dock at the ferry terminal near Dolphin Point at the north end of Vashon Island. A surfaced public boat-launch ramp immediately east of the ferry landing provides water access for hand-carried boats—it is not suitable for launching trailered boats. While paddlers are exploring, cars can be left at the ferry terminal parking lot, 1 block straight uphill from the ferry dock between 103rd and 104th Avenue SW.

The Mosquito Fleet

Today, Vashon and Maury islands are connected to the mainland by Washington state ferries. In early days the islands were served by Puget Sound's Mosquito Fleet, a collection of private boats that carried passengers back and forth, brought goods to the islands, and took away marketable products. The individual enterprise of the boats of the Mosquito Fleet eventually gave way to the more organized efforts of commercial shipping. By the 1920s the islands were served primarily by the Black Ball Line, a privately operated fleet that carried both people and cargo, landing at a long wharf on the north end of Vashon Island near Dolphin Point.

Over the years the rising rates of the private ferries caused irate islanders to pressure the state into taking over the line. In 1951 a large portion of the Black Ball fleet was purchased by the state of Washington, which then went into the ferry business; however, the state was never able to operate the boats any more cheaply or efficiently than private industry had.

Ever since the islands were settled there has been talk of building a bridge—or two bridges—across the channel to the Kitsap Peninsula (as was done on Bainbridge Island to the north), or east across East Passage to the mainland proper. The project has never proceeded past the talk stage, and today rising construction costs, coupled with the islanders' growing appreciation of isolation, make it unlikely that such a bridge will ever be built.

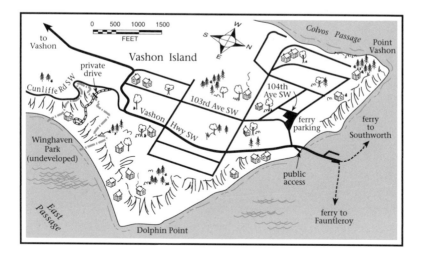

Old pilings near the ferry terminal, as well as the steep walls of the headland all the way from Point Vashon to Dolphin Point, are frequently explored by scuba divers. Gain access to the shore at the launch ramp, but do not dive among the pilings of the ferry wharf; it is unlawful to dive within 100 feet of a state ferry terminal. The beach below the access ramp is privately owned. Beach access is permitted, but do not remove any marine life.

Winghaven Park (Undeveloped, Vashon Island Parks)

Park area: 12 acres; 400 feet of shoreline
Access: Land, boat
Facilities: Picnic tables, sani-can, designated Cascadia Marine Trail campsite
Attractions: Beachcombing, clamming

Just a short distance south of the Vashon ferry landing is a small, undeveloped property. To reach it from the ferry terminal, go uphill ¾ mile on Vashon Highway SW to where the highway makes a sharp turn to the west. At that corner head south on Cunliffe Road SW. There is no public road access to the park; the upper section of an old road down through it is private and is blocked at the park boundary. Park on Cunliffe Road, but pull well off the narrow road. Watch for a boot path that scrambles down from Cunliffe Road ¼ mile from Vashon Highway SW, about 30

A crumbling concrete balustrade at Winghaven Park adds an air of mystery to the scene.

feet north of the driveway to 12115 Cunliffe Road SW. The path meets the old road just inside the park boundary, then descends down a steep narrow ravine for ¼ mile through dense woods, passes a small dam-created pond, and arrives at a marshy area above a grassy flat.

The park is an abandoned estate that was deeded to the county. The home that once was here has been removed, and now only a pair of picnic tables grace the lawn where it stood. A deteriorating bulkhead with ornate concrete balusters stretches along the bank above the beach. Engulfed in blackberries and weeds, the remains of an elaborate fountain sit at one end of the bulkhead, a reminder of prouder days.

Below the remnants of the garden a 400-foot-long sandy beach looks across East Passage to West Seattle. Empty shells give evidence that clamming is worth a try. Private residences mark the park boundaries on both sides; do not trespass.

The park is easy to identify from the water by two old wooden pilings just offshore and the remains of the ornate brick and concrete balustrade that can be seen on top of the bulkhead onshore. Small, shallow-draft boats can easily land on the gentle beach, and Cascadia Marine Trail camping is permitted.

Hitchings Property (Undeveloped Vashon Island Parks)

Another old waterfront estate deeded to the county is located midway down the east side of Vashon Island. It is even more difficult to reach than at Winghaven, and the beach is less appealing; however, it is a less-frequented spot to while away an afternoon.

Access is via a brushy, boot-beat path down the steep bank from the end of SW Soper Road. From Vashon Center head east on SW Bank Road, and in ½ mile turn north on SW Soper Road. When the road becomes gravel in ½ mile look for a turn-around loop, and don't drive below it! The narrow road that descends a few hundred yards more to a gate has no turn around, and is difficult to back up. The beach path starts at an abandoned road spur on the left side of the gate.

From the water, the property is located at the small point 1 mile south of Point Beals, just south of a line of pilings extending out from shore. A battered concrete bulkhead separates a small pocket of cobble from the barnacle-encrusted boulder beach.

East Passage DNR Beaches

The DNR manages two beaches fronting on East Passage, one on Vashon Island and one on Maury. They are accessible only by boat, as both have private uplands.

The first, Beach 85, a very narrow cobble beach, 1,500 feet long, is located ½ mile south of Point Beales on the east side of Vashon Island, facing Three Tree Point. Backed by a steep bluff, it extends south to where a number of residences are grouped around a pair of creeks that empty into a slight cove. There is little marine harvest here, except for sea cucumbers and rock crab.

Beach 83, 2,000 feet long, is located at the south end of Tramp Harbor on the north side of Maury Island. The sand and cobble beach starts a mile east of Portage, the isthmus between Vashon and Maury islands. Little harvestable marine life is found on the tide-swept shore.

Point Heyer

At the northern end of Tramp Harbor the broad, flat expanse of Vashon Island's Point Heyer projects into East Passage. An artificial reef, marked by red-and-white-striped buoys, lies 1,000 feet southeast of the point, in 45 to 100 feet of water. The massive rocks and chunks of scrap concrete that form the reef provide habitat for such popular food fish as rockfish, perch, lingcod, and cabezon. The state Department of Fish and Wildlife has placed a string of these reefs at approximately 10-mile intervals along Puget Sound to enhance local saltwater fishing.

The gently sloping beach at Point Heyer, known locally as KVI Beach, is open to public access, subject to revocation of the privilege by that radio station, which owns the point and has a large transmission tower on the property. Parking near the access path at the intersection of SW 204th Street and 78th Place SW is limited to one or two roadside spaces. Be aware that neighbors are quick to have illegally parked cars ticketed and towed. A saltwater lagoon, serving as home and hotel for shorebirds and waterfowl, lies between the bluff and the beach grass and sand of the point. The thick collection of silvered driftwood at high tide levels indicates that this would be an exciting place to visit during stormy weather.

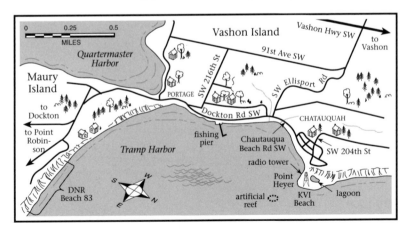

KVI Beach has driftwood, sand, and sun for play and lazing.

Tramp Harbor Fishing Pier (King County Parks)

Access: Land, boat
Facilities: Fishing pier, picnic table, sani-can
Attractions: Beachcombing, picnicking, fishing, scuba diving

What once was an old, decaying commercial pier on Tramp Harbor has been nicely refurbished by King County into a public fishing pier. To reach it, turn east from Vashon Highway SW onto SW 204th Street, which becomes SW Ellisport Road as it winds downhill to Tramp Harbor. At a T-intersection turn south on Dockton Road SW, which parallels the beach. The pier is reached in ½ mile.

The 300-foot-long dock ends in a square platform with a few sturdy benches and a picnic table. A pair of holes in the deck surrounded by pipe railings give fishermen a chance to drop a line in the midst of the pilings. A sani-can sits on a concrete platform adjacent to the shore end of the dock.

Stairs leading down to the rock- and boulder-strewn beach offer scuba divers access to the gently sloping shore. The old pilings that support the pier carry a thick coating of anemones and other marine life. Mooring of boats to the dock is prohibited.

Point Robinson Park (Vashon Island Parks) and Lighthouse

Park area: 10 acres, 600 feet of saltwater shoreline on East Passage
Access: Land, boat
Facilities: Picnic tables
Attractions: Picnicking, beachcombing, views, lighthouse, fishing, scuba diving

Point Robinson on Maury Island is known primarily to boaters as the site of a lighthouse and Coast Guard station, a spot where storm warnings are posted, a weather reporting station, and (incidentally) a fine place to go salmon fishing. Less well known is the pretty little park that perches on the hill above the lighthouse.

To reach the park and light station from the ferry landing, drive south on Vashon Highway SW through Vashon Center. Turn east onto SW Quartermaster Drive 7½ miles from the ferry, and follow this road around the north end of Quartermaster Harbor to the community of Portage, at the isthmus that joins Vashon and Maury islands.

In ½ mile, just beyond the radio transmission towers, Dockton Road SW bears south and SW Point Robinson Road goes straight ahead. Follow the latter to its intersection with SW 240th Street, then continue east to a T-intersection with SW Luana Beach Road. Turn south on SW Luana Beach Road and reach the park and the gate to the Coast Guard station

For over 100 years a light of one form or another at Point Robinson has guided mariners.

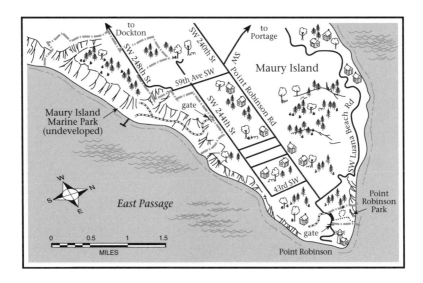

in ½ mile. The parking lot at the light station is open to the public daily until 4:00 P.M.

The day-use park, which is primarily a picnicking area, has parking for 10 cars at most. Tables are tucked away in the woods beside the parking lot and along a short trail that loops through the trees on the north side of the park. Between these two wooded sections a narrow swath of grassland sporting a field of aesthetically placed boulders is complemented by an arrangement of cast concrete slabs, an example of the county's commitment to using one percent of park development funds for art.

A poorly maintained trail leads down through the grassy meadow to the beach. All of the broad sandy beach below the park and clear around the point by the lighthouse is open for public use—beachcombing, picnicking, sunning, sand castle building, what have you.

Maury Island reaches out to the mainland, constricting East Passage to less than 2 miles across at this point. The first navigational light placed on Point Robinson in 1887 consisted of a lantern attached to a wooden arm. In 1894 a wooden tower was built housing a lantern augmented by a mirrored lens. A high-powered Fresnel lens made in Paris was installed in the present lighthouse when it was constructed in 1915. This modern light is visible for 15 miles in clear weather.

The foghorn, too, has had a succession of improvements, beginning as a hand-operated steam whistle and culminating in today's electronic horn. In marked contrast to the old lighthouse is the 100-foot-high metal tower that has been erected next to it to support a high powered radar antenna, part of the Puget Sound Vessel Tracking System.

The light station was one of the last in the state to be manned, but it too has succumbed to automation. The Coast Guard Auxiliary offers tours of the light station on Saturday and Sunday from noon to 4:00 P.M. and by appointment on Wednesday from noon to 4:00 P.M.

Maury Island Marine Park (Undeveloped, King County Parks)

Park area: 340 acres, 1¼ miles of saltwater shoreline on East Passage
Access: Boat, land
Facilities: None
Attractions: Hiking, clamming, paddling, boating, beachcombing

What may someday be one of the finest marine parks on the South Sound lies southwest of the tip of Point Robinson. It is here that King County recently purchased 340 acres of spectacular waterfront property on Maury Island. For more than 50 years the property had been used as a gravel quarry, shipping bargeloads of gravel throughout the area. Some of the old quarry is already so overgrown that it appears nearly natural; vegetation will soon reclaim the rest. The large 200-foot-long dock that was once used to load the barges still remains.

The real gem of the park is the 1¼-mile-long, gradually sloping beach facing on East Passage—one of the best to be found hereabouts. The beach is backed by a madrona-clad, 400-foot-high bluff. Park property that extends as much as ½ mile inland holds the promise of future hiking trails. Views extend south across the channel to the bluffs of the mainland and beyond to the icy mass of Mount Rainier.

Plans are underway for the development of the property, but you can visit this diamond in the rough now. Until development begins, access to the beach is via a hike down a steep ½-mile-long single-lane gravel road. The road is gated, and motorized vehicles are not permitted. To reach the gate, take SW Point Robinson Road from Dockton Road SW to its junction with SW 240th Street. In a few hundred yards turn south onto 59th Avenue SW, and in ¼ mile head east on SW 244th Street. At a Y-intersection in another ¼ mile take the south fork; the gate is reached in 50 feet. Hike the road downhill from here.

Quartermaster Harbor

Access: Boat, land
Facilities: Marina, fuel, supplies, restrooms
Attractions: Clamming, fishing, canoeing, kayaking

Separating Vashon and Maury islands, Quartermaster Harbor is a tranquil 5-mile-long haven for boaters, probably the best such place in southern Puget Sound. It may be that Lieutenant Wilkes, who surveyed this region, had run out of individual names of crewmen by the time he reached

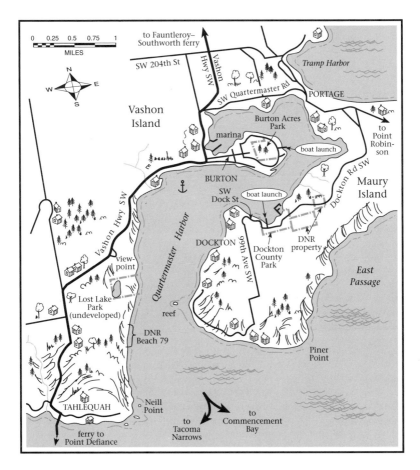

this bay, so he named it generically after his officers as a group. Another story is that he thought the harbor was so beautiful that he named it as a suitable resting place for the spirits of his crew.

Aside from a buoy-marked shoal, extending 300 yards offshore west of Piner Point, the harbor is a comfortable 4 to 6 fathoms deep all the way to the Burton Peninsula. Excellent anchorages can be found near Dockton and on the southwest side of the Burton Peninsula. At the end of the harbor, where it hooks to the south behind the peninsula, a marina provides moorage and other services to boaters. Parks at Burton and Dockton provide land access to the harbor.

You may see a number of herons nearby, or wading in the shallow waters of the harbor. Large heron rookeries are at Judd Creek, and on Melita Creek, at the head of the bay directly across from the Burton Peninsula.

At the head of the bay, a low isthmus, scarcely 200 yards wide, ties Vashon to Maury Island. Indians using Quartermaster Harbor as a

Looking northeast, up Quartermaster Harbor, to Portage

shortcut between East Passage and Dalco Passage portaged their dugout canoes across this neck of land. The small community now located here thus is named Portage.

Here, also, the resident Shomamish Indians, part of the Suquamish tribe, raised nets on poles to snare low-flying waterfowl as they landed or departed from the harbor. The nets, fashioned from thin, braided strips of bark and plant fibers, are reported to have been over 300 feet in length. This hunting technique thoroughly puzzled early European explorers, who were unable to visualize a use for the tall poles they saw standing in areas such as this.

Quartermaster Harbor Public Beaches

The long, protected waterway of Quartermaster Harbor is ideal for canoe exploration of nooks and crannies. In addition to the county parks, two short strips of public beach on the Vashon side of the harbor are good stops for lunch breaks and perhaps some clamming. DNR Beach 79 is 1 mile north of Neill Point at the entrance to the harbor. The 627-foot beach, which is rocky above with a wide stretch of sand at low tide, is said to hold some clams. It is accessible only by boat, because the uplands are private.

A second beach farther north along this same shore belongs to Lost Lake Park, an undeveloped Vashon Island Parks holding. The property, located ½ mile north of the DNR beach, has about 1,500 feet of waterfront. Extending inland for ¼ mile to the base of a steep cliff, the unimproved park encompasses a swampy bog, the source of its name. Again, no land access is available; boats can land on the gently sloping shore.

Burton Acres Park (Vashon Island Parks)

Park area: 68 acres, 250 feet of saltwater shoreline on Quartermaster Harbor
Access: Land, boat
Facilities: Boat launch (ramp), picnic tables, hiking trails, restrooms, nature trail
Attractions: Fishing, hiking, canoeing, kayaking

The blunt thumb of the Burton Peninsula projects into the north end of Quartermaster Harbor, creating a harbor within a harbor. The wooded heart of the small peninsula is a park—a former campground now limited to day use.

To reach the park drive south on Vashon Highway SW for 7¾ miles to the small community of Burton. At the Burton grocery turn east on SW Burton Drive, and in ½ mile turn south on SW Bayview Drive. Follow this road 1 mile to the tip of the peninsula, where it becomes SW Harbor Drive just south of the Burton Acres Park boat launch. Next to the launch ramp is a parking lot and a small lawn above a gravel beach. Restrooms are located alongside the road near the entrance.

The bulk of the park lying west of the launch ramp is densely wooded and at a glance seems impervious; a closer look reveals a series of old trails weaving their way through the overgrown campground. Some of the trailheads are difficult to find; careful observation and some brushwhacking may be necessary to locate them, but once found they are easy enough to follow. Watch closely for an unmarked trailhead immediately opposite the

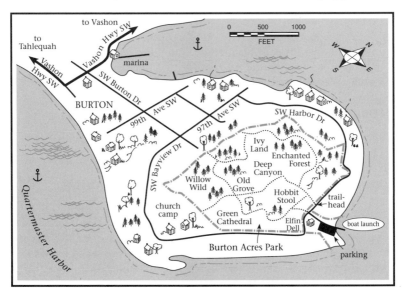

A madrona at Burton Acres Park overhangs Quartermaster Harbor.

launch ramp entrance or the marked trailhead on the west side of SW Harbor Drive about 50 feet farther north.

A rustic sign at the southern park boundary, near a church camp, has a map of the trails and tells the fanciful names of the forest areas through which they wend—Elfin Dell, Willow Wild, Enchanted Forest, Deep Canyon, Old Grove, Hobbit Stool, and Green Cathedral. Look sharp for leprechauns!

A Tacoma Eagle Scout troop recently brushed out the trail system and installed numbered posts that identify flora found along the major north–south path. An information board near the launch ramp trailhead has an identification brochure.

Dockton County Park (King County Parks)

Park area: 23 acres; 1,000 feet of saltwater shoreline on Quartermaster Harbor

Access: Land, boat

Facilities: Swimming beach, dock with floats, boat launch (ramp), picnic area, children's play area, restrooms, showers, hiking trails, disabled access

Attractions: Swimming, fishing, picnicking, canoeing, kayaking, hiking

Today it is difficult to envision Dockton as it looked in the 1890s when it was the site of a thriving shipyard. Huge vessels were built here, as well as many of the boats of the Mosquito Fleet—a flotilla of small craft that ferried goods and people to all points of Puget Sound.

In 1892 a 315-foot-long floating dry dock was installed at Dockton. The only such facility on the sound, it provided a place where large steamships coming in from foreign ports could make repairs. At that time over 400 workers were employed in the Dockton shipyards. Despite having one of the finest harbors on South Puget Sound, Dockton had one failing—it was on an island. Originally all of the communities on the sound relied on water traffic to supply materials and labor for their industries, but with the arrival of the railroad in December 1873, mainland industries gained a major advantage. Suddenly Dockton seemed remote by comparison. Unable to compete, it became a ghost town in a few short years. Today all that remains of the Dockton shipyards are a few deteriorating pilings in the cove. The onshore property is now a pleasant, water-oriented King County park.

To reach Dockton drive south from Portage on Dockton Road SW for 3¾ miles to the park. There is a paved parking area alongside the road at the park entrance and additional paved parking within the park; an older gravel parking lot on the south side of the road accommodates overflow traffic.

At the south end of the park beach is a public boat-launch ramp, marked by pilings and a boarding float alongside its water end. In the middle of the beach is a shallow, roped-off swimming area; a lifeguard is usually on duty during the summer.

A long pier leads to floats for fishing, swimming, and boat moorage. The floats were rebuilt and expanded in 1986 and can now accommodate about 75 midsize boats. There is a three-day moorage limit; moorage fees are charged nightly.

For land visitors and boaters ready to stretch their legs, the inland portion of the park and a quarter-section of adjoining DNR property have

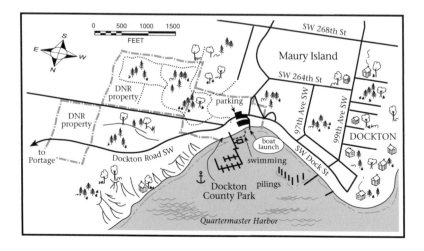

Spacious docks at Dockton County Park offer moorage for the day or for longer stays.

a pair of hiking trail loops, totaling over 2 miles, through second-growth forest of alder, bigleaf maple, and madrona. The park trailhead is at the northwest corner of the overflow parking lot; trails are open to hikers and equestrians.

Tahlequah

The ferry for Point Defiance leaves from Tahlequah at the south end of the island. The crossing takes only 15 minutes, but, because of usually light traffic, the boat has long pauses at the terminals instead of shuttling back and forth continuously. Consult a current ferry schedule to avoid a long wait. The dock adjacent to the ferry landing, once available for fishing, is no longer open for public use.

West Side DNR Beaches

Two stretches of beach owned by the DNR on Colvos Passage, on the west side of Vashon Island, are public, but they are accessible only by boat because their uplands are bordered by private property. Each offers a brief respite to boaters in small craft who want to stop for a while and watch traffic go by in busy Colvos Passage.

Both beaches are cobblestone-covered at their upper reaches; sand at low tide provides some opportunity for clamming. The more northerly, Beach 77, only 760 feet in length, is 500 feet north of the green navigational light located between Cove and Point Peter, directly across Colvos Passage from Fragaria. The second, Beach 78, is longer, 1,780 feet, and is located across Colvos Passage from Olalla, just south of where Green Valley Creek empties into saltwater.

Lisabuela Park (Vashon Island Parks)

Park area: 5.5 acres; 300 feet of saltwater beach on Colvos Passage
Access: Land, boat
Facilities: Picnic tables, sani-can, designated Cascadia Marine Trail campsite
Attractions: Paddling, picnicking, beachcombing, clamming

This tiny beach haven on the shores of Vashon Island, southeast across Colvos Passage from Olalla, has a grass lawn for picnicking and a secluded little wooded pocket where Cascadia Marine Trail paddlers are permitted to camp. The gentle gravel beach might offer opportunities to dig for

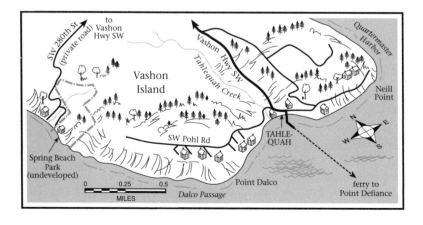

clams at a minus tide. From the water the park can be identified by an offshore piling and a conspicuous "Cable Crossing" sign on the beach.

To reach the park by land, south of Vashon Center turn west from Vashon Highway SW onto SW 216th Street. In ¾ mile head south on 111th Street SW, which bends west in another ½ mile and becomes SW 220th Street. Follow 220th for 2 miles to a right-angle turn south, where it changes to SW Lisabuela Road and drops steeply downhill for ¼ mile to the beachfront park.

Spring Beach Park (Undeveloped, Vashon Island Parks)

Park area: 45.8 acres; 1,400 feet of saltwater beach on Colvos Passage
Access: Boat
Facilities: None
Attractions: Beachcombing, clamming

Another Vashon Island public area on Colvos Passage is located at Spring Beach. The park begins just south of the small residential enclave of Spring Beach and runs south along 1,400 feet of sandy beach. The property extends uphill and includes a stream flowing down one of the steep, wooded ravines.

At present there is no public access by land; the road dropping down to the beach from the end of SW 280th Street is private. The waters offshore in Colvos Passage are subject to tide rips, so use caution approaching in a small boat.

Colvos Passage

This 13-mile-long, straight channel is a busy saltwater highway, providing a more direct route down Puget Sound than East Passage. Weekends find hundreds of cruisers and sailboats in the passage, making their way to their favorite recreation destinations, or merely enjoying the pleasure of being out. In midweek the channel is frequently used by commercial craft—tugs, barges, fishing boats—plying north and south with their cargoes.

Colvos Passage is especially favored by northbound traffic because the tidal current continually ebbs to the north. It even maintains a weak ebb tide during the major south-flowing flood tide in East Passage. Tide rips may be encountered near the north entrance, especially when a strong flood tide meets opposing strong south winds. Less severe tide rips also occur at the south end of the channel.

Public areas along Colvos Passage are skimpy: only a few DNR beaches, two small county parks, and an undeveloped county park property. This is more than compensated for by Blake Island Marine State Park, one of

A sailboat airs out its spinnaker in Colvos Passage, near Fragaria.

the state's favorite marine recreation areas, at the north entrance to the channel. Marking the south end is Gig Harbor, a former fishing village on a well-protected harbor, which proudly displays its historic and ethnic origins.

The heavily wooded shores of Colvos Passage are occasionally dotted by private homes, but there is no significant commercial development along its length on either the Vashon Island or Kitsap Peninsula side. Beaches are narrow and drop off steeply to a depth of 60 fathoms.

Blake Island Marine State Park

Park area: 476.5 acres; 17,307 feet of shoreline
Access: Private boat, Tillicum Village concession boat
Facilities: 12 floats, 21 mooring buoys, 54 campsites, picnic tables, 3 picnic shelters, picnic sites, fire rings, horseshoe pits, children's play equipment, 12 miles of hiking trails, nature trail, restrooms, showers, marine pump-out station, artificial reef, restaurant, disabled access
Attractions: Picnicking, boating, camping, hiking, clamming, beachcombing, swimming, fishing, scuba diving, Indian dances

Captain Vancouver's ship's log reports that Indians brought a deer they had killed on nearby Blake Island to the *Discovery*. The crewmen, intrigued with the idea, also went ashore to try their hand at hunting. Thus they became the first "tourist" visitors to the island—millions have since followed. One of the most heavily used of Washington's marine state parks, Blake Island now receives some 300,000 visitors annually. Deer are still to be seen—but not hunted.

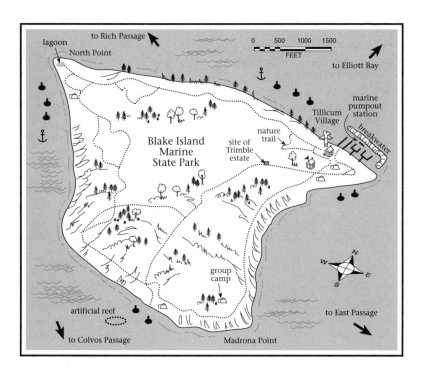

By boat, Blake Island is 6 nautical miles from Seattle's Elliott Bay, 9 nautical miles from Shilshole Bay, and 1 nautical mile from Harper or Southworth. Approaches to the east, west, and south sides of the island are clear. A shoal extends from the north side of the island for about ½ mile. At the northeast corner of the island, a narrow, dredged channel, with markers on pilings, leads to a small harbor protected by a rock breakwater. Here a series of floats have space for about 50 pleasure boats to tie up, and several times that many to raft alongside during busy weekends.

The first two floats at the entrance to the harbor are reserved for tour ferries and park boats. The outside of the first visitor float is reserved for 30-minute loading and unloading only. When the visitor floats overflow or when boaters desire more privacy, numerous buoys west of the breakwater and on the east, south, and west sides of the island give additional moorages. Good anchorages can also be found near any of these sites, depending on the wind direction.

A word here about courtesy. It is sometimes the practice to raft off other boats on the floats; however, no boat is required to permit others to tie alongside, and many people resent the intrusion of pounding feet

Opposite: *The popular boat basin at Blake Island Marine State Park is often jam-packed in summer.*

Blake Island History

It is claimed that Blake Island is the birthplace of Chief Seattle. It was an ancestral camping ground of the Suquamish Indian tribe, whose territory covered the eastern part of the Kitsap Peninsula from Port Madison to Gig Harbor. Their population, which was over 500 in 1844, had been depleted to 180 by 1909, attesting to the devastating effectiveness of pioneer settlement.

Blake Island is named for George Smith Blake, who was one of the officers of the Wilkes surveying expedition of 1838–42. Only a quirk of fate and the vision of a wealthy Seattle lawyer preserved this priceless real estate, located so close to major Puget Sound cities, from private exploitation. In 1900 that lawyer, William Pitt Trimble, bought the entire island with the intention of making it into an elaborate private estate. Over the next decade he transformed the northeast point into such a dream, complete with extensive botanical gardens and an elegant residence. When his wife died accidentally in 1929, Trimble lost all interest in the project and left the island, never to return.

The property was acquired in sections by the state of Washington, beginning in 1964, and it became a park in 1974. Several plaques near the campground relate the history of Trimble's undertaking and point out vestiges of the once-beautiful estate.

and sand-covered children crossing their boats. Ask permission before tying onto another boat. If refused, leave, and do not feel too resentful.

For those who do allow rafting, it is often a nice opportunity to make new friends and exchange sea stories. Those rafting off should be considerate of their host's privacy and boat. Friends who meet at the park might consider tying up together, leaving dock space for others.

Tillicum Village, a replica of an Indian longhouse operated by a private concessionaire near the boat moorage area, is a major tourist attraction. Tour boats ferry visitors year round from Seattle's Piers 55 and 56 to the island for a catered salmon buffet, traditional Indian dances, and a quick view of the island. Boats run two or three times daily during the summer, less frequently from October to May. Visitors who arrive by private boat may take part in the dinner or just view the dances. In either case there is a fee, but it is well worth it.

Hikers or campers who lack boat transportation may avail themselves of the tour boat by making reservations with Tillicum Village and Tours in Seattle. It is possible to arrive on one boat and leave on a later one, permitting a longer visit to the park. Check with the tour service if you wish to do this.

But what is there to see and do on the island? For those who enjoy the out-of-doors with a large dash of marine atmosphere, the list is long. The region around the boat harbor and campground is often crowded, but with a general air of laid-back conviviality. Cruising friends rendezvous in the boat moorage; families play Frisbee on the lawn; lovers stroll the beach. For those seeking solitude there are shadowed forest trails and distant pocket beaches on the outskirts of the island. Because of its popularity the park can be enjoyed at a more leisurely pace and with more solitude if a visit can be scheduled midweek or off-season rather than on crowded summer weekends and holidays.

A grassy play area, picnic tables, shelters, fire rings, campsites, restrooms, and park ranger headquarters fill the area above the moorage. The west and south points of the triangular island have two more camping areas with fire rings, picnic tables, and a number of mooring buoys offshore. A group camp, available by advance arrangement with the park ranger, is located in the timber near the south end of the island.

The island's western point and the beach south of the campground have sloping, sandy beaches that are wonderful for swimming and wading. At low tide lucky diggers may find a few clams, although heavy use has seriously depleted their numbers. The south and southwest beaches

When entering the boat basin at Blake Island watch navigational markers in the dredged channel carefully.

are mainly cobbles beneath steep embankments of clay, while the north side is rimmed by steep cliffs that drop off to rocky slabs above low-tide sand.

Off the south end of the island, the Department of Fish and Wildlife has placed an artificial reef, hoping to attract first fish, then fishermen. The old tires and broken concrete of the reef provide nooks and crannies where rockfish can hide to protect themselves, their eggs, and their young. Organisms such as anemones, tube worms, and hydroids establish their permanent homes here and form a food chain. Such reefs have been found to be especially effective in providing spawning grounds for lingcod; there is hope that technology may be able to rebuild the Puget Sound population of this once-abundant species. Scuba diving is permitted, but check local regulations before diving. Strong tidal currents make this a dive only for the experienced.

An extensive trail system leads around the island's perimeter and cuts across the middle. Because most of the trails are old service roads, they are wide, with relatively gentle grades. The perimeter trail to the north starts immediately beyond the longhouse and meanders through the forest of Douglas-fir, spruce, and cedar, with occasional views of the beach and sound, before arriving at the open beach adjacent to the west campground. Pause here to explore driftwood, sandy shores, and a lagoon that is filled or not, according to the tides.

Returning to the timber, the trail climbs upward to the high point of the island and then continues down through the trees until it once again meets the shore on the bank above the south campground. From here it dodges back and forth between the forest and the embankment before returning to the main campground. The total distance of the perimeter trail is 4 miles. During moderate to low tides, hikers can alternate between trail and beach walks for variety.

For those who merely want a sample of the island wilderness and some insight into its history, there is a path to the site of the Trimble estate, 300 feet or so inland from the main campground, and a self-guiding nature trail, which begins

Salal plants, such as these found at Blake Island, produce berries which were used as food by early Indians.

just a short distance off the perimeter trail, west of the longhouse. The nature trail, broad and flat through open timber, identifies the local flora and tells how they were used by the Indians. Remnants of logging operations that took place during the 1850s can also be spotted by sharp eyes.

All of the trails offer chance encounters with the local animal population—deer, squirrels, chipmunks, garter snakes, and magnificent specimens of the ubiquitous slug. The local deer are quite small because of overpopulation; the island is capable of supporting only about 50, but well over 100 live here and compete for available food. Do not offer them "people food"—doing so makes them dependent on humans and further decreases their chance for survival.

The nighttime view of Seattle from Blake Island is breathtaking. The lights of the city stretch from north to south, their glow reflecting in the water, but still far enough away not to obscure the brilliance of a star-filled sky. The Space Needle is visible, as well as the lights of airplane traffic at Sea-Tac and the blaze of ferries shuttling silently back and forth across the sound. The sights will linger with you long after you have left the island.

Southworth Public Access

The Fauntleroy ferry serves the Kitsap Peninsula via Southworth, with an intermediate stop at Vashon Island. The ferry dock is located at the easternmost protrusion of the Kitsap Peninsula, Point Southworth. Immediately north, separated from the ferry landing by a wire fence, a short stretch of beach provides a public access that can be used to put in canoes, kayaks, and other hand-carried boats.

To reach the beach access, turn north on the first side road after leaving the ferry and follow the road that parallels the ferry landing (Sebring Drive) back to the water. The street dead-ends into a sandy stretch of beach at a break in the fence. There is no parking here, and only limited turn-around space, but boats can be launched after being carried across the beach. Adjacent property is private.

Harper State Park

Park area: 3 acres; 777 feet of saltwater beach on Puget Sound
Access: Land, boat
Facilities: Boat launch (ramp)
Attractions: Boating, beachcombing

Although its only facility is a launch ramp, this property is administered as a state park. To reach it from the Southworth ferry landing, follow Route 160 (Port Orchard and Bremerton) for 1 mile to where it meets Stoholton Road SE. From here turn north, staying on Route 160

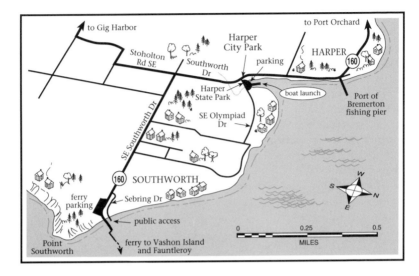

(Southworth Drive) for ¼ mile to where SE Olympiad Drive forks to the east across a saltwater finger.

At this spot the gravel beach serves as a primitive launch ramp, usable only at high tide. Pause to explore this interesting mudflat at low tide for clams and other sea creatures before going on to Harper. Parking is immediately east of the intersection.

Harper Fishing Pier (Port of Bremerton)

Access: Land
Facilities: Fishing pier, latrines
Attractions: Fishing, scuba diving

Harper, 1½ miles west of Southworth, was the original site of the ferry terminal. After the terminal's relocation to Southworth, the abandoned wharf at Harper was acquired by the Port of Bremerton and made available to the public as a fishing pier.

The fishing pier at Harper is popular with both anglers and scuba divers.

From the Southworth ferry landing follow the previous directions to reach Harper State Park. Continue a few short blocks north of the Olympiad Drive intersection to where the highway takes a sharp turn west at the Harper Fishing Pier. Parking is limited to space for two or three cars along one side of a short stub road just north of the bend in the highway.

The old pilings of the ferry landing support a thick growth of anemones, barnacles, mussels, and other marine creatures. Starfish, crabs, and a multitude of fish come to feed on the abundant life. The water is only 30 feet deep at its maximum; the bottom is sandy and gently sloping, making it an excellent spot for anglers, novice snorkelers, and scuba divers.

Olalla

Access: Land, boat
Facilities: Boat launch (ramp), latrines, groceries, fuel (service station)

Very few points for public use or access are available along the west shore of Colvos Passage. The only small boat launch on this side is at Olalla, midway down the 13-mile channel.

To reach it by land from the Southworth ferry terminal, go west 1 mile to Stoholton Road SE, then south and west, following the main highway to where it becomes SE Sedgwick Road. In about 1 mile Banner Road SE intersects from the north. Continue south on Banner Road SE; 1 mile farther south the road intersects with SE Fragaria Road.

Remain on Banner Road SE for 4 miles more as it dips and rises several times over hills and valleys—paved and pleasant, but a real workout for cyclists. The highway swings east and twists down to Olalla Bay, with long views down Colvos Passage.

Olalla consists of a combination grocery store/gas station/post office; the latter has been in operation since the late 1800s. Fishing supplies and boat fuel are also available here. A small paved parking area at the northeast end of the bridge over Olalla Bay sits just above a surfaced launch ramp. Toilets are provided at the parking lot.

The entrance to the bay is quite shallow, suitable only for small boats—in fact, it becomes a mudflat at minus tides. A rock lying outside the entrance on the north side dries at half tide.

During the 1880s the shores of the bay were the site of an Indian village. Olalla means "berries" in Chinook jargon and undoubtedly referred to the abundance of that staple food to be found in the vicinity.

At one time the community was larger, with a wharf for fishing boats and a large store offering merchandise to both fishermen and settlers. The remains of the old Olalla Trading Company is south of the bay. An elegant old mansion on the hill above Olalla—further evidence of the community's former prosperity—was built in 1914.

The community of Fragaria, which lies east of Banner Road, at the

Clam diggers head for the beach at Olalla.

end of Fragaria Road, on the shore of Colvos Passage, received its unique name from Ferdinand Schmitz—the same man who gave all that nice park property to the city of Seattle. Fragaria is the scientific name for wild strawberries, which at one time grew profusely in this region. All beach property at Fragaria is private.

Sunrise Beach County Park (Pierce County Parks)

Access: Land, boat
Facilities: Picnic tables, pit toilet
Attractions: Beachcombing, picnicking

About 1 mile north of Gig Harbor, Pierce County has acquired property with 500 feet of beachfront on Colvos Passage. The park, dedicated to the homesteaders of the property, Rudolph and Matilde Moller, is only modestly developed, with a few picnic tables on a small grassy knoll above the beach.

To reach the park, take Harborview Drive around the northwest shore of Gig Harbor. At 96th Street NW turn east to intersect Crescent Valley Drive NW in ½ mile. Go south for ¼ mile, then east on Dana Drive NW, which becomes first 94th Street NW, then briefly 24th Avenue NW, before ending up as Moller Drive NW. In 1½ miles, at the intersection with Sunrise Beach Drive NW, a sign indicates "Sunrise Beach County Park." Follow this road as it heads east and snakes downhill. In ½ mile a dirt road leads east to a field flanked by sheds and the residence of the park caretaker. A gated dirt service road drops another 100 yards downhill to the small picnic area above the beach; a short trail on the right leads to the beach.

The cobble beach, scattered with boulders, runs below a 40- to 50-foot-high jungle-like embankment. Houses and bulkheads define the north and south boundaries of the public beach. The park offers only beachcombing, saltwater views, and a primitive picnic site, but it has ample resources for future development.

Small boats can easily be beached here. Buoys offshore are private.

Gig Harbor

Access: Land, boat
Facilities: Groceries, fuel, marine repair, boat launch (ramp, slings, hoists), boat rental, guest moorage, hotels, bed-and-breakfast inns, restaurants, museum, viewpoints, stores, disabled access
Attractions: Fishing, boating, shopping, sightseeing, canoeing, kayaking, picnicking, local history

If ever there was a classic boating town, Gig Harbor must surely be it. It is the home port of the South Puget Sound commercial fishing fleet, and the beautiful, protected harbor at the confluence of Colvos and Dalco passages is the destination of thousands of pleasure boats annually. The town is a tourist's delight. Fascinating shops sell an array of goods, including arts and handicrafts (heavy on the nautical influence); taverns and restaurants range from casual to elegant; a museum displays pioneer history. Summer is a brightly colored kaleidoscope of people and boats.

By car Gig Harbor is just east of Highway 16, 4½ miles north of the Tacoma Narrows Bridge, or 18 miles south of the Southworth ferry terminal. By water it lies 20 nautical miles south of Seattle's Elliott Bay and 7 nautical miles from Tacoma's Commencement Bay.

The water entrance to Gig Harbor off the southern end of Colvos Passage is neither conspicuous nor generous. A 250-yard-long sandspit constricts the entrance to less than 200 feet wide. Its tip is marked by a small lighthouse. The narrow entrance channel is only 10 feet deep at its center at mean low tide

A charming little navigational light marks the entrance to Gig Harbor.

and sometimes has strong currents as the tides change. Heavy traffic through the channel can cause navigational gray hairs for skippers of deep-draft boats when high-powered cruisers challenge for the right to the middle of the channel.

A small public park in the heart of Gig Harbor commemorates its first settler, Samuel Jerisch. Sandwiched between major marine and commercial developments on the southeast side of the harbor, Jerisch Park has restrooms, a large deck with benches and picnic tables from which to watch the harbor traffic, and a public float for visiting boaters. From the water the park can be located by the large, conspicuous flagpole situated at its center.

The area surrounding the 250-foot-long public float and for a distance of about 20 feet to the southeast has been dredged to a depth of 5 feet at mean low water. The bottom beyond that has not been dredged and is much shallower; use care entering and leaving at low tide. The channel on the northwest side of the float next to the covered moorages is about 4 feet deeper. The square concrete float at the end of the dock is reserved for loading and unloading; uncrewed boats are not permitted to tie up

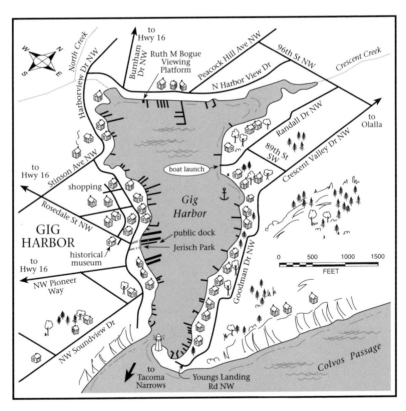

Fishing Days on Puget Sound

One of the earliest settlements on the sound was begun on the west side of Gig Harbor by Samuel Jerisch, a Yugoslavian immigrant. Jerisch and two partners, Peter Goldsmith and John Farragut, arrived at Gig Harbor in 1867, after rowing a flat-bottomed skiff all the way south from British Columbia. Although his partners decided to return north, Jerisch liked the area and decided to stay. He and his wife, a 15-year-old Canadian Indian woman, were the only settlers in the area until others began arriving in 1883. Jerisch started the local fishing industry by selling smoked fish and dogfish oil to pioneers in Steilacoom and Olympia. The oil, rendered from livers of the abundant dogfish, was used for burning in lamps.

By the end of the century a large commercial fleet of Slavonian, German, and Scandinavian fishermen was based in Gig Harbor. These men developed the purse-seining method of netting large schools of salmon. Teams of two four-man, flat-bottomed skiffs would row to the fishing grounds; while one boat remained in position at one end of the large net, men in the other would row around a school of fish and trap it. The filled nets were then hauled in by hand. There are accounts of salmon runs so large in those days that the laden nets could not be lifted into the boats. At times the men from Gig Harbor would follow the salmon runs as far north as the San Juan Islands, living in camps onshore until the season was over.

The catch was marketed locally to be served as fresh table fare, and to canneries and salteries in Seattle, Tacoma, Everett, Anacortes, and numerous other cities along the sound, where it was processed for distant markets. Often the fish were sold to passing steamers or to cannery tender boats, which then delivered them to the canneries, permitting the fishermen to return to the salmon banks to reset their nets.

The summer of 1903 saw the introduction of the first gasoline-powered purse seiner and also an automatic fish-processing machine that cleaned salmon more quickly and more cheaply than hand labor. It was the beginning of a new era.

here. Fees for overnight use of the dock may be deposited at a collection box at the head of the dock; maximum stay is 24 hours. Rafting is not permitted.

Several marinas are located along the south side of the harbor, as well as at its extreme west end; some provide guest moorage. Grocery stores, restaurants, and interesting shops are within easy walking distance of all moorages. Some restaurants have moorage floats for diners. The center of the harbor has excellent anchorages in 3 to 7 fathoms of water.

The mile-long bay was discovered by men of the Wilkes Expedition. Several small boats—gigs, as they were commonly referred to in those days—had been dispatched from the mother ship for purposes of exploration. A sudden storm forced them to seek refuge within the harbor, which thus received its name.

The Gig Harbor Historical Museum, displaying artifacts and mementos from Gig Harbor's early days, is located in the basement of the old building of St. Nicholas Catholic Church. Displays include Indian artifacts and historical memorabilia from the early fishing and logging industries. Pictures and posters show early-day Puget Sound steamboats. The museum is an easy walk from the waterfront. To reach the church from Jerisch Park, go 2½ blocks uphill on Rosedale Street, then left 1 block on Stinson Road. It is open Wednesday through Saturday from 1:00 P.M. to 4:00 P.M., or by appointment.

The classic view of Gig Harbor, with a tranquil, boat-filled bay and Mount Rainier rising above, can be seen from a viewing platform just south of the small business strip along North Harbor View Drive. The site is dedicated to Ruth M. Bogue, a longtime Gig Harbor public servant. A series of planked wooden decks with benches and colorful flower boxes extends over the beach. Shore access is via a staircase from one of the decks. The scene is especially beautiful in late afternoon and evening, when the setting sun sets the icy mountain aglow.

A diver unloads his catch of scallops at Gig Harbor.

The last rays of the setting sun light up Mount Rainier and boats moored in Gig Harbor.

Launching for trailered and hand-carried boats is available at a ramp on the north shore of Gig Harbor. The ramp can be reached by driving northeast on North Harbor View Drive along the northwest end of the bay. Where Harbor View intersects 96th Street NW (also called Vern–hardson Road west of this intersection), turn east, cross Crescent Creek, then turn south on Randall Drive NW. In ½ mile this road dead-ends into the single-lane concrete launch ramp. The ramp extends well out into the water and is usable at all tide levels. Parking is available alongside the road on Randall Drive and also adjacent to 89th Street NW. The north end of the harbor is a shallow tideflat—nice for investigating with canoe or dinghy.

The lighthouse that sits on a strip of public beach at the entrance to Gig Harbor can be reached from a public road end. Follow the above route to 96th Street NW, turn south on Crescent Valley Drive NW, then southeast on Goodman Drive NW, which ends at Youngs Landing Road NW. There is limited parking in the area. At the end of Youngs Landing Road, a staircase leads down past private residences to the beach on the east side of the spit. Only the beach and the staircase at the street end are open to public passage—respect the privacy of the adjoining property. The small concrete lighthouse was built in 1989 by a community improvement association.

CHAPTER THREE

TACOMA

The city of Tacoma is the metropolitan focal point of South Puget Sound, attracting visitors by both land and water. Within walking distance of the waterfront are neighborhoods of interesting Victorian homes dating from the 1800s, excellent examples of public architecture (both old and new), and an outstanding state historical museum. Recreation-minded visitors will find a wide spectrum of parks to enjoy, including massive Point Defiance Park, which boasts impressive historical displays.

COMMENCEMENT BAY

The Puyallup River drains into South Puget Sound at Tacoma's Commencement Bay. The broad alluvial fan formed here by centuries of river deposits serves as a vast staging area for the industries that are the city's trademark.

First noted on the charts by the Vancouver Expedition, Commencement Bay was named by the 1841 Wilkes Expedition, which used it as a base of operations and dispatched several small boats from here. Cartography efforts commenced from this point, and thus it was named "Commencement Bay" on the charts.

Browns Point Park (Tacoma Metropolitan Parks)

Access: Land, boat
Facilities: Picnic tables, restrooms, 2 mooring buoys
Attractions: Picnicking, wading, swimming, kite flying

The northeast perimeter of Commencement Bay terminates at Browns Point, a former Coast Guard facility that today is a small park administered by the Tacoma Metropolitan Park District. The community of

Opposite: *Marinas lie in the shadow of the Tacoma Dome on Thea Foss Waterway.*

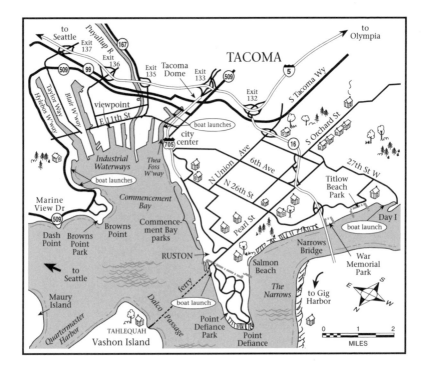

Browns Point can be reached from either the north or south via Marine View Drive.

Leave Marine View Drive at Le-Lou-Wa Place NE, signed "To Browns Point," and follow Le-Lou-Wa, then Tok-A-Lou Avenue NE ¾ mile northeast to the park at the point.

The park consists of a large lawn with scattered picnic tables and a few graceful old trees. The grass gives way to a gravel beach rimmed with driftwood at its high-water mark. At the extreme tip of the point a white concrete lighthouse still serves as a navigational aid. The beach that wraps around the point offers ideal sunbathing and pleasant wading in its shallow waters, and the frequent stiff breezes across the point lure kite aficionados. Park facilities are limited to day use only.

The caretaker resides in the old Coast Guard quarters. A one-room building north of the caretaker's residence, which houses the Points Northeast Historical Society, contains a collection of historical photos and prints. The tiny museum is open on Saturday from 1:00 P.M. to 4:00 P.M., or by appointment.

Two mooring buoys on the north side of the point accommodate visitors arriving by boat. The boat-launch ramp immediately south of the park is gated and private—for use by local improvement club members only.

Tacoma Waterways Industrial Area

Access: Land, boat
Facilities: Marinas, boat launches (ramps, slings), restaurants, fuel, guest
  moorage, supplies, restrooms, walkways, viewing tower

Dredging and landfill have converted the once-swampy Puyallup River delta and neighboring tideflats into a many-fingered industrial complex that hosts such diverse enterprises as grain elevators, pulp mills, electrochemical plants, boat building, commercial fishing, and pleasure-boat marinas. The sensory impact of the area is overwhelming—batteries of smokestacks spew steam, behemoth ships lie offshore waiting to load or offload their cargoes, chains of railroad cars whump and bump as they are coupled and uncoupled, and everywhere is the roar and clang and buzz of Tacoma earning its living.

When approaching the waterways by boat, refer to current navigation charts for waterway bridge clearances and the location of fog and visual signals. A 5-knot speed limit is enforced in all the waterways and within 200 yards of Commencement Bay shorelines. Pleasure boating should

Cyclists stop at the public viewing tower on the Tacoma industrial waterways.

be done cautiously, with an eye for the movement of commercial ships. Boats under sail in the bay might legally have the right-of-way but should not argue the point with a freighter. Paddlers in canoes or kayaks should use care not to endanger themselves, nor to impede the movements of commercial boats.

For boats in need of services, several marinas provide all necessary supplies and repairs; many have guest moorage. Two of these facilities are located on the northeast side of Commencement Bay on Marine View Drive, between Browns Point and the entrance to the Hylebos Waterway. Both have launch facilities, fuel, repairs, and marine supplies. A relatively new marina on the northeast side of the Hylebos Waterway west of 11th Street has both tenant and guest moorage, showers, restrooms, and a limited selection of groceries and supplies. Additional marinas situated within Hylebos Waterway on the northeast shore have marine repairs, floats, and some guest moorage.

Other large marinas on the southwest shore of Commencement Bay provide full services for boaters, including guest moorage and launching for trailered boats. There are two guest moorage floats on Thea Foss Waterway, one near "The Dock" (a large 2-block-long converted warehouse on the west side of the waterway, near its entrance), and a second below a seafood company near the end of the South 15th Street ramp. Both are within easy walking distance of downtown Tacoma.

For the recreational visitor there is little within the waterways except an opportunity to gape at the penultimate industrial uses of marine resources. Fishing and scuba diving are discouraged because of the concentration of chemicals that drain into the water.

A viewing tower built by the Port of Tacoma adjacent to its administrative buildings provides the public with a close look at the industrial waterfront activities. The two-story tower sits at the end of the Sitcum Waterway, overlooking the huge container cargo cranes at the Sealand Terminal and the twirley cranes and alumina domes at Terminal 7. Displays on the tower's various decks provide detailed explanations of the working waterfront. To reach the tower, turn off East 11th Street onto Milwaukee Way just northeast of where the 11th Street Bridge crosses railroad tracks, then follow signs that indicate a public access point.

Thea Foss Waterway Walkway

All Tacoma waterways seem in an eternal state of transition; the Thea Foss Waterway is no exception. Old fire-gutted docks and warehouses at the south end of the waterway are being replaced by freeway ramps and new construction.

A walkway along the west shore surveys the ever-changing scene. The 15-block-long route begins at East 23rd Street where it bends north to become Dock Street. Anchoring the south end of the walkway is a pretty

Sailing on the Thea Foss Waterway in the heart of Tacoma

little pocket park with an overlook and a few benches. The route may alter as freeway construction is completed, but in general it follows the waterfront, climbs up and down staircases, treads a boardwalk, and finally ends at Northwest Point Park. Along the way waterfront activity is ever-fascinating.

Northwest Point Park (Tacoma Metropolitan Parks)

Access: Land
Facilities: Beach, play boat, boat launch (hand carry), picnic tables
Attractions: Fishing, paddling, picnicking, beachcombing, sunbathing, wading

The north end terminus of the Thea Foss Waterway Walkway is another pretty little beachfront park. What was once a debris-laden memory of past Tacoma waterfront commerce has been transformed into a long grass-covered park, rimmed by tree-shaded picnic benches on one side, and artificial tidepools in the rip-rap at water's edge. At the north end of the park a half-moon pocket of sand and beach grass tapers gradually into Commencement Bay. The spot demands wading and sand castle building and also offers easy access for launching kayaks and other hand-carried water craft. Long-term development plans include a beachfront boardwalk and four cable-supported fishing piers extending out over the bay. Pray for funding!

Tacoma City Center

Access: Land, boat
Facilities: Marinas, fuel, marine repair, boat launch (slings), boat rentals and charters, guest moorage, groceries, supplies, hotels, stores, restaurants
Attractions: Fishing, shopping, sightseeing, museums, hiking, picnicking

There is a lot to see in Tacoma, whether you tour by car, by bicycle, or on foot. Even on a boat tour of Commencement Bay, the city is fascinating, with many architecturally unique municipal structures easily visible from the water. A 3- to 4-mile circuit via land encompasses most of the city's landmarks; allow plenty of time for dallying in parks, shops, and museums. Described here are but a few of the points of interest; others are left to surprise and delight the tourist.

South from the main business district, one of the city's newer public buildings, the Tacoma Dome, vies for attention with one of its oldest, ornately domed Union Station, dating from 1911. This grand old railroad

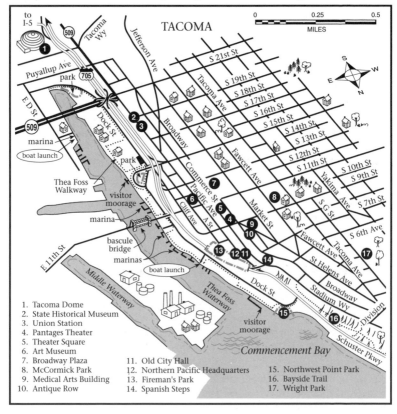

TACOMA

1. Tacoma Dome
2. State Historical Museum
3. Union Station
4. Pantages Theater
5. Theater Square
6. Art Museum
7. Broadway Plaza
8. McCormick Park
9. Medical Arts Building
10. Antique Row
11. Old City Hall
12. Northern Pacific Headquarters
13. Fireman's Park
14. Spanish Steps
15. Northwest Point Park
16. Bayside Trail
17. Wright Park

station, which had been abandoned since 1984, has been renovated and now functions as a federal court house. Portions of the building are open to the public, including the impressive marbled rotunda that features five large installations of Dale Chihuly glass. Memorabilia from the railroad's heyday are on display in the lower level. Portions of the concourse level afford views of Tacoma's waterways.

The gracefully soaring arches of the newly constructed State Historical Museum adjacent Union Station beautifully echo the older building's architecture.

Downtown Tacoma is a treasury of old buildings, some beautifully preserved and turned to new uses. The Pantages Center at South 9th and Broadway began its career in 1918 as a vaudeville theater; after years of serving as a movie house, it has now resumed its role as a theater for the performing arts. Old City Hall, built in 1893 at 7th and Pacific, now houses a complex of shops and restaurants.

Numerous city parks are scattered throughout the downtown district. Some are mini-parks with a few benches, a cool fountain, and some flowers, but Theater Square, adjacent the Pantages Center, incorporates an intriguing chain of waterfalls that cascade alongside a ramp that switchbacks down to the block below. Broadway Plaza is a 6-block-long strip with fountains, sculpture, play equipment for youngsters, and glass canopies to protect visitors from the elements.

Another of the larger parks, Firemen's Park at South 9th and A Street, commemorates a fire station that was once located in the area. Built on a lid over the Schuster Parkway, it has outstanding views of city waterways and Commencement Bay. The pride of Firemen's Park is an authentic Alaskan Indian totem pole, 83 feet tall, claimed to be the tallest in the world. A permanent photo exhibit at scattered points along the length of the park pictures and describes old-time Tacoma.

Waterfalls at Theater Square offer a cool break on a hot summer day.

Early Tacoma

The rivalry between the cities of Seattle and Tacoma has long been recognized, yet Tacoma itself grew out of a different struggle between cities. Two separate towns were established on Commencement Bay. The first, on the southwest shore of the bay, was surveyed in 1868 by M. M. McCarver, who named it Commencement City. About the time Anthony Carr platted a second settlement at the head of the bay and named it Tacoma, McCarver decided that he preferred that name for his town and initiated a political tug-of-war over the word. The two settlements were variously called Tacoma, Tacoma City, Old Tacoma, and New Tacoma—all derived from the Indian name for Mount Rainier, the peak that dominates the South Puget Sound view.

The original choice of the name Tacoma is generally credited to Theodore Winthrop, a writer who visited the Pacific Northwest in 1853. Although in his book *Canoe and Saddle* he jests about many strange-sounding Indian names, Winthrop thought the native word for Mount Rainier was beautiful and urged that name upon this new city growing in the mountain's shadow. One of the massive glaciers flowing from the summit of the mountain now bears, in turn, the name of this early author.

Along with the name dispute, the two towns competed for population, industry, and commerce. The rivalry was finally ended in 1883 when the state legislature permitted the two growing communities to merge and become a single city, named simply Tacoma.

Wander on to 27-acre Wright Park at 4th and South G Street, a botanical pleasure with colorful gardens and a greenhouse conservatory. Immediately north of here, across Division Street, is one of the city's earliest residential areas. Sandwiched between duplexes and contemporary homes are many Victorian homes from the turn of the century, with turrets, gables, ornate wooden gingerbread, and beautifully leaded windows. Some are a bit tattered, but many are lovingly maintained.

Overlooking Commencement Bay at Tacoma Avenue and North 1st, Stadium High School is housed in what was originally intended to be a French Provincial hotel in the grand manner. Begun in 1891, construction on the building ceased during the depression of 1893. It subsequently burned, and in 1906 the abandoned structure was renovated as a high school. It has served as such ever since.

The adjoining Stadium Bowl is also a major source of architectural pride. Opened in 1910, it filled a beautiful natural ravine facing out on the bay.

The city's lumber industry—which today, with shipping, is an economic mainstay of the region—was born on Commencement Bay in 1852 in a clattering, water-powered sawmill. When the Indian War made life on the bay unhealthy, and the competition of steam sawmills to the north made this primitive mill unprofitable, the owner, Nicholas DeLin, sold the property and the business foundered. The promise of a railroad brought a flow of settlers to the region, and with them came money for capital investments. By 1869 a new steam sawmill had been built on the site of DeLin's old mill—the first of several to flourish along the waterway.

The rapidly developing purse-seining industry created a demand for boats, and McCarver's little settlement, now called Old Town, became a boat-building center. By the 1920s this industry had outgrown the facilities of Old Town and moved to the tideflats near the current Tacoma Waterways Industrial Area; the boat yards were replaced by sawmills. Eventually the old buildings along the south shore of Commencement Bay suffered the ravages of fire and decay, leaving the Old Town area with a collection of deteriorating wharfs and pilings—ghostly memories of once-thriving industries.

Other business ventures contributed to the growing town. Fisheries demanded barrels to ship their catches to distant markets, and the ready supply of lumber from Tacoma's mills made this a natural site for a cooperage. Out near Point Defiance, William R. Rust bought a faltering milling and smelting operation and turned it into a money-making proposition, getting the town of Ruston named after himself in the process.

The aging athletic facility was totally renovated in 1979 at a cost of $2.5 million; just two years later, during a period of heavy rains, a storm sewer backed up and a large part of the hillside washed away—and along with it, a large part of the stadium. The stadium was subsequently restored yet another time.

Bayside Trail

A cool, green interruption in the gray tedium of the city, this 2½-mile, woodsy trail is sandwiched between Schuster Parkway and Stadium Way. The city-end trailhead is on Stadium Way at its intersection with South 5th Street; there is ample parking along the street. All trail accesses are marked with unobtrusive carved wooden posts; watch closely when driving by or you may miss them.

Midway trail accesses are along Stadium Way at Division Avenue, where there is parking for a couple of cars at the trailhead, and at Stadium Way

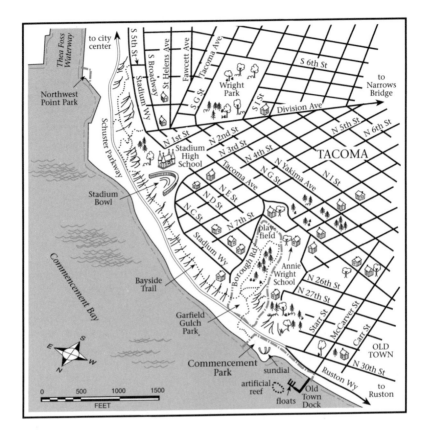

and North 4th, off a paved road (no turn around) that heads down into the end of Stadium Bowl, immediately west of the old Washington State Historical Museum parking lot. Leave cars in the parking lot or along the street. The access trails that descend to Schuster Parkway cannot be used to begin hikes, because stopping cars is not permitted along the busy highway.

Skirting the bayside bluff, the trail offers some brief views of Commencement Bay before ducking into the forest. Blackberry bushes and maple trees provide a nice green covering. One glade is filled with towering columns of slender maples, their trunks entirely draped in ivy. Although the view of the city is lost, its sounds are not; the jangling of industry and the crunching and bumping of railroad cars blends with the soft twitter of birds. At one time wooden shelters were spaced along the route to provide places to rest and picnic; all have been destroyed, and their sites, unfortunately, are now garbage pit remnants of transient campsites.

Near its midpoint the trail picks up a wide brush-bound swath that once was the bed of a railroad serving the industrial waterfront. After swinging along the bay for 1½ miles, the trail bends into the green swale of Garfield Gulch Park, where the final mile of trail loops up one side of the ravine and back down the base of it. Here the sounds of the city are finally muted by distance and dense vegetation, and the hiker is more conscious of the calls of birds and the rustle and creak of the forest. Maples 200 feet tall soar skyward, ivy entwines, and flowers carpet.

At the head of the gulch, a spur trail leads to another trail entrance at North D Street and Borough Road. Good parking is found along the street. Nearby is an open, grassy park with play equipment for children, a softball diamond, and a basketball court.

For those wanting further exercise and a different view of Commencement Bay, leave the gulch trail at its lower intersection beside Schuster Parkway, follow the street under the overpass, cross the railroad tracks, and head left to Commencement Park, just a block away.

Ruston Way Waterfront Parks (Tacoma Metropolitan Parks)

Access: Land, boat
Facilities: Fishing pier, artificial reef, guest float, mooring buoys, picnic tables, restrooms, children's play areas, historical displays, scenic viewpoints, fitness course, concession stands, restaurants, disabled access
Attractions: Fishing, boating, picnicking, beachcombing, sunbathing, swimming, wading, jogging, bicycling, skating

You must visit Ruston Way parks, if for no other reason than to marvel at the many ways Tacoma recreates—strolling, walking, jogging, or being carried grandly in a backpack. Wheeled recreation runs the gamut from unicycles to bicycles, tricycles, three-person pedi-cabs, wheelchairs, roller skates, and in-line skates. The sparkling, marine-oriented parks, fishing piers, and other recreational attractions are interspersed with a few restaurants, concession stands, shops, and small buildings that house professional offices. Sunny benches beckon to passersby, and on hot days occasional pockets of sandy beach invite swimmers and waders. The wide,

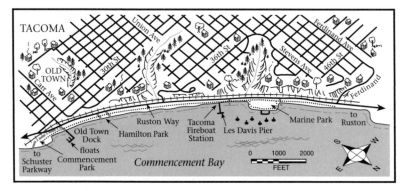

Fishing at Les Davis Pier on Ruston Way

level sidewalk provides a long, scenic excursion. Hikers can connect this path to the Bayside Trail, as described previously, for even more exercise.

Ruston Way is reached from downtown Tacoma by following Schuster Parkway, which ends at the southeast end of the waterfront. McCarver Street joins the midpoint of Ruston Way, and Pearl Street intersects its northwest end. Parking is in numerous lots distributed along the street.

In the early days of Tacoma the southwest shore of Commencement Bay, along Ruston Way, was its maritime and industrial heart, lined with wharfs, warehouses, and factories. As commerce moved to the tideflats at the head of the bay, many of the old piers and buildings located here fell into disuse. Some burned and were left as mouldering hulks—visual and commercial blights.

In recent years urban renewal programs have removed rotted pilings and ratty piers and rebuilt some 2 miles of waterfront along Ruston Way. Only a few short segments of the old waterfront remain as of 1996, and these are also scheduled for renewal.

Boaters have not been neglected in the restoration. There are guest floats alongside Old Town Dock, and six mooring buoys have been located offshore from Marine Park. They are exposed in heavy weather but offer a nice spot for an overnight stay in the calm weather more typical of the area.

Restaurants that have taken advantage of the pier restorations offer waterfront dining, ranging from casual to formal. Many of these restaurants also have floats that welcome visiting boaters.

Commencement Park. Tacoma's string of waterfront parks begins with Commencement Park, at the west end of Schuster Parkway. At the top of the park's grassy knoll, a huge metal sculpture is sure to pique curiosity. Is this some sort of religious monument, possibly part of a Druid ceremony? Not quite, but close—it's a giant ring sundial, a unique center of interest for the park.

The embankment encircling the sundial has benches, a nice view of Commencement Bay (and above it Mount Rainier), and an interesting display describing the history and geology of the area. Toddlers can conduct their own geological explorations in the pair of sandboxes tucked along the outer edge of the knoll.

The east end of the beach is gently sloping sand—nice for wading, sunbathing, or swimming. The sand fades into rock and boulder shoreline that extends west 2 blocks to the opposite end of the park.

Old Town Dock. Adjoining Commencement Park on its west end, at the intersection of Ruston Way and McCarver Street, is Old Town Dock, which has forsaken its commercial beginnings and now is a public fishing pier. An artificial reef placed in the vicinity helps increase the fishing odds. Covered benches and tables at the far end of the pier encourage picnicking and lolling. For boaters wishing to drop by and stroll uphill to Old Town or tie up for the night, concrete floats off the east side of the pier have moorage space for half-a-dozen boats.

Three blocks uphill is Old Town (known as Commencement City in early days), where Tacoma was born. A few of the early buildings remain, including the Slavonian Union Hall, a reminder of the fishermen who brought purse-seining methods to the sound from Europe.

Major construction underway at Marine Park

Hamilton Park. Continuing past Old Town Dock, in 2 blocks Ruston Way arrives at tiny Hamilton Park—a grassy mound above a rock bulkhead, with a solitary picnic table, benches, and a jogger's exercise station. Beyond is a currently undeveloped section of waterfront that is slated for restoration and development.

Tacoma Fireboat Station. The Tacoma Fireboat Station is located near the end of North 38th Street. Fast, modern, 70-foot-long hovercraft fireboats are moored here, while a retired old-style fireboat now sits on land as an attraction for sightseers.

Les Davis Pier. Northwest from the fire station is the 300-foot-long Les Davis Pier. The end of the T-shaped fishing pier has a rail drilled to hold fishing rods and mounted with fish-cleaning plates. Puget Sound weather is acknowledged by six small shelters—four protecting benches and the remaining two covering cleaning stations. Concessions, bait and tackle, and restrooms can be found at the shore end of the dock.

Marine Park. Marine Park runs northwest along the shoreline. A series of small, sandy pocket beaches is tucked below the rock bulkhead that fronts the narrow park. As it continues along Ruston Way, the grassy ribbon has benches, picnic tables, and more fitness course stations. A pier has been filled in to form a wide grass lawn that lures sunbathers and Frisbee tossers. Picnic tables and flower-filled planters form a pretty border. A U-shaped boardwalk extending out above the beach holds benches that offer water views north across the bay and up Colvos Passage and west across the industrial waterways to Mount Rainier. The park (and the waterfront redevelopment) finally come to an end at North 49th and Ferdinand Street, just southeast of the site of the old Asarco smelter in Ruston.

Point Defiance Park (Tacoma Metropolitan Parks)

Park area: 698 acres; 18,500 feet of shoreline
Access: Land, boat
Facilities: Zoo, aquarium, botanical gardens, tennis courts, volleyball court, picnic shelters and tables, hiking trails, logging museum, Fort Nisqually historical restoration, children's fantasy land, children's playground, restaurant, shops, marina, boat launch (ramp, elevator), boat rental, boathouse, scenic viewpoints, disabled access
Attractions: See above and choose for yourself

This is without a question the greatest park on all of Puget Sound. With nearly 700 acres, it is the largest of Tacoma's parks—even larger than nearby, wonderful Northwest Trek. In fact, it is the second-largest metropolitan park in the country, surpassed only by New York City's Central Park. But it is not mere size that makes Point Defiance great. The park's diversity provides something for every age and nearly every recreational predilection. It seems incredible that the park can offer so much and still retain much of its wilderness character.

If one were to criticize the park at all (although to some this may seem blasphemous), it would be on the grounds that it does too much, even for its size. On sunny weekends Point Defiance is hard-pressed to accommodate the crowds it attracts. Cruising young people, engaged in modern courtship rituals, take over the pond and lawns near the entrance, and motorcycles and blaring stereos invade Owen Beach. Traffic is heavy, and parking lots and restrooms throughout the park are jammed. As with any well-loved park, to truly savor all it has to offer, visit on an off day, or off-season.

Point Defiance has been in the business of being a park for a long time. Originally the site of a military reservation, 640 acres of the peninsula were set aside for the public in 1888, and a boathouse was built here in

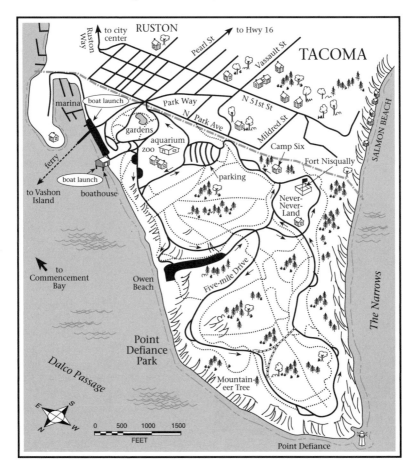

1890. In 1905 the city was given clear title to the land for use as a park. An aquarium opened here in 1936. Developments, improvements, and additions have been made regularly since that time; the most recent was a multimillion-dollar series of renovations to the zoo and aquarium.

For visitors from outside the Tacoma area, the park is most easily reached by taking Exit 132 (Bremerton, Highway 16) from I-5. In 3½ miles take the 6th Avenue Exit (Ruston, Vashon Ferry). At 6th Avenue go 2 blocks to the west, where Pearl Street leads north 3¼ miles to the park entrance.

Nearly all park roads are one-way loops. The outer drive is a 5-mile scenic route that includes strategic pull-offs at the end of the peninsula with dramatic views across South Puget Sound and the Tacoma Narrows. The end loop is restricted to use by bicycles and foot traffic on Saturdays from 9:00 A.M. to 1:00 P.M. All manner of cyclists take advantage of this opportunity, including entire families all the way down to kiddies vigorously pedaling with training wheels.

Just inside the entrance to the park is a large lily pad pond with adjoining formal gardens. The Japanese garden to the right of the road features traditional landscaping and a pagoda.

Beyond this is the zoo—not huge by big-city standards, but tastefully done with a fine sense of what is interesting and pertinent. The newly remodeled facility has a strong emphasis on animals native to the Pacific Rim, in their natural surroundings. For visitors whose interests lie with the marine aspects of the sound, the aquarium is a "must-see," with a well-displayed collection of the fascinating creatures that inhabit the beaches or lurk in the nooks and crannies beneath the water.

Beyond the zoo a side road drops down to Owen Beach, and the scenic tour begins, first inland among primeval forest, then skirting the bluff edge to occasional viewpoint pull-outs. At the very tip of the point a sign relates the origin of the name Point Defiance—it was here in 1841 that Lieutenant Charles Wilkes looked out across the confluence of the channels and noted that cannons placed here and at Gig Harbor across the way could defy the world. Although the point itself was never armed, the original use of the peninsula as a military reservation was based on that idea.

A sea otter at the Point Defiance Zoo

From Point Defiance the view sweeps north, up Colvos Passage.

Miles of hiking paths crisscross the woodland; most are marked, but all eventually intersect the road. A hiking circuit of park uplands, following trails and roads along the outer periphery, covers only about 7 miles but can take forever, with time allowed to stop and explore all there is to see. For the observant nature lover, the pleasures are legion: a dismembered pine cone marks the presence of a squirrel; a concentration of droppings near the base of a tree indicates the favorite perch of an owl; wildflowers nod in moss-encrusted crannies.

Because the entire park is on a bluff jutting 200 feet above the sound, beach access from above is quite limited. The only ways to reach the shore are at the boathouse and at Owen Beach. Old de facto paths down the steep sandy bank west from Owen Beach are dangerous and cause needless erosion; the park discourages their use.

On the west side of the point, near the end of Five-mile Drive, are more man-made attractions. Never-Never-Land has scenes of fairy-tale fantasies, expertly created in wood and concrete in a natural forest setting, that manage to avoid most of the schmaltz of commercial kiddylands and are fun for grown-ups as well as children.

Next door is Fort Nisqually, a replica of a Hudson's Bay trading post circa 1833. Here, too, youngsters can put their imagination to work by climbing the ladders of the two-story blockhouses and conjuring up visions of hostile Indians lurking outside the walls; the major difference between this and Never-Never-Land is that the setting is real. Two buildings—the granary and the proctor's house—are original structures, moved here from the actual site of the fort near Dupont, 11 miles to the south. The log palisade wall with its blockhouses, as well as several buildings within the walls, are authentic re-creations. The proctor's house is now a museum filled with interesting historic artifacts.

The Hudson's Bay Company flag flying from the parade ground pole points out that this first settlement on Puget Sound was a British post on then-British soil. On the north side of the grounds rests the boiler from the steamer Beaver, which was brought to the Northwest in 1837 by the British to assist in their attempts to discourage American maritime intrusions into the area.

Down the road ¼ mile from Fort Nisqually is yet another museum, but of quite a different sort. Camp Six is an outdoor display of actual machinery and railroad equipment used during the days of steam logging. Bunk rooms atop flatcars, a fire car, a yarder, loaders, a spar pole,

Fort Nisqually, at Point Defiance Park, is a re-creation of a stockade used during the Indian War.

donkey engines, and a massive 300-ton Lidgerwood skidder are located along a short section of railroad track looping through the woods. Housed in a shed is the Fabulous Shay Number 7, the first geared locomotive in the western forests, invented by F. O. Shay in 1880 and built in 1928. Steam-powered train rides around a short section of logging train track through the nearby woods are a popular feature.

So much for inland attractions; Point Defiance also has its share of water-oriented facilities for fishing, boating, and various beach-associated diversions.

A road dropping downhill from the park entrance to the shore at the northeast end of the park ends at the loading ramp for the Vashon Island ferry. Immediately east of the ferry ramp is a paved, three-lane, public boat-launch ramp with an adjacent lot for parking boat trailers. Be aware that this lot is for trailers only; vehicles must park in another lot west of the ferry ramp, where there is also additional trailer parking.

The marina east of the launch ramp provides fuel, propane, and ice, plus overnight moorage at four long floats attached to a concrete pier. Beyond the marina the Tacoma Yacht Club has extensive private floats; its distinctive clubhouse is on the end of a long breakwater (built of slag from the Tacoma Smelter) that protects the marina and yacht basin.

West of the ferry terminal is an immense, 3-block-long boathouse, a replacement for one that burned down in 1984. The east wall of the boathouse carries a series of permanent posters describing the long and checkered history of the facility. An octagonal-shaped restaurant on a large deck at the east end of the boathouse has views of the comings and goings of the Tahlequah ferry, as well as other boat traffic in Commencement Bay and Dalco Passage.

The boathouse includes a bait and tackle shop, snack bar, boat rental shop, and fuel float. The interior of the two-story building is a warren of long corridors lined with lockers for small-boat dry storage. Open elevators at the outer edge of the deck are for boats to be launched and hauled out; ramps leading down to several floats permit hand launching of small boats. At the end of the pier, adjacent to the boat elevator on the west end, fishermen congregate, making one wonder how any fish could possibly escape the minefield of hooks dangling below.

West of the boathouse the shoreline can be walked, with some cooperation from the tide, for 2 miles to the end of the point. An abandoned road below the timbered bank parallels the beach for a ¾-mile stretch to Owen Beach. Any marine life on the tidelands has long since been carried away by beach users, but low-tide excursions offer the rewards of discovering water-washed agates, engineering sand castles, or simply skipping rocks from the sand and gravel expanse.

Owen Beach, which can also be reached by road from above, is a ¼-mile-long band of soft sand edged by driftwood. The break in the high bank caused by a ravine permits the sun to arrive early and linger late. In summer, sunbathing is a major activity, in addition to swimming, wading, picnicking, fishing, and snoozing. An aged bathhouse is no longer functional, but it is preserved as a historical structure; a picnic shelter and numerous picnic tables are nearby.

West of Owen Beach the cliffs of sand and clay sweep swiftly upward for 200 feet. As it heads toward the end of Point Defiance, the sandy beach narrows, disappearing entirely at high tide. The only trail leading up the steep bluff is a ¾-mile trail from Owen Beach. Beyond here rising water may dictate a retreat.

A light and foghorn mark the rocks extending from the end of the point, a favorite spot for both shore and boat fishing. South of the point beaches are even more narrow, with no upland exits of any sort for tide-trapped beach walkers. Beware.

THE NARROWS

South of Point Defiance the waters of all the southern reaches of Puget Sound are funneled through a deep, narrow, 4-mile-long underwater canyon. Timid sailors approach the tidal currents of the Tacoma Narrows with trepidation; knowledgeable sailors treat it with respect. Even for boaters who have traveled it many times, the mile-wide channel, with its churning water and spectacular bridge, must cause a quickened heartbeat and a tightening of the hand on the helm.

From any point of view the bridge is awesome, with a central span more than ½ mile long, a vertical clearance of 180 feet at its center, and two giant pylons towering nearly 500 feet above the water of the narrows.

The tidal currents in the narrows display the perverse nature of many of the currents in South Puget Sound waterways. An underwater shelf near the east end of the Tacoma Narrows Bridge blocks tidal currents that flow south and tends to make them run in a counterclockwise circle at the north end of the narrows. Consequently, ebb tides are stronger on the east side of the channel, and flood tides stronger on the west side. Boaters will make better way if they follow the west shore when headed south and the east shore when headed north. Currents in excess of 5 knots can be encountered at the south end of the channel; tidal current charts should be consulted for specific daily predictions.

Immediately south of Point Defiance Park, on the east shore of the narrows, is the small community of Salmon Beach—a string of houses perched on pilings and displaying a spectrum of architectural anachronisms. "Quaint" is definitely an understatement. The houses are also unusual in that their only land approach is by steep (private) trails descending the clay cliffs. The community offers no recreational possibilities, but it is definitely worth seeing for passing boaters.

With spinnakers billowing, sailboats race under the Narrows Bridge.

War Memorial Park (Tacoma Metropolitan Parks)

Access: Land
Facilities: Formal garden, disabled access
Attractions: Scenic viewpoint, scuba diving

Its name indicates that the purpose of this park is to honor war veterans. While it does accomplish that with its memorial plaques and floral gardens, the park's main points of interest are its close-up views of the Tacoma Narrows Bridge and the access it provides to scuba diving sites.

To drive to the park, take the Jackson Avenue Exit, the last exit from Highway 16, east of the bridge. Follow North 10th Street along the north side of the highway to the park. Past the park entrance, the road ducks under the bridge to reach the flower gardens and viewpoint on the south side, high above the water.

The bridge pilings and rocky ledges along the east side of the 150-foot-deep channel create a spectacular underwater site for scuba divers.

Bridging the Narrows

During the early part of the century, vehicle traffic across the narrows traveled by ferry from Titlow Beach to the landing at the mouth of Wollochet Bay. As the city grew, and with it demands for residential real estate, the idea was born to build a bridge across the channel to open up development of the Gig Harbor area.

And so one was built. Economic constraints made it necessary, however, to cut a few corners here and there. When the bridge was open for use in July 1940, it seemed a bit flimsy. In fact, persons driving on it during a crosswind had the interesting (and unnerving) experience of feeling it buck like a horse and seeing cars ahead of them drop down into a valley and reappear at the crest of a hill. By the time winter came the bridge had already been nicknamed Galloping Gertie. On November 7, 1940, as a nice little winter storm brewed up out of the south, winds reached 42 miles per hour. The overstressed span finally snapped, dumping a couple of cars (whose drivers had run for their lives) and an unfortunate dog (who had been left behind) into the channel.

Determined to do it right the second time, engineers took 10 years to redesign and rebuild the span, while ferries resumed service between Titlow Beach and Wollochet Bay. In October 1950 the new bridge—Sturdy Gertie—was completed.

Crannies harbor octopus and wolf eels, as well as a wide variety of fish. Only the experienced should attempt to dive here, due to the swift current and eddies. To reach the water, park at the viewpoint and walk the gated road that heads down to the Western Slopes Treatment Plant, or hike a primitive trail from the southeast edge of the parking area at the gate. The beach can be accessed from a continuation of this trail that leaves the last switchback above the plant, or at the plant itself. Either route leads to the railroad tracks, which must be crossed to reach the shore. Watch for trains when crossing the track: rail traffic here is frequent and fast!

Tacoma Narrows DNR Beaches

Three public DNR beaches are located along the west shore of the narrows. Beach 36—2,600 feet long—runs northwest from the navigational light on Point Evans. The cobblestone beach, which tapers to gravel at low tide, supports a few clams and some red rock crab. Beaches 1 and 1a, 2,300 feet long and 900 feet long, lie below sandy cliffs northeast of Point Fosdick. These, too, are cobble with some clams and rock crab.

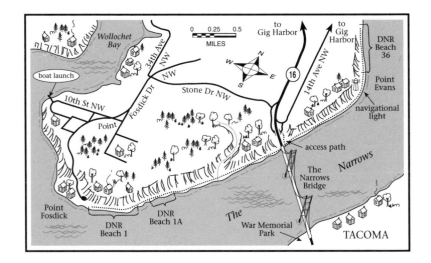

All three beaches can be reached on foot via a steep, slick, boot-beaten path that descends a brushy ravine beneath the west end of the Tacoma Narrows Bridge. From there follow the shore north or south to the DNR beaches. To reach the path, drive west in Tacoma on Highway 16; take the first right after crossing the Tacoma Narrows Bridge (Stone Drive NW), and circle right under the bridge. Here there is limited parking next to a Department of Transportation storage area for at most four to five cars.

The walk can be made at all but high tide. All uplands are private. The narrow beaches lie below near-vertical bluffs that range from 100 to 300 feet high with no upland access. Plan beach walks carefully to avoid being endangered by high water.

Titlow Beach Park (Tacoma Metropolitan Parks)

Park area: 58 acres; 2,800 feet of shoreline
Access: Land, boat
Facilities: Picnic shelters and tables, kitchens, swimming pool, wading pool, tennis courts, volleyball court, horseshoe pits, fitness trail, softball diamond, children's playground, lagoons, beach, restrooms, community center, underwater reef, outdoor shower, disabled access
Attractions: Picnicking, fishing, swimming, beachcombing, jogging, scuba diving

This nice little metropolitan park has many attractions for local residents—tennis courts, a swimming pool, picnic facilities, and a pair of lagoons filled with ducks clamoring to be fed—but it is just as interesting for tourists, offering a couple of miles of trails, a long beach, and, just offshore, some of the best scuba diving on South Puget Sound.

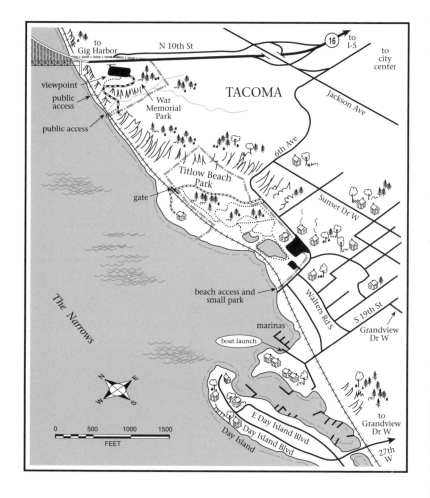

To reach the park follow Highway 16 toward the Tacoma Narrows Bridge. Take the Jackson Avenue Exit from Highway 16, and follow Jackson Avenue south for 1 block to 6th Avenue. Turn west on 6th Avenue and follow its twists downhill for ¼ mile to Titlow Beach.

The park's trail is actually a fitness trail with several loops for different levels of ability and way stations for stretching muscles. It is also a pretty nature walk, skirting the edges of the lagoons and then wandering on through shrubbery and timber. The longest loop trail is 1¼ miles; side trails can make it longer. Enjoy the sights, but slow-paced walkers should yield to joggers.

The main body of the park is separated from the beach by Burlington Northern railroad tracks, and a high wire fence along the tracks prevents direct access to the beach. A trail heading north parallel to the tracks ends at a road. On the beach to the left are the buildings and launch ramp of a private boat club, all fenced and gated—no beach access here either. The road to the right loops back to the park.

The only place where the beach portion of the park can be reached is at the south end of the park where 6th Avenue curves west, crosses the railroad tracks, and dead-ends just above the water. Here is a tiny park with benches, picnic tables, an outdoor shower for scuba divers, and interpretive displays describing the subtidal and intertidal zones and the species to be found there. Barnacle-encrusted pilings standing in disarray just offshore are remnants of the old ferry dock that was used by the ferry that ran between here and Point Fosdick before the Tacoma Narrows Bridge was built.

The beach is rocky—not inviting for either swimming or sunbathing—but it does offer tideland exploration north for ½ mile to the park boundary. Fishing is good from either beach or boat. Small boats can be carried from cars for launching, but use care as tidal currents can be very strong. The waters offshore have been declared a marine sanctuary—no fauna, flora, or archeological objects may be removed from the area (food fish regulated by the Department of Fish and Wildlife excepted).

Old pilings, such as those offshore at Titlow Beach, harbor different

Decrepit pilings at Titlow Beach are all that remain of the old ferry dock.

Octopuses like this large specimen photographed at the Seattle Aquarium are often found in South Puget Sound waters.

types of underwater life that can tolerate the brighter light and occasional low-tide exposures. Brightly colored hydroids, lacy white sea anemones, and feather-duster worms make the pilings resemble exotic gardens. Although many of the plankton-feeding animals found on pilings are permanently attached, some sea anemones are capable of moving slowly along on their single foot.

Red Irish lords, cabezons, and schools of shiny little pile perches graze among the pilings, nibbling on soft-bodied invertebrates. In summer the water near Titlow Beach may have heavy concentrations of red jellyfish, which can give swimmers and scuba divers a nasty sting.

Day Island

Access: Land, boat
Facilities: Marinas, fuel, ice, marine supplies, boat launch (ramp)
Attractions: Fishing

Several commercial marinas located just south of Titlow Beach, near the entrance to the Day Island lagoon, have some marine and fishing supplies for visiting boaters, but all moorages are permanent. A launch ramp

Octopuses and Others

The dark, subterranean caves of Puget Sound shelter what is believed to be the world's largest concentration of octopuses, as well as the largest individual specimens. While some species measure mere inches, males of the *Octopus dofleini* species commonly grow to a diameter of 7 feet. Individual specimens have been reported that measured in excess of 20 feet and weighed nearly 100 pounds.

Its bizarre appearance is no doubt responsible for its bad reputation, but in fact the octopus is a shy creature with intelligence that is rare for this level of invertebrate. This not-too-distant cousin of the clam is believed capable of curiosity, friendliness, fear, anger, and even a sense of humor. Many scuba divers who once looked on the octopus as a challenging trophy now respect it as a fascinating underwater compatriot.

At one time octopus wrestling was considered a worthwhile sport along Puget Sound, but many of the unfortunate creatures that were captured died later. They may now be taken only for food use, and divers are not permitted to use a spear or any device that will mutilate the animal.

Another inhabitant of the murky caves of the sound is the wolf eel, whose ferocious expression and formidable size (up to 8 feet) command instant respect. Although this fish is known to be very timid, divers rarely try to develop a meaningful relationship with a wolf eel, for the eel's strong jaws can inflict a serious injury.

operated by one of the marinas provides small-boat access to this side of the narrows, for a fee. To reach it from 6th Avenue, turn south on Walters Road South for ¼ mile, then turn west on South 19th Street for a couple of blocks to the marina areas.

Day Island, which is joined to the mainland by a marshy spit and a permanent bridge, encloses a long, shallow lagoon. The channel into the lagoon shrivels to a mere 1 foot deep at low tide, and the enclosed bay itself is not much deeper. The slender island is totally residential, with no public water access.

CHAPTER FOUR

CARR INLET

Once past the Tacoma Narrows, South Puget Sound spreads out into a jigsaw puzzle of inlets, with short-cut passages running behind and between islands. Carr Inlet, which takes a hard right past Fox Island and heads north, is perhaps the most recreation-oriented of the waterways. There are two large state parks on its shores, as well as an island-based marine state park and a smattering of other public accesses.

The inlet was named for Lieutenant Overton Carr of the Wilkes Expedition, not (as one might expect) for Job Carr or his brother Anthony, who both played an important part in Tacoma's early history. Peter Puget and his crew were, of course, the first Europeans to see the channel. One

Mount Rainier rises above Carr Inlet.

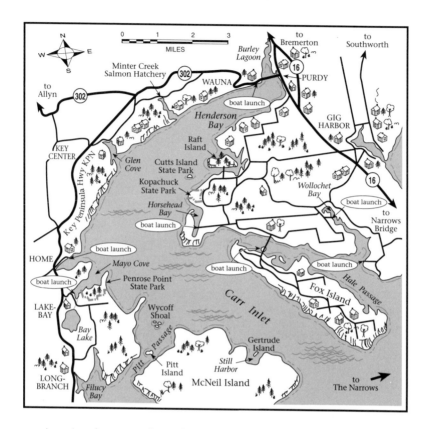

can imagine the sense of wonderment felt by this small band of men after rowing through the stricture of the narrows as an entire inland sea opened up to them.

HALE PASSAGE AND FOX ISLAND

Mile-wide Hale Passage separates Fox Island from Wollochet Bay and the Kitsap Peninsula mainland. This favorite fishing area offers chinook salmon year-round in the channel and off both ends of Fox Island. Steep walls around the island support some of the most beautiful seascapes to be found on South Puget Sound and make it a favorite scuba diving ground, but the strong currents on the north and east sides require intermediate to advanced diving ability. Heavy boat traffic in the channel is an additional hazard.

The fixed bridge at the north end of the channel has a restricted clearance of 31 feet, preventing passage of many sailboats. A shoal that bares at low tide lies 350 yards east of the bridge on the south side of the channel and is marked by a buoy on its northeast side.

Wollochet Bay

Access: Land, boat
Facilities: Boat launches (ramps)
Attractions: Fishing, scuba diving, canoeing, kayaking

While egocentric white men usually choose geographic place names to honor friends or patrons or politicians, the more literal-minded Indians chose place names with descriptive significance. Mount Rainier, with its massive glaciers, was known to Indians as Tahoma, or "father of the waters." Chilacum (later anglicized to Steilacoom) meant "place with the pink flowers." And Wollochet, which was named VanderFord's Harbor by Charles Wilkes, literally translated, was the inelegant "bay of the squirting clams."

The few clams and oysters remaining today along the 2½-mile-long bay are on private tidelands, for the shores are now a Tacoma suburb. The only public accesses are two boat-launch ramps, one near the entrance to the bay on the east side, and a second near the much shallower northwest end of the bay. Both are more suitable for launching hand-carried boats than trailered ones. The access near the bay's entrance, just around the corner from the old ferry landing at Point Fosdick, was a site used by steamers in the late 1800s to deliver freight and mail to the Wollochet area.

To reach this access (if approaching from the north on Highway 16), turn on Wollochet Drive NW at the Gig Harbor interchange and drive south 2 miles to East Bay Drive NW. Turn southeast and follow East Bay Drive NW south for 4 miles along the east side of the bay as the road

A board sailor tests the wind in Wollochet Bay.

progressively changes names to 25th Street NW, 34th Avenue NW, Stone Way NW, and Point Fosdick Way NW. Beyond Stone Way ½ mile, turn west from Point Fosdick Way onto 10th Street NW and follow it downhill ½ mile to a paved boat-launch ramp at Berg Drive NW and Berg Court NW. Beaches on either side of the ramp are conspicuously posted as private. There is no place to turn a trailer around near the ramp, and the only parking is alongside the road a few blocks uphill from the ramp.

To reach the ramp from Tacoma, turn right immediately after crossing the Tacoma Narrows Bridge and follow Stone Drive NW to its intersection with Point Fosdick Drive NW, then drive south to the 10th Street NW intersection.

To reach the second public access, on shallower water, follow Wollochet Drive NW to its junction with 40th Street NW, and continue south on Wollochet Drive along the west shore of the bay. Turn east on 37th Street

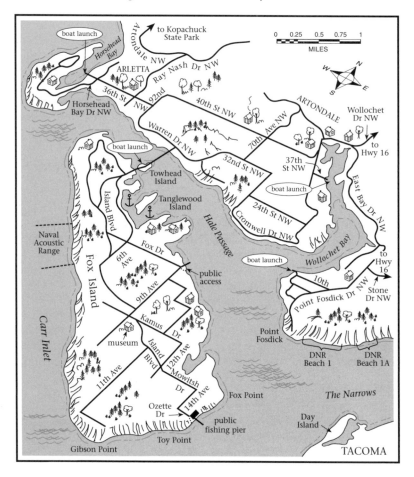

NW, which leads steeply downhill to a paved launch ramp at the street end. There is no turn-around space and no street-side parking east of Wollochet Drive.

Fox Island

Access: Land, boat
Facilities: Boat launch (ramp), museum, fishing pier
Attractions: Fishing, scuba diving

Early settlers on Fox Island were farmers and fruit growers, who lived a self-sustained life with little need to visit the mainland. The ferry that ran from Titlow Beach to Point Fosdick also served Fox Island during its early years. The construction of the bridge across Hale Passage in 1954 ended the island's isolation, and it became a popular suburban residential area with beachfront homes and acreages for people employed in Tacoma and Gig Harbor. With the exception of a fishing pier on the south end of the island, there are no public recreation areas, either inland or along the shores; the few public beach accesses are used primarily by fishermen and scuba divers.

From the Gig Harbor Exit on Highway 16, highway signs (and realtor advertisements) mark the 3-mile route to Fox Island via Wollochet Drive NW, 40th Street NW, 70th Avenue NW, 32nd Street NW, and Warren Drive NW to the Fox Island bridge, at the north end of Hale Passage. The south bridge abutment actually touches down not on Fox Island but on tiny Towhead Island, which is joined to the larger island by a sandspit. The public-access area located on Towhead Island has a surfaced boat-launch ramp and parking for a dozen vehicles with trailers.

Scuba diving is excellent among the numerous concrete bridge pilings and around the bouldery reef to the east. Sea perch feed on the dense piling growth, while cabezon and lingcod seek the protection of reef crannies.

A second small island, Tanglewood, lies east of the bridge near the Fox Island shoreline. The island was once used by Indians who placed their dead in canoes lodged in tall trees, according to their custom. Early white settlers called it Grave Island, but a fruit grower who planted orchards there at the turn of the century gave it its present name. Boaters can find good anchorages on either side of Tanglewood Island in the quiet, protected cove known to early settlers as Sylvan Bay, but all shorelands are private.

The site of the old Fox Island ferry terminal provides another access for scuba exploration of underwater walls along Hale Passage. From the bridge, follow the main road, Island Boulevard, for 1½ miles to Fox Drive and turn east on it. In 1 mile the old ferry dock sits off a sharp right-angle turn. The dock is posted as private. On the east side of the dock a metal stairway leading down to the beach provides saltwater access. Limited parking is available just west of the dock.

A longtime Fox Island landmark was "The Concrete Dock" midway between Fox Point and Gibson Point on the southeast end of the island. The old monster of a dock, originally built for ferry access to the island, was an instant failure because the location was too exposed to weather and tidal currents. The landing was relocated to the east side of the island. The Department of Fish and Wildlife has removed the old dock and, as of 1996, is in the process of replacing it with a new fishing pier. Fishermen and scuba divers have traditionally congregated in this area to harvest the bounty of South Puget Sound. Chinook salmon and an abundance of bottomfish are found offshore from Fox Point to Gibson Point and on to Toliva Shoal. For divers an extravaganza of marine life grows on limestone ledges and canyons down to a depth of 100 feet.

To reach the pier by land, follow Island Boulevard for 3¼ miles from the bridge to its intersection with 9th Avenue, turn south and drive ¼ mile, then turn east on Kamus Drive for another ¼ mile. Take the right-hand fork here, again Island Boulevard, which eventually becomes Mowitsh Drive at the intersection with 12th Avenue in another ¾ mile. Follow the public road as it turns south onto 14th Avenue, which

A log cabin, totem pole, and old wagon are among the many relics displayed at the Fox Island Historical Museum.

The Legend of the Mud Babies

According to Indian legends, a beautiful young maid often played on the beach near the west end of Fox Island. A handsome young brave who was the son of the Old Man of the Sea wooed her and claimed her as his bride. He took her away to live with him in Tolivia Shoal, his home under the sea. Although she returned to visit her parents a few times, each time her appearance took on more of the form of the sea creatures with which she lived. Her parents finally told her not to return. However, when she becomes lonesome for her old home, she is said to come back to the beach and fashion pebbles and mud into bird and animal shapes, as she did when she played there as a girl. People walking the beaches can sometimes discover these strangely shaped mud babies.

becomes Ozette Drive just before it dead-ends at the fishing pier parking lot, 2 miles from 9th Avenue. Parking space here accommodates a couple dozen cars; restrooms adjoin the lot. Paths lead to the fishing pier and down to the beach. The buoy in the channel between here and Steilacoom marks Toliva Shoal.

On the west side of Fox Island, in Carr Inlet, the U.S. Navy maintains an acoustic range. The test area, marked by buoys, is restricted and should be avoided by boaters.

Fox Island played a major role in the early history of South Puget Sound. Back in 1855, when the terms of the Medicine Creek Treaty were established, the island seemed suitably remote and undesirable enough to be assigned to the Nisqually and Puyallup tribes as a reservation. By the mid-1860s, with the Indian War a fading memory to white settlers, much of the island property was sold by the Indians, who left the confines of the reservation for the mainland. One 135-acre parcel of prime land was reported to have been exchanged for a horse and saddle.

Fox Islanders' interest in the area's past is reflected in a historical museum, housed in a large, new building behind the fire station. Follow Fox Island Boulevard to the intersection of 9th Avenue and Kamus Drive, and continue south on 9th Avenue for 50 yards beyond the intersection to the signed entrance of the museum parking lot. The museum is open Monday, Wednesday, and Saturday from 1:00 P.M. to 4:00 P.M.

EAST SHORE

Because of their easy access from Tacoma via the Narrows Bridge, and from Gig Harbor, recreation areas on the east shore of Carr Inlet are somewhat more heavily used than those farther down the sound. The shoreline is heavily residential, with many homes having docks with boats poised for a quick escape to favorite boating or fishing grounds.

Highway 16, which rushes quickly from the Narrows Bridge to Purdy, at the end of the inlet, provides the major avenue of land access.

Horsehead Bay

Access: Land, boat
Facilities: Boat launch (ramp)
Attractions: Fishing, canoeing, kayaking

Geological tombolos, which are quite common throughout Puget Sound, are sandspits, built up over a long period of time by wave action, that permanently join former islands to nearby islands or to the mainland. The long hook of land enclosing Horsehead Bay at the northwest end of Hale Passage is an example of this phenomenon. It is actually the land formation itself that is shaped like a horse head, but over time the name has been transferred to the slender bay it protects.

Beaches surrounding Horsehead Bay are all private, but a public launch ramp on the east shore provides water access. To reach the ramp from Highway 16, follow road signs for Fox Island, but at 70th Avenue NW, instead of turning south continue straight ahead on 40th Street NW. In 1½ miles the road bends south and becomes 92nd Avenue NW. At an intersection in ¼ mile turn west on 36th Street NW and continue past Arletta to where 36th Street NW intersects Horsehead Bay Drive NW.

Roadside parking is available along the west side of Horsehead Bay Drive in the vicinity of the intersection. The launch ramp itself is located where the extension of 36th Street NW drops steeply down to the water. A turn-around area (no parking) is provided immediately above the ramp. All surrounding property is private.

Kopachuck State Park

Park area: 103 acres; 1,500 feet of shoreline
Access: Land, boat
Facilities: Picnic sites, 5 picnic shelters, 41 standard campsites, group camp, restrooms, trailer dump station, 2 mooring buoys, artificial reef, designated Cascadia Marine Trail campsite, disabled access
Attractions: Camping, picnicking, beachcombing, clamming, wading, swimming, scuba diving, hiking, canoeing, kayaking

This park has a cool, forested campground and one of the best public beaches to be found on South Puget Sound—all that and summer eves lovely enough to inspire poetry as the setting sun spreads its glow across Carr Inlet and finally drops behind the black phalanx of Olympic peaks.

Kopachuck State Park can be reached by leaving Highway 16 from either of two Gig Harbor exits that are also signed to the park. Follow signs marking the 6-mile route along back roads to the park entrance.

All campsites lie on an upper road that loops through a timbered flat some 150 feet above the beach. Views of the beach and Carr Inlet are blocked by the tall forest. A restroom with showers is in the center of the campground loop. A trail from the west edge of the campground road intersects the lower road and eventually leads down to the beach.

A lower road loops around the group camp area and ends in a huge day-use parking lot. Wooded picnic sites and a restroom sit just below the parking area, and a gated service road drops steeply down to the beach. At the lower end of the service road are more restrooms (with showers), small picnic shelters, and some picnic tables with views of the beach. A primitive Cascadia Marine Trail campsite is located just above the beach at the south park boundary.

The hiking trail through the uplands that interconnects with campground road is short, but pleasant. Sun filters through tall fir and alder onto paths lined with salal, false Solomon's seal, and sword fern. Fall brings the promise of some huckleberries—if you get there before the birds.

The long beach is rocky and strewn with driftwood at the high-tide level, but low tide exposes a stretch of gently sloping sand. In summer, water flowing over the shallow tideflat warms to temperatures bearable for wading and swimming. Clam populations are somewhat depleted, but visitors may like to try for a tasty meal. The park is one of several on the sound where geoducks are being reintroduced; the beds are being

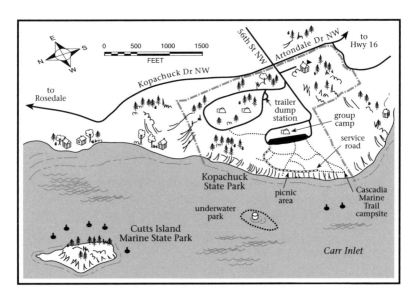

Clam diggers try their luck on the Cutts Island beach, offshore from Kopachuck State Park.

protected from harvest for several years until the clams reach adequate size and number. Be sure to check regulations and restrictions posted along the service road before heading for the beach with shovel and bucket.

Offshore, two mooring buoys accommodate visiting boaters. Only boats light enough to be carried down from the parking lot can be put in at the park. The nearest ramp for trailered boats is at Horsehead Bay, 1½ nautical miles to the south.

About 200 yards offshore the seabed drops off steeply to the 9-fathom level. This area has been designated as an underwater park for use by scuba divers. An old barge that has been sunk in 50 feet of water increases the opportunities for underwater exploration.

Cutts Island Marine State Park

Park area: 5½ acres; 2,100 feet of shoreline
Access: Boat
Facilities: 10 mooring buoys, artificial reef, pit toilet, no water
Attractions: Beachcombing, clamming, swimming, scuba diving, canoeing, kayaking

By virtue of being accessible only by boat, Cutts Island is designated as a marine state park. However, it lies so close to the mainland that it

A sailboat makes use of one of the mooring buoys at Cutts Island Marine State Park.

seems to be more of an annex to Kopachuck State Park. The ½-mile distance between the two parks is an easy paddle, but use a little caution—in a heavily loaded boat it can be farther than it looks.

With its distinctive tuft of scraggly firs above a 40-foot sheer cliff of eroding glacial till, Cutts Island qualifies as the most scenic of South Puget Sound state parks. Wide, level tideflats surrounding the island are rocky on the east, merging into sand on the west. A long sandbar extending from the northeast point of the island reaches nearly to Raft Island at extreme low tide. Clamming may be more productive here than at Kopachuck State Park, but the rocky beaches demand greater effort for the reward.

Ten mooring buoys are located around the south and east sides of the island. Overnight camping is not permitted because the area is without water and restrooms. A single latrine toilet at the south end of the island is for use by the desperate.

Cutts Island is shown on some early navigation charts as Deadman's Island, as it was once used as a burial ground by Indians who would place their dead in the trees to mummify—a wonderful tale to relate to wide-eyed kids as evening mists settle over the anchorage.

HENDERSON BAY

The last navigable part of Carr Inlet, Henderson Bay, ends abruptly at a rock jetty crossed by the highway. Beyond here the inlet trickles out into the drying mudflat of Burley Lagoon. These tideflats north of the jetty support commercial oyster production, and the owners are as hostile to visitors' encroachments as were the Indians when Lieutenant Peter Puget and his men visited here. The beach on the south side of the jetty is public, however, and is a popular source of oysters and clams at low tide, as well as a prime spot for boardsailing. There is ample parking space on the wide shoulder along the south side of the highway.

In recent years an added early spring attraction has been a group of gray whales that have appeared for a few days in the bay for a side excursion during their annual coastal migration. News media usually announce when the whales are seen.

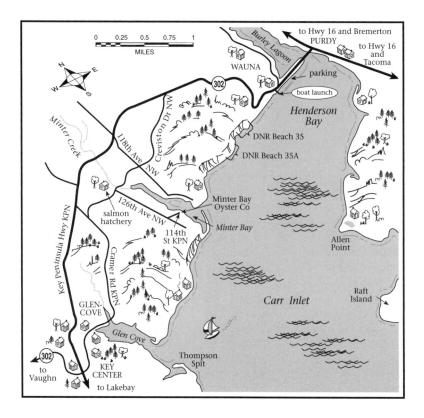

Wauna

Access: Land, boat
Facilities: Boat launch (ramp)
Attractions: Fishing, boardsailing

A boat-launch ramp at Wauna, at the west end of the jetty, provides ready access to Henderson Bay. Leave Highway 16 at Purdy and drive west across the jetty on Highway 302. Immediately west of an old store, a steep road leads down a concrete launch ramp to the water. Parking is available (but limited) in the immediate vicinity.

Two public DNR beaches, accessible only by water, are situated along the north side of Henderson Bay, approximately halfway between Wauna and Minter Creek. Beaches 35 and 35A, which are both private above mean high tide, have some littleneck clams and geoducks at the sandy, low-tide reaches.

Minter Creek Salmon Hatchery

If you have ever hauled a silvery beauty out of the waters of Puget Sound, or merely enjoyed one at the dinner table, you will undoubtedly be interested in seeing how they begin and what Washington State is doing to improve the harvest. Take Highway 302 west from Purdy for 4½ miles, then turn south on 118th Avenue NW. In ½ mile turn west on Creviston Drive NW and continue another ½ mile to Minter Creek and the state salmon hatchery.

The hatchery, which has recently been rebuilt and modernized, produces over 10 million salmon annually. Salmon production starts at a roofed area on the west side of the rearing ponds, where eggs are stripped from female salmon, fertilized, and placed in incubation frames in tanks housed in the building behind the ponds. The newly hatched salmon remain here until the yolk of the egg is absorbed and they start feeding. The fingerlings are then transferred to a series of outside holding tanks, segregated by age and type of salmon. One of the major hazards to fish rearing prior to the remodeling was predation by birds, raccoons, and otters; the new raceways (rearing ponds) are higher off the ground, well fenced, and protected from above by frames and wires, which significantly reduces hatchery losses.

The hatchery is open to visitors between 8:00 A.M. and 4:30 P.M. daily. Crews can be watched as they feed the fish, tag them, and check the tag coding used to track the released fish for information feedback.

Minter Bay, just below the hatchery, dries to a mudflat at low tide. It is the site of commercial oyster beds; no public access is available to the bay, although the oyster company is open to public visits and sales midweek during working hours.

Board sailing on Henderson Bay, near Wauna

Glen Cove

Midway along the west shore of Carr Inlet, 2 miles southwest of Minter Creek, is Glen Cove, a small inlet that has a few protected anchorages in shallow water. The intimate cove makes an ideal destination for canoes and kayaks put in at Kopachuck State Park, 3 nautical miles away, directly across the inlet. There are no public launch facilities for trailered boats on the cove, but a breach in the bank on the south side of the cove near the Glen Cove Hotel permits launching of hand-carried boats at high tide levels. The small adjacent parking area is county property.

The Glenn Cove Hotel, on the southwest side of the cove, is a Registered National Historical Landmark, now operated as a bed-and-breakfast inn. It was built in 1897 by Nick Peterson; the depression of 1893 forced closure of logging and brickyard enterprises in the area and made the innkeeper business an attractive alternative. The ornate hotel was built with hand-crafted workmanship and was elegantly furnished. It has been restored to its Victorian prime and is open for paid tours during afternoons on weekends.

WEST SHORE

Life slows along the Key Peninsula shoreline of Carr Inlet. Homes are fewer than on the eastern shore, and the ambiance is more rural. Land access is from Highway 302 via the Key Peninsula Highway KPS, which runs to its southern tip.

Von Geldern Cove

Farther down the west shore of Carr Inlet, 14 miles southwest of Purdy via the Key Peninsula Highway, is the village of Home, whose quiet, rustic demeanor belies its early history as a nineteenth-century "hippie" colony. Home was founded in 1896 as a Utopian community populated by outspoken exponents of anarchy, free speech, yoga, spiritualism, nudity, and free love. After fourteen years of harassment by less free-thinking politicians and newspaper editors, the colony disbanded, accused of anarchist bombings and victimized by a sanctimonious press.

A concrete launch ramp on the Home waterfront provides public access to Joe Bay and Von Geldern Cove. Just north of the bridge over the end of the cove, turn on A Street. In ½ mile, at the junction with 8th Avenue North, is a pull-out at the launch ramp with parking space for about a dozen cars. The bay is extremely shallow west of the launch ramp, and a long shoal extends from the north shore into the entrance to the cove.

Mayo Cove

Access: Land, boat
Facilities: Marina, boat launch (ramp), groceries, guest moorage

Penrose Point State Park shares Mayo Cove with the village of Lakebay. To reach the small community, continue south from Home on the Key Peninsula Highway KPS for ¾ mile to its intersection with Cornwall Road KPS. Turn east and wend steeply downhill to Delano Road KPS and the head of the cove, where there are a few residences and a marina that is built on pilings over the water. Lakebay derives its name from Bay Lake, 1 mile to the south, which drains into Mayo Cove.

A boat-launch ramp located north of the marina pier is reached from the end of a narrow road near some adjoining houses. The lower portion of the ramp is covered with sand and is only marginally usable unless you are using a four-wheel-drive vehicle. The marina offers fuel, bait, guest moorage, and a limited selection of groceries.

The water approach to the marina and the floats at nearby Penrose Point State Park can be tenuous for deep-draft boats at low tide. A sandspit that projects well into the cove from the northeast must be given adequate berth before turning into the head of the cove itself. The best anchorages are near the northeast shore of the cove.

Penrose Point State Park

Park area: 152 acres; 11,751 feet of shoreline
Access: Land, boat
Facilities: 83 campsites, group camp, picnic tables, picnic shelters, fire rings, restrooms, showers, nature trail, hiking trails, trailer dump station, float, 8 mooring buoys, disabled access
Attractions: Camping, hiking, fishing, clamming, swimming, beachcombing, canoeing, kayaking, nature trail

One might think that Penrose Point had been designed by Mother Nature specifically as a waterfront park, so ideally suited is it to its role. Despite its relatively small size, the park has nearly 2 miles of gentle beaches, along with ample uplands for a forested campground and a couple of miles of hiking trails. Inside the long arm of the point lies Mayo Cove, offering ample anchorage for boats, well protected from gusty southerly winds. Low tide reveals the best feature of the park—a ½-mile-long sandbar paralleling the point, with clams and seaweed and all sorts of squiggly things to investigate.

To reach the park from Lakebay, turn south on Delano Road KPS and

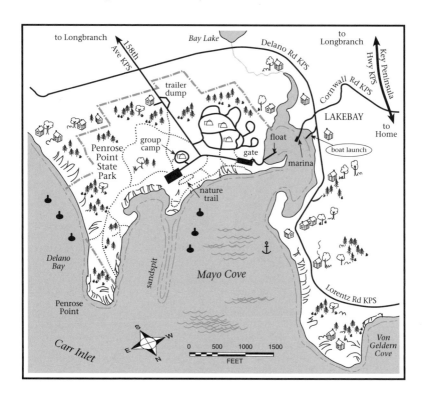

Alders and huge maple and cedar trees tower above picnickers at Penrose Point State Park.

drive 1 mile to its junction with 158th Avenue KPS. Turn left (north) and in ¼ mile reach the state park entrance. The route is well signed.

Inside the park entrance a branch road to the left leads to the campground, while the main road goes straight ahead. At a T-intersection turn right and pass the group camp to reach the day-use area—a broad, grassy lawn with picnic tables, fire rings, and plenty of space to spread picnic cloths or blankets on the ground. Additional tables and a picnic shelter are nearby in the shade of stately firs. The adjacent beach is sandy and shallow—ideal for a summer dip.

From the T-intersection the left fork of the road heads west to a parking area on the bank above the small harbor. More picnic tables and another shelter are located in a broad grass strip between the parking area and the high bank above the cove. A service road drops down to beach level where there is a float with space for six to eight boats, another shelter, and more picnic tables. Three buoys sited in deeper water offshore from the drying sandspit and five more on the east side of the park give added moorage.

A network of about 2 miles of trails weaves through the timber and brush between the access road and the beach. A nature trail loops through the woods above the beach near the entrance to the picnic area parking lot. A dozen numbered stations along the way are keyed to an informational brochure available at the bulletin board by the picnic area or from the park ranger.

Paths between the group camp and ranger station are broad and well marked, as is the one that leads to the east-side beach. Spurs from the latter that head to the west-side cove and out to the end of the point are more primitive, but most eventually lead somewhere if followed persistently. Major trail junctions are marked by posts labeled A through F, but the beach ends of these trails are unmarked and very obscure. The main attraction of the trails, however, is not where they lead, but what can be seen along the way—huge Douglas-firs, a trickling creek, nodding trilliums, a marsh blazing with skunk cabbage blossoms, birds, squirrels, and who knows what else.

A beach on the east side of the park is headed by a high bank and impenetrable brush but it is accessible by trail from marker A at the picnic area parking lot. The extreme end of Penrose Point is not part of the park. On the east, the boundary of this private property is marked by a pipe embedded in concrete on the beach near where a trail emerges from the woods. Boaters moored on this side of the park or beach walkers looking for an upland return can locate this trailhead about 200 yards north of the most northerly mooring buoy. There is also a large, white pole marking an underground cable located where the trail breaks onto the beach.

A few oysters, clams, and mussels may be found on beaches on either side of the park, but the best intertidal exploration is the ½-mile-long sandspit in Mayo Cove that is exposed at a minus tide. Because this is a heavily used clamming beach, the mollusks are somewhat depleted and digging can be a lot of work for a little success.

If you take beach life of any sort, do so only if you intend to consume it. State law requires that holes dug in the beaches must be filled. Do not rely on the incoming tide to do the job for you, because small invertebrates exposed to the sun may die in the meantime. Regulations about taking shellfish are usually posted on a bulletin board near the restrooms by the picnic area.

CHAPTER FIVE

Nisqually Reach

Beyond the Tacoma Narrows are two east–west water thoroughfares, separated by Anderson Island, that lead to the Western Inlets. One route threads between McNeil Island and Anderson Island via Balch Passage, then doglegs to the left into Drayton Passage between Anderson Island and the Key Peninsula. The second route, somewhat longer but broader, swings south of Anderson Island before heading northwesterly to Johnson Point.

Although this chapter describes all of the waterways and abutting lands in this midsection of South Puget Sound, the name Nisqually Reach technically applies only to the portion of the wide southern channel where it

Ferryboats link Anderson and Ketron islands to Steilacoom.

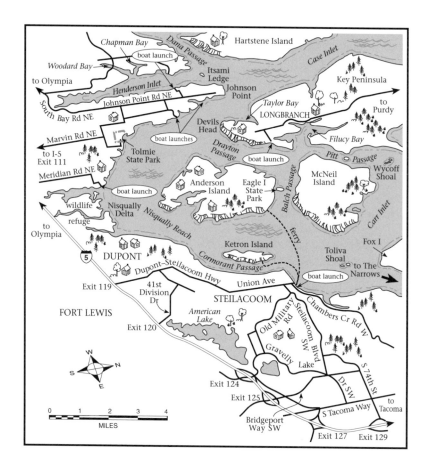

curves in a 180-degree arc along the head of the Nisqually Delta. By land, nearly all the area is but a short hop from exits on I-5, which skirts its southern shore.

These channels are noted for outstanding salmon fishing, especially where tidal eddies around points of land and channel entries build feeding grounds. As a result, a number of commercial and public launch facilities are available along adjoining shorelands; some marinas also have boats for rent. In several areas fishing is also excellent from shore or docks.

Four islands are located here: McNeil, which houses a former federal penitentiary currently being operated by the state; Ketron and Anderson, which are entirely private; and tiny Eagle Island, which is a marine state park. A second state park, Tolmie, is located on the mainland between Nisqually Head and Johnson Point.

On the southern shores of Nisqually Reach, a broad salt-marsh delta, formed where the Nisqually River flows into the sound, is a national wildlife refuge. Here flocks of waterfowl pause to rest and feed in their migratory flights along the Pacific coast. The refuge is a resource for wildlife education and recreation and the scene of bird hunting during the fall.

THE STEILACOOM REGION

This area could certainly be considered the cradle of Puget Sound settlement. In 1824 a contingent of Hudson's Bay Company representatives, scouting the West Coast for possible trading post sites, visited the Nisqually Indian village of Chilacum, at the present location of the town of Steilacoom. On the recommendation of this survey the area's first white settlement, Fort Nisqually, was established near the mouth of the Nisqually River in 1833 by the British-owned business. After that fort was destroyed by Indians it was relocated, in 1843, to a site 5 miles south of Chilacum on a hill overlooking Nisqually Reach near Sequalitchew Creek.

Six years later two American ministers and their families built a Methodist mission near the fort. The first white baby on Puget Sound, Francis Richmond, was born here in February 1842.

The Treaty of 1846 settled the American–British jurisdictional dispute, making all of Puget Sound country part of the United States' Oregon Territory. In 1849, in an effort to protect settlers from hostile Indians, a detachment of troops was sent here; they occupied some abandoned buildings on a hillside above Chambers Bay. Fort Steilacoom, which was built on this site, remained a major protective stronghold for white pioneers throughout the Indian War. It was abandoned by the Army in 1870 when such protection was no longer necessary.

Steilacoom

Access: Land, boat
Facilities: Groceries, stores, fuel, marine repair, boat rental, boat launch (ramp), fishing pier, restaurants, historical museums, ferry
Attractions: Boating, fishing, sightseeing, picnicking, shopping

With shattered dreams of economic importance and residential prominence, Steilacoom looks wistfully back to a time when it was the most important settlement on South Puget Sound. In 1851 Captain Lafayette Balch first built a wharf and general store on the slight bay near the site of the Indian village of Chilacum. Balch had brought the lumber and goods for the enterprise by ship all the way from his home state of Maine. He named his new settlement Port Steilacoom, but a rival commercial development, Steilacoom City, was established slightly to the west just a few months later by John B. Chapman. Eventually the competing entrepreneurs joined forces, and in 1854 the town of Steilacoom became the first to be incorporated in the newly formed Washington Territory.

The town, in fact, claims a long string of territorial "firsts": the first Protestant church north of the Columbia (1853), the first jail (1858), and the first public library (1858). By the end of the 1850s it was the fastest growing community on Puget Sound, the home of a busy shipping industry, and center of settlement for pioneers who chose to live near the protection of Forts Nisqually and Steilacoom during these times of Indian unrest.

The pin that popped the Steilacoom bubble was its rejection, in 1873, as a terminus for the Northern Pacific Railroad. Businesses fled to the north to become part of the Tacoma boom. In 1895 an electric trolley line from Tacoma to Steilacoom gave the city new hope as it became a popular seaside resort for vacationers from Tacoma and Olympia. When the railroad did finally come to Steilacoom in 1912, it dealt the city a near-death blow, for it located its tracks along the shore and destroyed the waterfront summer homes, resorts, and recreational beaches, effectively separating the town from the beach.

Steilacoom can be reached by car by leaving I-5 at Exit 129 (South 74th, South 84th) 4 miles south of Tacoma. Go west on South 74th Street for 1 mile to South Tacoma Way, then south another mile to Steilacoom Boulevard SW (Historical Road Number 1). Here turn west and follow Steilacoom Boulevard into the heart of town. An alternate route leaves I-5 at Exit 124 (Gravelly Lake Drive). Drive north on Gravelly Lake Drive 1¼ miles, west on Washington Boulevard SW for 1½ miles, then northwest on Old Military Road, which becomes Stevens Street just inside the city limits.

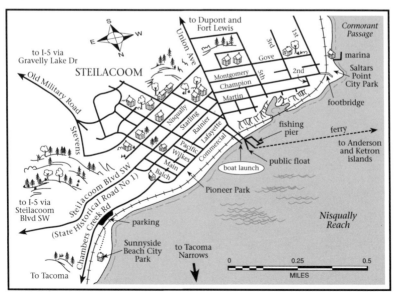

By boat, Steilacoom is 6 nautical miles southwest of the Tacoma Narrows Bridge. Anchorages offshore are not recommended because the holding ground is poor and currents can be quite strong. Small boats should use extreme care when the direction of the wind opposes that of the current; at such times offshore tide rips can be quite dangerous.

Today the town's prime claims to importance are as the terminal for the ferries to Anderson, Ketron, and McNeil islands, as a suburb of Tacoma, and as the site of the state mental hospital on the nearby grounds of the old fort. For visitors, Steilacoom's major attractions are the numerous old homes that can be viewed on a walking or bicycle tour of town. A very active historical museum association is responsible for the preservation and restoration of many of the pioneer buildings, three of which are listed on the National Register of Historic Sites.

One of the most fascinating of these historic structures is Bair Drug and Hardware, a combination museum and soda parlor located on the corner of Wilkes and Lafayette, about 3 blocks uphill from the ferry landing. Visitors can stroll in to admire a multitude of goods—from mustache cups to patent elixirs—displayed just as they were in Victorian times. Historic items are not for sale, but sticks of candy and gummy jujubes are still sold, and the 1906 soda fountain still dispenses phosphates and ice-cream sodas. The clerks will cheerfully relate the history of the store to those interested. A monument commemorating the site of the first Protestant church north of the Columbia River has been erected just behind the drugstore.

A museum that displays artifacts from pioneer times is located in the

Indian artifacts are displayed at the Steilacoom Tribal Cultural Center.

basement of the town hall, a block north of Bair Drug on the corner of Main and Lafayette. It is open Tuesday through Sunday from 1:00 P.M. to 4:00 P.M. The meeting room of the town hall, also open to the public, has an interesting series of enlarged photographs taken during the early days of the town.

A second museum features displays, photos, artifacts, and archeological recoveries relating to Indian tribal history. This facility is located at the corner of Lafayette and Pacific in the old Oberlin Congregational Church, now the Steilacoom Tribal Cultural Center.

One of the national historic sites, the Nathaniel Orr Home, dates from 1857 and has been fully restored using many of the original furnishings. Located at 1811 Rainier Street, it is open for viewing during the summer on Sunday from 1:00 P.M. to 4:00 P.M.

An elegant Queen Anne-style mansion, The E. R. Rogers Home, at 1702 Commercial Street, was a private home when it was built in 1891. It later became an inn; today it is open as a fine restaurant. Nearby, at 1706 Commercial Street, the charming cottage that was the William Webster Home, built in 1854, is the oldest structure still existing in Steilacoom.

Pioneer Park, on a grassy bluff along the north side of Commercial Street between Wilkes and Main streets has inviting benches that provide a pleasant spot to stop and have a picnic lunch or simply to enjoy the splendid view down Carr Inlet and beyond to the high peaks of the Olympic Mountains. A large wood-decked overlook has an interpretive sign identifying the geographic features within view. This park was once the site of a two-story log house that in 1853 was used as the town's first school. A second nearby park, dedicated to longtime community activist Charles R. Buchanan, links Pioneer Park to the Steilacoom Tribal Center with a pair of decks and a stairway through evergreens, lilacs, and Oregon grape.

At the foot of Union Avenue is the landing for the Anderson Island ferry. On the east side a small float is open for loading and unloading small boats. Next to it a narrow passage under the railroad tracks ends in a launch ramp (fee) for trailered boats. Parking for boat trailers is permitted immediately south of the railroad tracks, and a parking lot for cars is available across the street.

The Clyde B. Davidson fishing pier extends out along the west side of the ferry dock. The lighted pier is a popular spot for crabbing as well as fishing.

Sunnyside Beach Park (Steilacoom City Parks)

Access: Land, boat
Facilities: Beach, picnic tables, restrooms, open shower, volleyball courts, children's play area, disabled access
Attractions: Swimming, picnicking, scuba diving, fishing

On the northern outskirts of Steilacoom, at a slight bulge in the shoreline, is Sunnyside Beach. To reach it from Union Avenue, follow Lafayette Street northeast out of town for 1½ miles to a parking lot on the west side of the road next to the railroad tracks. Walk across the tracks to reach the beach. A gravel path leads to the restrooms and permits beach access for disabled persons.

A large, grassy area shaded by tall poplar trees forms the heart of the park. The long, sandy beach, dappled with driftwood, is ideal for summer

The beach at Saltars Point Park is reached via a wooden footbridge.

sunbathing and swimming. There are no boat-launch facilities, but light-weight boats can easily be carried from the parking lot to the beach for put-ins and paddling nearby water.

The park is sometimes a starting point for scuba divers who wish to explore the steep canyons of the channel and the multitude of old pilings along the shore. Toliva Shoal, a rocky reef 2 miles to the north marked by a red-and-black navigational buoy, is a popular diving and salmon fishing site, although there are strong currents and tide rips in the vicinity.

Saltars Point Park (Steilacoom City Parks)

Access: Land, boat
Facilities: Picnic shelter, restrooms, marina
Attractions: Picnicking, fishing, sunbathing

A second Steilacoom city waterfront park is located at Saltars Point, west of the ferry terminal. From Union Avenue drive west on Martin Street, turn south on 2nd Street, then west on Champion Street to 1st Avenue. There is only street parking. A wooden footbridge at the corner of 1st and Champion leads over the railroad tracks and down to the small day-use park.

Although the park has a picnic shelter and a single picnic table, driftwood provides ample places to spread a portable feast. The gravel beach drops off quickly, making it a fine spot for beach fishing.

Immediately west of the park beach is a marina that has bait and tackle, rental boats, fuel, and a snack bar. The bridge over the tracks provides the only land access to the marina.

There is no fence separating the park from the railroad tracks. Keep an eye on the kids, as trains do whiz by.

Ketron Island

George Vancouver slept here, as did Peter Puget. They both landed on this slender island during their reconnaissance of Puget Sound, and Vancouver fittingly called it Long Island. It was later renamed by the Wilkes Expedition for Hudson's Bay trader William Kittson; from there the name degenerated to Ketron.

The ½-mile-wide channel of Cormorant Passage separates the island from the mainland. With steep cliffs bounding most of the beach perimeter and dense timber masking the few homes on top, the island has a decided aura of privateness. A Pierce County ferry makes four daily runs from Steilacoom to Ketron, but all roads are inland and there are no views for sightseers.

From the water, Ketron Island looks today much as it did when George Vancouver and his crew visited it.

Anderson Island

Access: Land, boat
Facilities: Freshwater swimming beach, picnic area, marine park, historical museum
Attractions: Bicycling, fishing, boating, swimming, hiking, historical point of interest

Anderson Island is so fiercely private that recreational use is virtually nonexistent; those facilities that do exist are primarily meant for use by residents. Mainland access is via a Pierce County ferry from Steilacoom, and that may well be the nicest part of the trip. Once on the island, you may drive, bicycle, or walk the roads, visit a museum, or take a pleasant hike to one public beach—and then go home, unless you are planning to stay at one of the island's nice bed-and-breakfast inns. Islanders are friendly folk who wave as they pass on the road, but they clearly do not encourage a large influx of tourists.

The ferry ride to the island takes only about 20 minutes, but the boat is scheduled at roughly one-hour intervals; plan ahead for proper timing

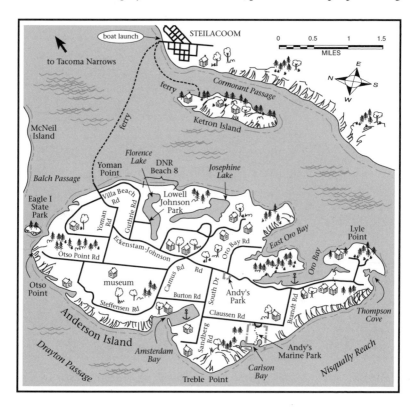

Anchorage in Anderson Island's Oro Bay

for your trip. The newest, largest ferry accommodates about 55 cars; older boats that are sometimes pressed into service hold about half that many. Purchase tickets in advance of boarding in the restaurant by the dock at Steilacoom. There is no fee upon departing the island.

A public DNR beach that has no upland access and must be reached by boat lies along the east side of the island beneath an abrupt cliff, ¼ mile south of Yoman Point. The combination of a sharp drop-off about 500 feet offshore and strong tidal currents makes this an unattractive anchorage, but boats can be beached when the tide is low enough to expose the 2,500-foot-long sand and gravel beach.

The only bay of any size that marks the shore of the island is Oro Bay, located on the southeast corner—and it is shallow and exposed to the rake of tidal currents and southeasterly weather. The western arm of the bay offers some protection, although it is quite shallow; Peter Puget sought shelter here from a storm. In good weather, it can be a pleasant anchorage that offers a knockout view of Mount Rainier. Enter between a pair of red-and-green buoys that mark the entrance along the north side of the bay to avoid a long submerged spit extending from the south side of the entrance. All the shoreline on the bay is private, so there is no way to go ashore.

Amsterdam Bay, on the northwest side of the island, is a smaller indentation in the shoreline, but it does offer some anchorages well protected from southerly winds. Local knowledge is necessary to attempt the narrow entrance to a larger, shallow inner bay, which is nearly isolated by a long sandbar. The entrance channel dries at minus tides.

Lowell Johnson Park. Visitors exploring the interior of Anderson Island will find a few interesting tidbits. Lowell Johnson Park is located on the north shore of Florence Lake. The gravel road leading down to the park is ¼ mile east of the intersection of Guthrie Road and Eckenstam–Johnson Road, just east of a Lutheran church. A sign arching over the road proclaims "The Old Swimmin' Hole." The park has a sand volleyball court in a large grassy bench above the beach, a couple of picnic tables in the cool shade of firs, two small swimming beaches with a small triangular dock, and a swim/dive float in a roped swimming area. It is a welcome respite to cyclists on a hot summer day.

Andy's Park. A tiny wildlife preserve with three picnic tables and a pit toilet is located at the junction of Oro Bay Road and Eckenstam–Johnson Road, where Schoolhouse Creek trickles through a boggy grassland. There is room for at most one car to park, so the park's primary attraction is as a lunch or snack stop for bicyclists. Most of the park is densely overgrown with Himalayan blackberries that discourage exploration of its perimeter.

Andy's Marine Park. The only public saltwater beach access on the island is at Andy's Marine Park. To reach it, 2¼ miles from the ferry landing turn west off Eckenstam–Johnson Road onto Sandberg Road. In

Wooden walkways lead across damp spots to reach the beach at Andy's Marine Park.

another ¾ mile turn south on Claussen Road, and in ½ mile look for a small gravel parking loop on the right side of the road. Here there is room to park five or six cars, a picnic table snuggled in the trees, and a sani-can. The ¾-mile-long trail that weaves through the woods to the west passes signs that identify local flora: wild rose, Oregon ash, blackberries, salal, honeysuckle, western red cedar, dogwood, salmonberry, and alder.

The narrow path snakes through head-high brush, with damp spots covered with puncheon and corduroy logs or log section steps. Most of the way is nearly flat until it reaches another picnic table on a tiny bench above the beach; a pit toilet is nearby in the woods. A log staircase switch-backs down to the water level, where a wooden float anchored across the neck of Carlson Bay, a freshwater lagoon, connects the trail to a gravel baymouth bar. Beach grass and driftwood line the narrow top of the bar; outboard a wide gravel beach tapers gently into Nisqually Reach. Because the park is a nature preserve, clamming or taking of oysters is prohibited.

Johnson Farm. The 40-acre Johnson Farm was purchased by a young Finnish immigrant couple in 1896 and was actively worked by two generations of Johnsons until 1975, when the last of the immediate family died. A granddaughter who inherited the property deeded 5.9 acres of the farm—along with its house, barn, milk house, water tower, and other outbuildings—to the Anderson Island Historical Society.

The house is furnished as it was during the early 1900s, and farm tools and machinery of the period can be found in the other farm buildings. One of the buildings houses the Historical Society Gift Shop and Museum, where historical memorabilia that have been collected from the island are displayed. The farm and museum are open for visitors on Saturday and Sunday from noon until 4:00 P.M. The museum is located on Otso Point Road, just south of the intersection with Yoman Road.

Eagle Island Marine State Park

Park area: 10 acres; 2,600 feet of shoreline
Access: Boat
Facilities: 3 mooring buoys, no water, no toilets
Attractions: Fishing, beachcombing, swimming, wading

Although the birds were once numerous in the area, Eagle Island was not named for our national symbol, but for Harry Eagle, a member of the Wilkes Expedition. Early American settlers along Puget Sound thought it patriotic to shoot an eagle on the Fourth of July; modern man uses subtler methods by destroying the eagles' habitat and poisoning their environment.

The small island sits in the middle of already constricted Balch Passage, between Anderson and McNeil islands. Large boats navigating the passage should stay well in midchannel between McNeil and Eagle islands.

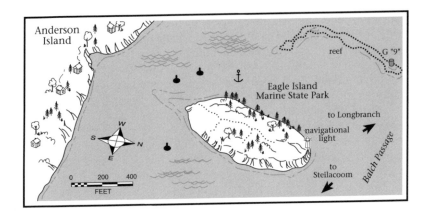

A buoy in the channel marks a reef extending from the west side of Eagle Island.

Even though you might not find eagles there today, you are likely to spot a hawk, and the island has the prettiest collection of gnarled madronas to be found anywhere on South Puget Sound. Overhanging the banks are firs with curving, pistol-butted trunks, caused by the tree growing upward as its roots were undermined and the trunk tilted downward.

A tracery of madrona branches frames a beach walker on Eagle Island.

Beaches are gravel, with little evidence of marine life. The southern point, which reaches toward Anderson Island, has fine-grained sand, worthy of any sand castle and soft enough for an afternoon of sunbathing. Mooring buoys are set on either side of the sandspit. Anderson Island is invitingly close, but all beaches there are private.

Trails lace the uplands, some more primitive than others, but all are certain to provide an hour's diversion of brushwhacking. The most scenic spot is on the bank on the southeast end of the island, where a break in the trees provides a nice view down Balch Passage and out to Mount Rainier.

McNeil Island

Take a 4,400-acre island in the heart of Puget Sound, complete with timber stands, fresh water, sandy beaches, herons, eagles, and seals—and, incidentally, a penitentiary—put it up for grabs to a host of special-interest groups, then stand back and watch the donnybrook. This scenario was played out 15 years ago when the federal government decided to close its penitentiary on McNeil Island.

The island was the site of a territorial jail in 1867 and became a federal penitentiary in 1870 to take advantage of its natural isolation, created by the swift tidal currents and bone-chilling waters of the sound. It was the oldest operating federal penal institution in the country until 1980, when the government closed it down because the facilities were too out of date and too costly for it to operate.

Recreational and conservation forces, as well as the descendants of the former owners, began a battle for the island. Ideas ranged from building a bridge across Pitt Passage for greater public access, to completely vacating the island and leaving it as a wildlife refuge. Washington's own prison requirements finally carried the day, and the buildings were taken over by the state penal system. In 1984 the federal government deeded 3,100 acres to the state Department of Fish and Wildlife, which now manages that portion as a wildlife preserve.

The island has had many names. Puget called it Pidgeon Island; for a short time it was called Wallace Island for Leander Wallace, who was killed by the Snoqualmie Indians in an attack on Fort Nisqually in 1849; a British survey tried to impose the name Duntze Island for the captain of the survey ship *Fisgard*. The name that finally stuck was given by the Wilkes Expedition in honor of William McNeil, captain of the Hudson's Bay steamer *Beaver*.

The prison complex is located on 30 acres on the southeast side of the island, and a large prison garden is near Hogan Point on the southwest; the remainder of the island is largely in its natural state. Signs along the shores warning boaters to maintain a respectful distance because of the prison have helped wildlife to thrive here unmolested. Still Harbor, which

Prison buildings at McNeil Island

deeply indents the northeast shore, is one of the last remaining harbor seal breeding grounds south of Whidbey Island. A colony of some 200 seals haul out to rest and sun themselves on Gertrude Island and the connecting sandspit. A great blue heron rookery is on one of the island creeks, and bald eagles nest nearby. Concentrated on the northern third of the island, away from the penitentiary, these precious wildlife assets are of the greatest concern to environmentalists.

PITT AND DRAYTON PASSAGES

Pitt Passage, separating McNeil Island from the Key Peninsula, is shallow enough to encourage prison inmates of early days to occasionally attempt wading across on a minus tide when the narrow portion south of Pitt Island drains to 6 feet deep (a new fence at the prison now precludes this). Tidal currents run fast through here, however, ranging to more than 2½ knots. For boats attempting the channel, the recommended passage runs east of Pitt Island. Signs on pilings mark shoals north and south of the island.

Due to its shallowness, it is not advisable to attempt Pitt Passage at low tide in boats with any draft. Be aware that, contrary to logic, the current ebbs to the north and floods to the south.

The short waterway of Drayton Passage bounds the northwest side of Anderson Island and joins Balch Passage to the west end of Nisqually Reach. It also exhibits some of the illogical tidal flows of the area by always ebbing weakly to the northeast, regardless of the ebb or flood direction in adjacent waters.

Pitt Passage DNR Beach

On the west side of Pitt Passage are some 2,000 feet of public tide-lands; DNR Beach 6 lies beneath a steep, 150-foot-tall clay bluff immediately south of a row of beach cabins, and stretches south to within ¾ mile of Mahncke Point. The gravel beach changes to sand when low tide exposes the long, shallow tidelands. Beachcombing offers cockles and possibly some clams. All upland approaches are private.

Drayton Passage Launch Ramp

Popular fishing and boating areas in and near Drayton Passage are accessible to trailered boats from a launch ramp on its western edge.

To reach the ramp, continue south from Longbranch on the Key Peninsula Highway KPS for 1¼ miles to 72nd Street KPS. Turn east, and in ¾ mile a single-lane concrete launch ramp dips into Drayton Passage. There is ample vehicle and trailer parking alongside the road, but all shorelines on either side of the ramp are private.

Longbranch and Filucy Bay

Access: Land, boat
Facilities: Fuel, water, marine supplies, groceries, guest moorage
Attractions: Fishing, canoeing, kayaking

Filucy Bay (pronounced "fih-LOO-chee") is every bit as pretty as its name, with tree-lined shores enclosing one of the best anchorages on Puget Sound. The protected bay is located where Drayton, Balch, and Pitt passages converge off the west tip of McNeil Island. A small cove at the southern extremity of the bay is protected by McDermott Point. The extreme

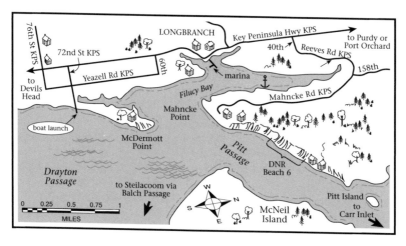

Morning comes to a quiet anchorage on Filucy Bay.

end of the point, the former site of a lighthouse, is currently high on the state parks' wish list for acquisition for a Cascadia Marine Trail site. The sloping gravel beach is fine for sunbathing and watching passing maritime traffic.

At the center of the bay, on the west side, is the village of Longbranch, which consists of a general store that carries a supply of groceries. A float at the marina here permits access to shore facilities. A long finger of the bay runs north for 1½ miles, offering ample space for a fleet of boats and solid anchorage in a mud bottom in 2 to 2½ fathoms of water.

Longbranch can be reached by land from either Purdy or Port Orchard by following the Key Peninsula Highway.

Wycoff Shoal

Just off the northwest end of McNeil Island, where Pitt Passage joins Carr Inlet, is Wycoff Shoal. Only a hazardous scattering of rocks is exposed at high tide, but low tide reveals sand and gravel bars where clams, geoducks, and sea cucumbers can be harvested. All exposed tideland is public. When it is submerged, the extremities of the shoal are outlined by five red-and-white cone markers.

Access to the tidelands is by boat only. The nearest launch ramps are at Mayo Cove and on Drayton Passage south of Longbranch.

THE NISQUALLY DELTA

A bonanza! The Nisqually Delta is a natural cornucopia on the shores of the busy water highway of Nisqually Reach, within eyeshot of the intensely private shores of Anderson Island.

The Nisqually Delta was a favored spot for Indians, who harvested the bounty of the grasslands, marshes, and streams, and who located a major village nearby at Chilacum on the bluff to the east. The Hudson's Bay Company established a post nearby at Fort Nisqually, and its subsidiary, the Puget Sound Agricultural Society, imported livestock. By 1847 some 6,000 sheep and 2,000 cattle were grazing the lush meadows on the banks of the Nisqually.

James McAllister, an early settler in the region, scratched out a farm on the banks of Medicine Creek, the lower reaches of which now bear his name. He took a place in history when he became one of the first whites killed during the Indian War of 1855–56.

Medicine Creek is best known as the site where the Indians were hornswoggled by Governor Isaac Stevens when he convinced the chiefs of the tribes living along the shores of South Puget Sound (except for Leschi,

Marshes surround the Twin Barns at Nisqually National Wildlife Refuge.

one of the chiefs of the Nisqually) to sign the Medicine Creek Treaty. The Indians were assigned to meager reservations, one south of the Nisqually River, another on a bluff between Tacoma and Point Defiance, and a third on Hartstene Island. A later treaty renegotiation (inspired by the Indian War) gave the tribes somewhat more favorable lands, including the rich prairies and salmon-filled streams south of the delta.

Although there are varying accounts of the meaning of the name Nisqually, the favorite one is that the word "squally" imitates the sound of the breeze blowing through the grassland and flowers. The name broadened to include the tribe of Indians living in this region.

Nisqually National Wildlife Refuge

Refuge area: 3,780 acres
Access: Boat, land
Facilities: Education center, trails, vault toilets, photo blinds, nature trail, disabled access
Attractions: Fishing, hiking, wildlife observation, canoeing, kayaking

The merging of freshwater and saltwater from river, streams, and the sound, coupled with broad grasslands, deciduous woodlands, and thick conifer forests, creates the uniquely diverse environment of the Nisqually National Wildlife Refuge. Daily tidal flows through the saltwater marshes

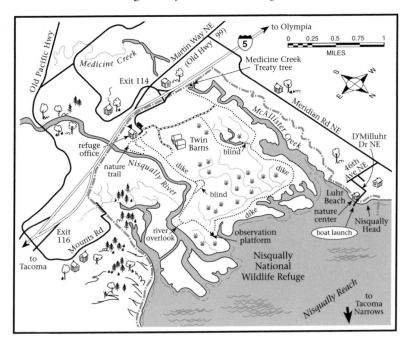

bring organic life, an important link in the food chain that includes some 50 species of small mammals, 125 kinds of fish, and 200 species of birds ranging from waterfowl to songbirds to raptors. They are all here to be discovered, enjoyed, and photographed.

To reach the refuge take Exit 114 (Nisqually) from I-5. From the off-ramp drive to the intersection signed "Nisqually Wildlife Refuge," and go east ½ mile to the refuge entrance. The gate is locked daily at sunset, so plan visits accordingly. Be sure to bring binoculars, a camera, and pos-sibly a bird identification guide. An entrance fee of $2 per person or

Canvasback ducks are one of the many species of waterfowl that mi-grate through the wildlife refuge.

group is charged. Persons with an authorized Golden Passport or duck stamp need not pay the fee. Boat access to the delta is available at the Luhr Beach boat ramp, described later.

In 1904 Alson Brown purchased the rich delta land and with horse-drawn scoops built dikes to hold back the saltwater. He started a large dairy farm; buildings still stand on the land today. Preserved as farmland, the Nisqually Delta has remained one of the most pristine river deltas in the United States. The threat of industrial encroachment pressed the area in the early 1970s because the Brown farm could no longer compete with modern farming giants. An environmental group, The Nisqually Delta Association, succeeded in their efforts to preserve it with the establish-ment of the Nisqually National Wildlife Refuge in 1974.

Substantial private holdings border the refuge, and proposed devel-opments there could have significant impact on its fragile ecology. Major real estate developments are underway on the bluffs immediately east and west of the delta. "Planned communities" will bring over 20,000 residents within a few wing-flaps of the delta, where 1,000 people now live. Although developers, including the Weyerhaeuser Company, assure environmentalists of their sensitivity to the ecology of the delta, concerns for the delta are multiple: the lights and noise from such a concentration of people might affect the sensitive nesting and wintering activities of birds; sewer and storm-water systems could foul the water of the delta or Nisqually Reach; pet dogs and cats from the residential developments could become predators within the wildlife refuge; more residents in the area will likely bring increased recreational use of the delta, making it more of a park than a wildlife refuge.

Canada geese nest in marshes of the Nisqually National Wildlife Refuge.

Several hikes start from the kiosk adjacent to the parking lot. Some sections of trails may be closed during nesting season. Hunting is permitted in some sections of the delta, and during hunting season some parts of the dike trail may be closed for the safety of hikers.

The longest hike in the refuge is a 5-mile loop atop the dike that surrounded the old farm. The trail, framed with a light growth of maple, alder, and cottonwood, and a feast of blackberries in season, parallels the banks of the Nisqually River along the east side of the farm, eventually breaking out of the woodland to wend between cattail-filled marshes. A ring dike, built in 1975 to help contain tidewaters while a break in the main dike was being repaired, holds a short side-loop trail. Here a photo blind permits unobtrusive observation of the marshland activities. Ahead are the Olympic peaks and behind—surprise!—Mount Rainier.

Turning west, the dike separates the marshes—inside are freshwater marshes and outside, saltwater. Both of these vast marshes serve as resting and feeding areas for migratory waterfowl and shorebirds. A 20-foot-high viewing platform, built in 1989 to commemorate the State Centennial, provides sweeping views over the delta and its bordering islands, Anderson, Ketron, McNeil, and Fox. Heading back south, the dike trail wanders through brush and grasslands parallel to McAllister Creek. The creek weaves through grass-topped hummocks, which mark its course at high tide, past open freshwater ponds where pintails and mallards raise their broods. Note the nesting boxes on low poles in some of the marshes; these are placed in hopes of attracting wood ducks, which normally nest in hollow trees. Another photo blind is adjacent to this side of the trail.

A shorter nature trail loops ½ mile through the riparian woodland to the edge of the Nisqually River and back. The trailhead is just north of the refuge office, a short distance down the dike trail. Interpretive symbol markers are keyed to a guide pamphlet that describes the natural attractions.

The huge Twin Barns, ½ mile north of the refuge office, once housed dairy herds, but are now used as an environmental education center. An elevated platform built on the end of one of the barns provides an overlook of the delta. En route to the barns, several outdoor study sites are identified by markers. Groups and classes interested in using the educational facilities should contact the refuge office for reservations.

Luhr Beach

Access: Land, boat
Facilities: Boat launch (ramp), vault toilets, environmental displays
Attractions: Boating, paddling, fishing, interpretation, birdwatching

One excellent way to view the Nisqually Wildlife Refuge is by canoe or kayak from the shallow waters of McAllister Creek, the Nisqually River, or the head of the estuary. The only public boat launch close to the area is at Luhr Beach, where a ramp is maintained by the state Department of Fish and Wildlife.

To reach Luhr Beach, take Exit 114 (Nisqually) from I-5 and drive ¼ mile south to Martin Way NE (old Highway 99). Go west on Martin Way for 1 mile, then north on Meridian Road NE 2½ miles more to 46th Avenue NE. Turn east on 46th and in ½ mile turn north on D'Milluhr Drive NE, which dead-ends at the launch ramp in ½ mile. The ramp, with a lone picnic table nearby, is open to use during daylight hours.

Just south of the ramp parking lot is the Nisqually Reach Nature Center. Environmental displays and a mounted bird collection in the building are open for public viewing Saturday and Sunday from 11 A.M. to 4:00 P.M. A covered fishing pier (use at your own risk) adjoins the building.

Mid- to high-tide is best for exploring the myriad channels of the delta. McAllister Creek and the Nisqually River lead far inland. Red Salmon Creek, near the eastern boundary, connects to the Nisqually. At low tide the exposed riverbeds and tideflats provide an opportunity to examine a wealth of intertidal life—worms, shrimp, jellyfish, clams—all part of the complex web of life in the delta.

Group raft tours of the delta may be scheduled in advance with the Nisqually Reach Nature Center. Contact them at 4949 D'Milluhr Drive NE, Olympia, WA 98516, (360) 459-0387. A fee is charged.

Tolmie State Park

Park area: 106 acres; 1,800 feet of shoreline
Access: Land, boat
Facilities: Picnic shelters, tables, restrooms, shower, 5 mooring buoys, 3½ miles of trails, artificial reef, disabled access
Attractions: Picnicking, beachcombing, swimming, clamming, fishing, scuba diving, hiking

Although limited to day use, this pretty little state park packs a lot of recreation into its 100-plus acres. To reach the park by land, take Exit 111 (Yelm, Marvin Road, Highway 510) from I-5. Follow Marvin Road NE north for 3¾ miles to 56th Avenue NE, turn east on 56th, and in ½ mile turn north on Hill Road NE. In ½ mile turn west onto 61st Avenue NE, the park entrance road.

By boat the park is about 15 nautical miles from the Tacoma Narrows Bridge, 2½ nautical miles from the Luhr Beach launch ramp. Five mooring buoys are located offshore.

The focal point of the park is a saltwater marsh that separates the wooded uplands from the long tideflat facing on Nisqually Reach. Informational plaques at several points in the park explain the natural forces

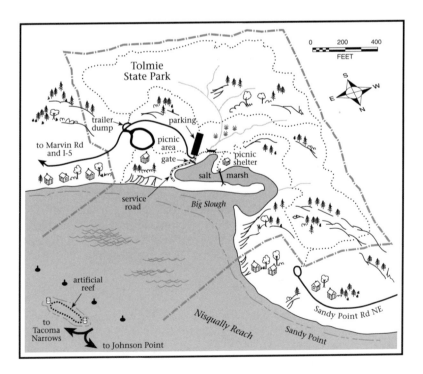

Ferns and moss-covered trees crowd the forest trail at Tolmie State Park.

that create such marshes and the unique ecology that makes them important to wildlife.

The park's broad, sandy beach is one of the best in the region for wading, swimming, and clamming. Three wooden barges that were intentionally sunk 500 yards offshore in 40 to 60 feet of water form an underwater park attracting a myriad of marine life, including large rockfish and cabezon. The underwater park location is marked by white can buoys with red stripes. The lack of any significant current makes this an ideal dive site.

There is no overnight camping in the park, but it does offer fine day-use picnic facilities. Just inside the park entrance, a small loop road with parking pull-outs fronts a grassy picnic area and restroom/picnic shelter. Picnic tables are nicely secluded from each other in cozy pockets among the trees and bushes. Near the lower parking area, just above the beach, are more picnic tables, a kitchen shelter, and adjoining restrooms with an outdoor freshwater shower and inside changing rooms to accommodate scuba divers.

A hiking trail winds through the forested uplands. The trail leaves the lower picnic area near the picnic shelter, meanders through woods of alder, cedar, oak, and fir, with a dense understory of ferns and shrubs. The route explores the perimeter of the park before returning to the end of the lower parking area. The full trail is about 2½ miles long, but for a 1-mile circuit a shortcut leaves the trail halfway along its route and returns to the parking lot. The trail is wide and easily followed; it is often too muddy for street shoes, although some muddy areas are bridged or have boardwalks. Elevation gained and lost en route never exceeds 100 feet. Log benches along the route encourage rest stops for listening to and watching birds, squirrels, and other woods creatures.

Two short trails leave from the upper picnic area; the one to the northeast drops steeply down a gully to the beach at the park's east boundary, while the one to the west heads gradually down to the beach area near the lower parking lot.

JOHNSON POINT AND HENDERSON INLET

A long finger of land, capped by Johnson Point, marks the confluence of Dana Passage, Nisqually Reach, and Case Inlet. Early Kittitas Indians established a large summer camp on Johnson Point and built fish traps just offshore to harvest the teeming salmon that gathered to feed at the merging channels. Today the region remains one of the most popular in South Puget Sound for sports fishing.

Originally named Moody Point by the Wilkes Expedition, after quartermaster William Moody, the point eventually became known for Dr. J. R. Johnson, who established a crude, log-cabin hospital in the vicinity.

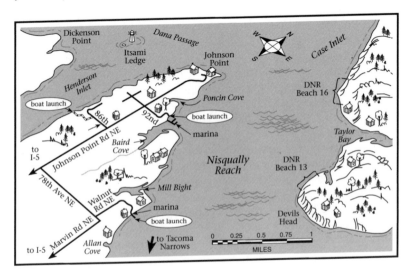

Pioneer Ezra Meeker found him here in 1853, attending to the health of the Indians and settlers.

With no public beaches and very limited access, Henderson is one of the less familiar South Puget Sound inlets. Wilkes named the bay for another of his quartermasters, James Henderson, but today it is also known by the more nondescript name of South Bay.

The mouth of the bay is disrupted by Itsami Ledge, a popular salmon fishing site, but a dangerous shoal; it is marked by a light atop the ledge. Seals can often be spotted in the vicinity, also taking advantage of the fine salmon fishing.

There are some protected anchorages in Henderson Inlet in 30 feet of water, just south of Cliff Point. The south half of the inlet tapers to the characteristic mudflats, home to some clams and oysters.

Johnson Point Marinas

Access: Land, boat
Facilities: Marinas, boat launches (ramps)
Attractions: Fishing, boating

There are no public beaches between Tolmie State Park and Johnson Point, but boat access to this favorite fishing area is available via two marinas on the east side of the point. To reach the first, leave I-5 east of Olympia at Exit 109 (Lacey, Olympia, Business Loop I-5). Go west on Martin Way NE for ¾ mile, then turn north on Sleater Kinney Road NE. In 3 miles turn northeast at the junction with South Bay Road NE. In

Marinas near Johnson Point provide quick access to nearby fishing grounds.

about ½ mile the road curves north at the end of Henderson Bay and becomes Johnson Point Road NE. Continue 4 miles to 78th NE; here go east 1 mile, then north on Walnut Road NE, and in ½ mile arrive at a marina located south of Mill Bight. Parking, a concrete launch ramp (fee), a float, marine repair, and fuel (gasoline) are available.

To reach the second marina, on Baird Cove, drive another 1½ miles on Johnson Point Road NE to 92nd Avenue NE. Turn east, and in ½ mile the road dead-ends at the marina, which offers floats, repairs, fuel, groceries, marine repairs, fishing supplies, a sling launch, and a launch ramp for a fee.

Another privately owned ramp offers the only boat launch on Henderson Inlet. Turn west off Johnson Point Road NE onto 86th Avenue NE. In ½ mile two parallel dirt roads head left. Turn down the first narrow road (marked "Private, subject to closure at any time") and follow it to its end in ¼ mile, where you will find a paved launch ramp, primitive restrooms, and a parking area for six or seven vehicles and trailers. This launch facility is mainly used on an annual-fee basis by locals, but occasional public use (for a fee) can be accommodated by the owner.

Devils Head and Taylor Bay

Across Nisqually Reach, east of Johnson Point, the Key Peninsula terminates in an abrupt 200-foot-high promontory called Devils Head. Immediately north of Devils Head the shore is indented by Taylor Bay. Cruising boats can find some limited anchorages near the mouth, although the bay shallows rapidly and all the shoreline is private.

Geographic names sometimes commemorate mundane as well as historic personalities, with Taylor Bay a case in point. It was named for "Old Man Taylor," a sailor who left an English ship and settled nearby.

Two public DNR beaches, accessible only by water, are located north and south of the bay. DNR Beach 13, with 1,300 feet of shoreline, lies between Devils Head and Taylor Bay. This is one of the nicest DNR tidelands in South Puget Sound, with a broad gravel bar fronting a grassy meadow. Back in the trees lies a weathered barn. As with most DNR beaches, property above the mean high tide level is private.

Immediately north of Taylor Bay lies DNR Beach 16. The narrow, 2,500-foot-long beach is driftwood and gravel at its upper reaches, with sand at low tide. Open to the sweeping waters of Nisqually Reach, beach life here is limited to some piddock clams and sea cucumbers.

Woodard and Chapman Bays

Two small fingers, Chapman and Woodard bays, fan out from the west side of Henderson Inlet, south of Dickenson Point. Hand-carried boats can be launched at the bridge that crosses Woodard Bay. This launch site

Fishing near Devils Head

is reached by driving north from Olympia on Boston Harbor Road NE 4½ miles to Woodard Bay Road NE, then northeast 2½ miles to the bridge over the bay. Roadside parking is available along the dead-end spur, Whitman Road NE, at the west end of the bridge. Look out for a swift current under the bridge at maximum tidal flow. At minus tide this portion of Woodard Bay dries; plan trips accordingly.

The first settler in the Henderson Bay area was Harvey Rice Woodard, for whom Woodard Bay was named. He filed a donation land claim for 320 acres on the bay in 1854, cleared some acreage, and moved his family to a farm on the site. The Indian Wars of 1855–56 drove Woodard and his family to the safety of Olympia, where they remained. Woodard sold off the property in segments to loggers, and eventually most of the property was acquired by the Weyerhaeuser Company.

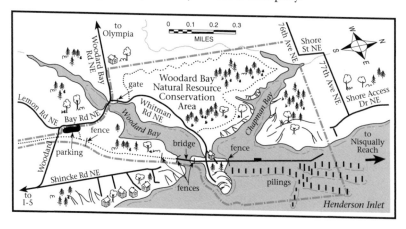

Woodard Bay is a quiet backwater that attracts paddlers.

The lumber company was attracted to the bay by its need to find an economical means of getting timber from its large forest holdings near Vail, in southern Pierce County, to its major lumber mills in Everett. The waters of Woodard and Chapman bays were deep enough that log booming and rafting could go on at any tide level, and the bays were well protected from storms. The company built private railroad lines to the bay and, beginning in 1928, unloaded an average of 140 railroad cars of logs a day here. The logs were secured into rafts and towed to the Everett mills.

By the 1970s the Everett mills had become obsolete, and the logs from Weyerhaeuser's timber lands were more profitably exported to the Far East via the Port of Tacoma. All log storage activity in Woodard Bay ceased in 1984, and in 1988 the state Department of Natural Resources purchased the land for a Natural Resource Conservation Area. Much of the area is fenced to protect the wildlife.

The old access road to the log-booming area, Whitman Road NE, is now gated just beyond Woodard Bay Road NE. The remainder of the road and a trail that explores the woodland on the west side of the property are open to foot traffic.

Whitman Road leads ½ mile north to a residence, now used by the DNR, that sits at the head of a grass field above the log-boom railroad track. The railroad bridge across the head of Woodard Bay, as well as the extension across the head of Chapman Bay to the old grapple unloader, are fenced off for safety. Hopefully the DNR will find funds at some future date to provide interpretive displays describing this unique log-booming operation.

The grass plot between the bridges has a few tired picnic tables that overlook the heads of both bays. The bay to the north was once laced with boomsticks tied to lines of pilings that held together rafts of logs awaiting transport to the Everett mills; only the pilings remain, a faint memory of the bay's past log-boom activity. Today harbor seals haul on out remnants of the old log-boom workings, bald eagles nest in snags, and clams and ghost shrimp regenerate in the shoreline mud of the bays. The area may be closed in spring when pupping seals are especially sensitive to intrusion and when pups tend to get separated from their mothers.

The backwoods trail leaves Whitman Road a short distance beyond the gate for a slick, muddy climb west, through woods, along the conservation area boundary.

A youngster tries his hand at fishing in Woodard Bay.

After passing through a tall, skinny, dog-hair growth of fir, the path meanders north through second-growth forest and thick underbrush, periodically passing trail-side benches. Pause here to listen to the chorus of bird calls in the surrounding woods. The trail continues north, passing stops above a deep creek drainage to the west, then rounds a corner where a bench overlooks the crooked finger at the end of Chapman Bay, where twice daily the tide makes it a mysterious green waterway, then twice daily a mudflat. Here the path heads east through oak, cedar, alder, and damnable stinging nettles—views of Chapman Bay always appear through the trees. After dropping past a swampy spot, the way returns to the road near the caretaker residence.

CHAPTER SIX

CASE INLET

The geological carvings of that capricious Pleistocene glacier stopped just short of gnawing away a 2-mile-wide, 400-foot-high neck of land that now separates the northern tip of Case Inlet from the remote end of Hood Canal. Had this final connection of waterways taken place, the story of South Puget Sound would surely be far different today—Hood Canal would be a major maritime thoroughfare, connecting ports along the inner margin of the Olympic Peninsula; the Kitsap Peninsula, at present tenuously fastened to the mainland, would be a giant Kitsap Island.

As it is, the wide channel of Case Inlet heads northward resolutely for 15 miles toward the heart of the Kitsap Peninsula and fizzles out in a mudflat. For the recreation seeker, however, this geological quirk is a blessing; the remote inlet remains the most pristine of South Puget Sound

Rhododendrons overlook Fair Harbor Marina.

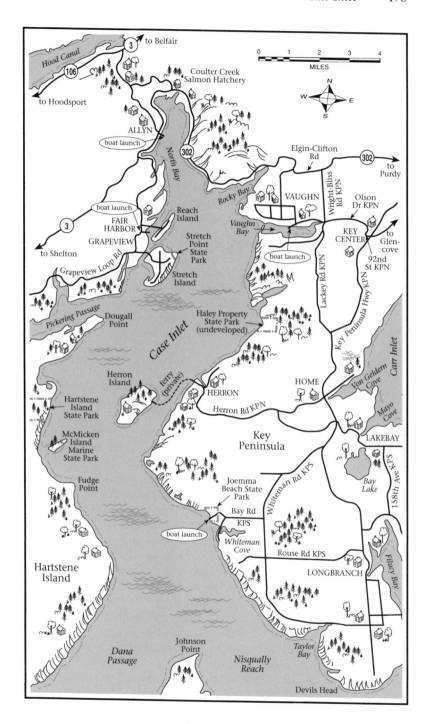

to Belfair

Hood Canal

106

to Hoodsport

Coulter Creek
Salmon Hatchery

ALLYN

boat launch

North Bay

302

Elgin-Clifton
Rd

302 to
Purdy

Rocky Bay

VAUGHN

Wright-Bliss
Rd KPN

Olson
Dr KPN

3

boat launch

FAIR
HARBOR

GRAPEVIEW

to Shelton

Reach
Island

Stretch
Point
State
Park

*Vaughn
Bay*

boat launch

KEY
CENTER

to
Glen-
cove

92nd
St KPN

Grapeview Loop Rd

Stretch
Island

Pickering Passage

Dougall
Point

Haley Property
State Park
(undeveloped)

Case Inlet

Lackey Rd KPN

Key Peninsula Hwy KPN

Von Geldern
Cove

*Carr
Inlet*

Herron
Island

ferry
(private)

HERRON

HOME

*Mayo
Cove*

Hartstene
Island
State Park

Herron Rd KPN

Key
Peninsula

LAKEBAY

McMicken
Island
Marine
State Park

*Bay
Lake*

158th Ave KPS

Fudge
Point

Joemma
Beach State
Park

Whiteman Rd KPS

boat launch

Bay Rd
KPS

*Whiteman
Cove*

Rouse Rd KPS

LONGBRANCH

*Filucy
Bay*

Hartstene
Island

*Dana
Passage*

Johnson
Point

*Nisqually
Reach*

*Taylor
Bay*

Devils Head

0   1   2   3   4
MILES

N
W   E
S

waterways. The only town is the small community of Allyn, situated where Highway 302 skirts the west shore of North Bay. Three parks offer public recreational facilities, while numerous coves and tiny bays provide shelter for cruising boats.

KEY PENINSULA SHORELINE

Inside Case Inlet and along the eastern shoreline, Mount Rainier, which dominates the skyline in Carr Inlet and Nisqually Reach, drops from sight behind the Key Peninsula. Now the tourist is rewarded with broad panoramas of the Olympic Mountains. On land, an especially fine view of the Olympics is from Highway 302 northbound between Vaughn Bay and Coulter Creek.

Joemma Beach State Park

Park area: 22 acres; 1,100 feet of shoreline
Access: Boat, land
Facilities: 19 standard campsites, picnic shelter, picnic tables, vault toilets, water, boat launch (ramp), dock and floats, 4 mooring buoys, hiking trail, designated Cascadia Marine Trail campsite, disabled access
Attractions: Camping, picnicking, boating, paddling, fishing, clamming, crabbing, hiking, beachcombing

The shoreline of Case Inlet skirts steep bluffs north of Taylor Bay for 2 miles before arriving at the next indentation, Whiteman Cove. Joemma Beach State Park, immediately north of Whiteman Cove, holds the only land-access campground on this side of Case Inlet. The park makes a nice overnight stop for campers and cyclists touring the Key Peninsula, as well as for boaters and paddlers cruising or fishing in the inlet.

To reach the park by land, follow the Key Peninsula Highway southwest from Purdy to an intersection 1½ miles south of the small community of Home. Here bear southwest on Whiteman Road KPS and follow it for 3¼ miles to Bay Road KPS, signed to the park (but only from the north). Head west on Bay Road to reach the park property line in 1 mile.

For boaters, the park offers an excellent 500-foot-long dock with space on floats for about 20 boats. Additional moorage is provided by four buoys north from the end of the dock. The floats are removed from late September to May to prevent storm damage.

For many years this spot, then known as Robert F. Kennedy Recreation Area, was a rustic gem, with primitive campsites and a dilapidated boat float that appealed only to the desperate. During 1990 the facilities were beautifully remodeled by the DNR. In 1995 it was transferred from the DNR to state parks and renamed Joemma Beach. Park neighbors had requested the park be given a local name; the final choice was

Till, deposited by ancient glaciers, forms the bluffs at Joemma Beach State Park.

a combination of the names of Joe and Emma Smith, who lived there between 1917 and 1932.

Two campground loops lie just inside the gate; the one to the south has 12 campsites along a tight loop that circles a wooded knob, the one to the north has another 7 sites in grass and open timber. Both loops have water faucets and vault toilets; each has one site designed and designated for disabled campers. Some sites have water views. Primitive Cascadia Marine Trail sites are located on the hillside between the northern loop and the picnic shelter.

A short hiking trail on the northeast side of the park wanders through

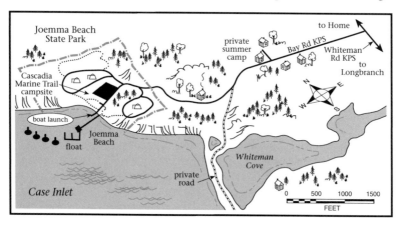

the second-growth forest, much of it logged by the DNR in the late 1980s; trailheads are located along the northern campground loop road.

The smooth beach, which slopes out gradually, is peppered with small rocks and has little exposed sand except at extremely low tides. To the north, steep bluffs of glacial till rise 150 feet. South, the rocky shore continues to Whiteman Cove, where the bluff tempers somewhat to 20 to 50 feet high.

George Vancouver and his crew are believed to have camped at Whiteman Cove in May 1792, after exploring the lower reaches of the sound. They neglected to name the cove, however, and it picked up its identity from an early settler who married an Indian woman and settled here and for many years was the only "white man" in the vicinity. Wave action built up a sandspit at the mouth of the cove, and over time it has totally blocked the entrance. Today the cove is actually a lagoon with a road-topped bar.

Herron Island

Just as Eagle Island is not named for eagles, Herron Island is not named for herons, abundant though they may be in the vicinity. The island's name honors Petty Officer Lewis Herron, barrel maker for the Wilkes Expedition. (It didn't take much to get a piece of real estate named after you in those days.)

The mile-long island on the east side of Case Inlet is completely private and is accessible only by the island's privately operated ferry. The mainland ferry slip is on Herron Road South, on a small point of land northeast of the island.

Boats of any draft navigating behind the island should be wary of a shallow sandbar protruding northeasterly from Herron Island, but midchannel depths between the island and shoreline are at least 2 fathoms. Tidal currents are swift in the shallow channel.

Haley Property State Park (Undeveloped)

Park area: 178 acres
Facilities: None
Attractions: Fishing, beachcombing, clamming

On the northeast shoreline of Case Inlet is a piece of property purchased by the state parks in the early 1980s from the Haley family, of Brown and Haley candy fame. Park development plans were stymied in 1992 by objections of local residents and the inability to gain an access easement. Neighbors who oppose the park may try to discourage its use, but the property is public.

The only public access is by boats that can be landed on the wide sand

and gravel beach. The property is located 2 miles north of the Herron Island ferry landing and ½ mile south of Dutcher Cove. A 30-foot-high light-colored bank marks the north side of Dutcher Cove; there are a few beachfront residences along the south side of the cove, just north of the creek. South of the creek the park property is identified by a wide, gently tapering beach below a gravel bar, topped by an old, weather-silvered totem pole at its north end.

The beach above the gradually tapering tidelands is open to clam digging. The heavily wooded, undeveloped property surrounds a drainage, whose stream was once dammed to form a freshwater lagoon just above the beach. The dam broke in a 1994 earthquake,

Raccoon tracks on the beach tell a tale of nighttime visitors.

and the lagoon disappeared. The surrounding woodland is home for a variety of wildlife, including otters, beaver, deer, foxes, and osprey.

Vaughn Bay

The north end of Case Inlet splits into three fingers. The largest of these, North Bay, continues on for another 3 miles; two smaller, shallower coves, Vaughn Bay and Rocky Bay, reach eastward. The ¼-mile-long sandspit guarding the west end of Vaughn Bay is a public beach from the top of the spit to the low-tide line on its western side. The sand and gravel bar offers a variety of clams and some red rock crab.

Access to the spit is by boat only, but a public launch ramp is nearby on the north shore of Vaughn Bay. To reach the ramp, drive west from Key Center on 92nd Street KPN, which in 2 blocks bends northwest as Olson Drive KPN. At its four-way intersection with Vaughn Road KPN (to the south), Wright-Bliss Road KPN (to the north), and Hall Road KPN (to the west), continue straight ahead on Hall Road for ½ mile to its intersection with Van Slyke Road at the community of Vaughn. The ramp is located 1 block downhill from the intersection; parking is very limited along the south edge of the street. The ramp is not usable at a minus tide.

The bay is shallowest along its north side, so after launching follow

Wires and netting keep away hungry birds at the Coulter Creek Salmon Hatchery.

the south shore to about 200 yards from the entrance spit and parallel the spit north to the entrance before heading out into Case Inlet.

Coulter Creek Salmon Hatchery

North from Vaughn Bay, Case Inlet tapers to North Bay and then to the tidal flats at the mouth of Coulter Creek. Immediately east of the highway intersection at Coulter Creek are salmon-rearing pens that serve as satellite facilities for the Minter Creek hatchery on Carr Inlet. The hatchery facilities are open to the public from 8:00 A.M. to 4:30 P.M. daily.

Adjacent to the road are two large concrete pens covered with netting to keep out enterprising birds. Nearby on pretty little Coulter Creek are a fish ladder and a low weir dam.

NORTH BAY AND ALLYN

The northwest end of Case Inlet is known as North Bay. Here Highway 3 from Belfair joins Highway 302 at the small community of Allyn. The west side of North Bay is extremely shallow, so boats of any draft should favor the east side of the bay until due east of the public pier at

Allyn. North from the public pier the bay dries to mudflats and commercial oyster beds at low tide.

South from the community of Allyn, nestled against the western shore of Case Inlet, are a pair of islands that, although largely private, do have some interest for land and water tourists. The more northerly, Reach Island, is also known by its realtor-hype name of Treasure Island. It is accessible by a bridge spanning the 200-yard-wide channel, but the entire island and shorelands are private.

Allyn

Access: Boat, land
Facilities: Boat launch (ramp), public pier, float, guest moorage, waterfront park, picnic tables, picnic shelter, sani-cans, groceries, fuel (service stations), restaurants
Attractions: Boating, fishing, picnicking

At the north end of town, a half-block downhill on Drum Street, the Port of Allyn has developed a very nice little waterfront park that includes a public dock and boat-launch ramp. A prominent sign beside the highway at Drum Street identifies the park.

A concrete boat launch is 300 yards north of the dock. The ramp is not usable at a minus tide, when the water retreats well out into the bay. Stretching between the dock and the ramp is a large dirt parking area fronted by picnic tables along the shoreline and a tall totem pole. North from the parking area, a tree-shaded lawn contains a covered pavilion and several more picnic tables. The 600-foot-long dock is a popular fishing spot for both visitors and residents. A float at the end of the dock has space for about eight boats (overnight moorage permitted, for a fee). Boaters in need of supplies will find grocery, drug, and hardware stores a few blocks to the south.

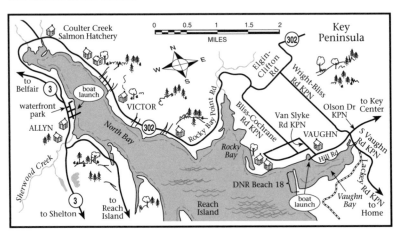

Reach and Stretch Islands

Access: Boat, land
Facilities: Marina, fuel, guest moorage, snack bar, boat launch (ramp)

Reach Island serves as protection for a small marina and launch ramp located south of the bridge on an inlet locally called Fair Harbor. To reach them by land from Allyn, follow Highway 3 south to a bridge over Sherwood Creek. Just beyond the bridge turn east on Grapeview Loop Road. In 2¾ miles the Treasure Island bridge road exits east; the marina is obvious in another ¼ mile. The two-lane concrete launch ramp north of the marina is public, operated by the Port of Grapeview, but there is no public parking nearby.

By boat the marina is best approached from the south, because at low tide the channel to the north holds only 1 foot of water. At high tide the 16-foot clearance of the Reach Island bridge is a hazard to be considered by sailboats. Boats entering the channels from either the north or the south should favor the west shoreline to avoid baring rocks midchannel and along the east side.

South of Reach Island ¼ mile is Stretch Island, which also has no public property accessible from land but does have a public DNR beach and a small state park that is accessible from the water. Stretch Island can be reached by land via a bridge ½ mile south of the marina.

At the turn of the century the island supported the beginnings of a western Washington wine industry and was known as Grape Island; the onshore community is Grapeview. As recently as the 1962 Seattle World's Fair, the island's St. Charles Winery produced a "Century 21"-label vintage.

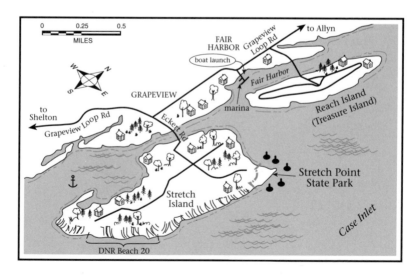

The winery closed in 1965; today grapes from Stretch Island vineyards are used primarily for juice and fruit leather, although a few boutique wineries operate here.

The passage behind Stretch Island, which dries at low tide, is also constricted by the 14-foot-high fixed bridge. Some protected anchorages can be found in the small cove on the southwest side of the island, although it is exposed to weather from the south. Just around the southern tip of the island on the southeast side, an 1,800-foot segment of tidelands is a public DNR beach accessible only by boat. The gravel beach below the steep clay bank offers some chances to gather oysters and mussels at low tide. Please respect private uplands and adjoining private beaches.

Stretch Point State Park

Park area: 4.2 acres; 610 feet of shoreline
Access: Boat
Facilities: 5 mooring buoys, no water, no toilets
Attractions: Picnicking, boating, beachcombing, clamming, fishing, swimming

The small northeast tip of Stretch Island is a minuscule chunk of marine state park. Five mooring buoys placed around the point are within arm's reach of shore at minus tides, but because of the rapid drop-off they have adequate depth for most boats.

A kayaker pauses at Stretch Point State Park.

The gravel beach wrapping around the point provides an inviting picnic or swimming stop for passing boaters. At the heart of the point is a small, tree-ringed saltwater lagoon.

The park has no drinking water or restroom facilities, so onshore camping is not permitted. There is no regular garbage pickup here; take all trash away with you.

HARTSTENE ISLAND SHORELINE

Because most Hartstene Island recreation sites are reached via the bridge over Pickering Passage, the island itself is included in the following chapter. However, those sites on the east shore of the island that can be reached by water from Case Inlet are described here.

Hartstene Island State Park and DNR Beach 24

Park area: 315 acres; 1,600 feet of shoreline; Beach 24: 5,400 feet of shoreline
Access: Boat, land
Facilities: Hiking trail, picnic tables
Attractions: Hiking, beachcombing, clamming, fishing, scuba diving

This small park with limited facilities provides easy access to one of the nicest beaches on South Puget Sound. To reach the park by land, from the Hartstene Island bridge go north on East North Island Drive 3¼ miles to the intersection with East Hartstene Island Road North. Here turn south, and in 1 mile turn east on East Yates Road. Follow the single-lane gravel road for 1 mile to an unmarked intersection. Turn right, and in another ¼ mile reach the state park parking area, where there is space for a dozen cars.

From the parking lot a ¼-mile trail leads through dense brush and

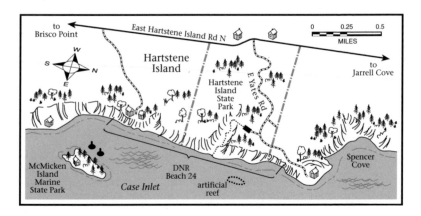

Sand dollars are abundant on DNR Beach 24.

second-growth trees that are fast reclaiming an old clearcut. Picnic sites, each with a gravel pad and picnic table, are strung along the path. At the edge of a 100-foot-high forested bank, another ¼ mile of trail drops steeply down a ravine to the beach. Log benches are provided for much-needed uphill rest stops along this steep section. The trail breaks out onto the gravel beach ¼ mile north of McMicken Island.

The mile-long piece of tidelands stretching north from McMicken Island is DNR Beach 24, although most of the uplands are private. The gravel beach beneath a steep bank tapers gently to sand and mud that contains some clams and oysters, as well as a profusion of sand dollars. At extreme low tide the beach can be walked all the way to McMicken Island. Portions of the shoreland are always soggy; wear boots or be prepared for wet feet.

For anglers, the most interesting feature of this beach is the artificial reef placed offshore in 25 feet of water. The reef, composed of old automobile tires, provides a haven for marine organisms that establish their homes on the rough surfaces, for tiny animals such as crabs and shrimp that seek shelter in the nooks and crannies, and for larger fish such as lingcod that come here to feed. Fishing and scuba diving in the vicinity are excellent. A buoy marks its location.

McMicken Island Marine State Park

Park area: 11.4 acres; 1,661 feet of shoreline
Access: Boat
Facilities: 5 mooring buoys, composting toilet, no water
Attractions: Fishing, boating, clamming, beachcombing, hiking, swimming

Little McMicken Island represents one man's bid for posterity and another man's duplicity. The island was originally settled by a Swedish sailor called Lundquist who named it after himself; his land claim ran afoul of government bureaucracy because the island's existence had never been recorded. A surveyor, dispatched to establish the reality of the property, preempted Lundquist and, alas, named it McMicken after himself.

The entire island is a state park, with the exception of a triangular, fenced-in acreage enclosing some cabins and sheds on the south side of the park. This fenced area is the private property of the island's previous owner, who retained a lifetime lease as a contingency of sale.

Although the island is joined to Hartstene Island at low tide by a sandspit, no public roads reach the uplands; approach is limited to boats or via foot from DNR Beach 24. Five mooring buoys, three on the north and two on the south, float offshore, while a good holding bottom offers anchoring on either side of the island. A large rock erratic, deposited by a Pleistocene glacier, is conspicuous at low tide on the south shore but is covered at high water; use care anchoring here at high tide. Also exercise caution when passing on the west side of the island because of the sandspit.

Sandy beaches on the west end are quite shallow and warm enough in

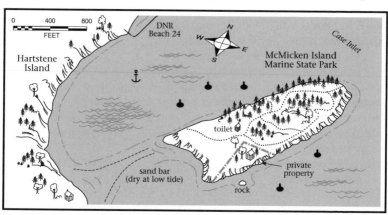

Driftwood on the shore at McMicken Island Marine State Park

summer to invite saltwater wading and swimming. During low tide clamming is sometimes good, with red rock crab and some oysters also available on the eastern end of the island. DNR tidelands stretching north from here are within easy dinghy reach of the park moorages. At a minus tide the connecting land is exposed enough to walk on.

A composting toilet is located just at the edge of the forest on the northwest corner of the island. There is no garbage pickup on the island, so be sure to carry yours away with you.

An unimproved trail system runs the length of the island through dense second-growth forest. One branch of the trail stays inland, while another skirts bluffs 50 feet above the beach on the southeast side. None of the trails have easy access to the shore. Signs warn that poison oak grows on the island. Beware!

CHAPTER SEVEN

PICKERING PASSAGE

The ½-mile-wide finger of Pickering Passage bends around the west side of Hartstene Island, connecting Case Inlet to the western channels of South Puget Sound. At its western end the waterway divides as it flows around Squaxin Island and becomes Peale Passage on the east and Squaxin Passage at its southwestern extremity.

Pickering Passage was first explored by Peter Puget in his initial thrust through the lower sound in May 1792, but neither it nor Peale Passage was named until the Wilkes Expedition.

Pickering Passage once offered an alternative route around Hartstene

Kayakers land at Hope Island Marine State Park.

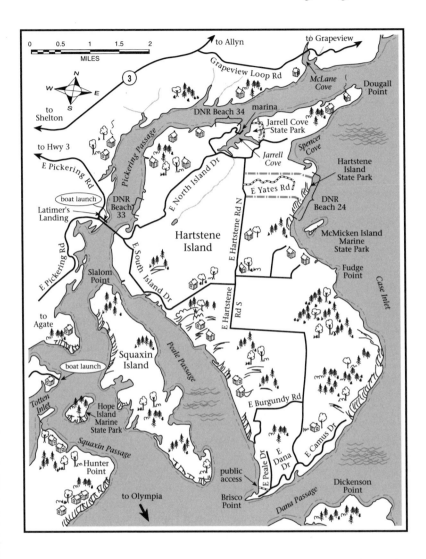

Island, when Hartstene was reached from the mainland only by ferry. The ferry has now been replaced by a fixed bridge across the passage at Graham Point, which restricts the route to boats with a vertical clearance of less than 31 feet.

Tidal currents in the passage contradict logic; the flood tide current flows south, not north, reaching velocities of as much as 2½ knots near its southern end. Look out for an unmarked shoal that extends well into the passage at the point where it joins Hammersley Inlet. This shoal and the bridge are the only navigational hazards in the waterway.

WEST SHORE

McLane Cove

This gunkholer's delight, at the north end of Pickering Passage, just off the tip of Hartstene Island, holds one or two secluded anchorages, although there are no public shorelands. An old highway bridge once crossed McLane Cove midway, but the present highway skirts its northern end. The cove is at least 20 feet deep up to the point of the old bridge crossing. Anchorages are wherever one pleases.

Latimer's Landing (Mason County Parks)

Access: Boat, land
Facilities: Boat launch (ramp), float, latrines

There are no public boat-launch facilities on Hartstene Island itself; however, an excellent boat-launch ramp is located at the west end of the bridge leading to the island.

Latimer's Landing, a Mason County Parks Department launch facility, is located just north of the west approach to the Hartstene Island bridge. Here, a single-lane concrete ramp, with an adjoining concrete boarding float, drops sharply into Pickering Passage. The ramp is usable at all tide levels. At the head of the ramp are a pair of latrines and a gravel parking lot ample for a dozen cars and trailers.

HARTSTENE ISLAND

Although it is almost as large as Vashon Island, Hartstene remains an area of sparse residences and summer homes, owing to its remote location in this far reach of South Puget Sound. Portions of the island are heavily logged, and a major real estate development, Hartstene Point, is on the northern end. A beach with picnic shelters at Dougall Point and a moorage basin around the corner at Indian Cove, all part of this development, are for use by members only.

The island's shoreline is totally private, with the exception of a few isolated DNR beaches and two state parks. A small commercial marina lies on Jarrell Cove, just across from the state park.

Beaches and other recreation sites that face on Case Inlet, on the east side of the island, are described in chapter 6.

Hartstene Island DNR Beaches—West Side

Two public DNR beaches are located on the west side of Hartstene Island, facing on Pickering Passage. The more southerly, DNR Beach 33, which is accessible only by water, is ½ mile north of the bridge, directly

The float at Latimer's Landing and the Hartstene Island bridge

across from the public boat launch at Graham Point. The 1,200-foot-long beach is narrow, with overhanging brush. The tidelands have potential harvests of a few clams and oysters.

Immediately west of the entrance to Jarrell Cove, DNR Beach 34 stretches for nearly ½ mile along Pickering Passage to the mouth of a tiny bay. A white post with a black top marks the western boundary—unless it has been removed by vandals. This beach, too, is narrow, but less overhung with vegetation, making walking more pleasant. Gravel throughout its length, with a small, muddy bight midway at low tide, the beach also has some oysters and clams.

Jarrell Cove

Access: Boat, land
Facilities: Transient moorage (with power and water), fuel, propane, trailer dump station, groceries, restrooms, picnicking

The only commercial marina on Hartstene Island fills the west side of the entrance to Jarrell Cove with floats that provide some 100 permanent and guest slips. The marina has fuel and groceries, as well as a couple dozen picnic sites on two tree-shaded grass benches overlooking the floats.

To reach the marina by land, drive 2¾ miles north from the bridge on East North Island Drive and turn on East Haskell Hill Road, which later becomes East Wilson Road as it drops down 1 mile to the marina.

Jarrell Cove State Park

Park area: 42.6 acres; 3,506 feet of shoreline
Access: Boat, land
Facilities: 20 campsites, group camp, floats, 14 mooring buoys, picnic shelters, picnic tables, restrooms, showers, water, trails, marine pump-out station, porta-potty dump, designated Cascadia Marine Trail site, disabled access
Attractions: Fishing, hiking, birdwatching, camping, picnicking, canoeing, kayaking

You might expect this remote little park on a far corner of the sound to be undiscovered, but it is one of the worst-kept secrets of the boating fraternity. On a sunny summer weekend it is often jam-packed, despite its generous mooring facilities. Off-season, however, the park is lightly used; that may be the best time to visit and quietly enjoy its charms.

To reach the park by land, turn north on East North Island Drive after crossing the Hartstene Island bridge and drive 3¾ miles to a Y-intersection with Wingert Road. Take the left fork, which in ½ mile reaches the park gate. By water, the entrance to the cove lies 1¾ nautical miles southwest of Dougall Point, or 3½ nautical miles northeast of the Latimer's Landing launch ramp.

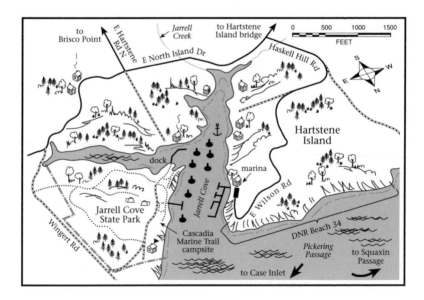

Jarrell Cove State Park offers quiet anchorages, as well as moorages on buoys and floats.

The heart of the park is a meadowy camping area on a bluff above the cove. Campsites are informal, with picnic tables and concrete fireplaces scattered about. There are no surfaced pull-offs or hookups for trailers or RVs. Use care driving heavy vehicles on the grass as much of the meadow is quite soft and cars can get stuck, causing irritation to the driver and damage to the grass. A few additional walk-in campsites are on the west side of the park, on a small bench just above the small float. The site at the far north end of this bench is a Cascadia Marine Trail site, reserved for visitors in hand-powered boats.

Many boaters come into the cove to take advantage of the park's excellent moorages and never go ashore. When the floats and mooring buoys are filled, good anchorages can be found farther into the cove, but be aware that the head of the cove is quite shallow. The small float on the northwest shore of the park can accommodate three or four boats. A larger float extends from the southwest corner of the park across the head of the western finger inlet. The float has about 10 feet of water alongside, and most of the buoys have 8 to 10 feet of water below them at a minus tide.

Jarrell Cove was named for Philora Jarrell, the first woman settler on Hartstene Island. The major body of the inlet thrusts southward for

Great blue herons are frequently seen at Jarrell Cove.

about ¾ mile, with numerous private homes along its shoreline.

Along the cove's eastern shore a narrow finger protruding inland invites exploration by dinghy. At high tide a thick growth of trees and vines hangs over the water's edge to form a little everglade, complete with mini-coves along its periphery. At minus tide its character changes completely as the finger drains to a mucky mudflat.

A heron rookery in the area is home to spindle-legged spectators who warily observe intruders. Heron nests, flat platforms of sticks, can be seen in some tall fir trees near the inlet. A variety of other waterfowl can often be spotted, depending on the season. Western grebes and mallards are in residence all year, while a wide range of migratory ducks can be seen in early spring and late fall.

Several trails, some official and others just plain tramped, wind through the dense forest around the park's boundary. One leads to the land side of a mini-cove, but beach travel is impossible at high tide and unappealing in the mud of low tide.

Brisco Point

At the far south end of Hartstene Island a county road dead-ends at the beach at Brisco Point. For those who wish to launch a canoe or kayak or other hand-carried boat, this access offers the possibility of an excursion up Pickering Passage with a car pickup at Graham Point or Jarrell Cove.

To reach the road, after crossing the bridge to Hartstene turn south on East South Island Drive and follow it 3½ miles to its intersection with East Hartstene Island Road South. Here turn south again and continue for 5¼ miles as it eventually winds downhill to intersect East Dana Drive and East Camus Drive just above Dana Passage. Turn west on Dana Drive, and in ½ mile meet Peale Drive at a multiple intersection.

The paved road continuing downhill to the southwest is private, but the steep gravel road dropping due west (Squaxin Drive) is a county road. It is narrow and has no turn-around space as it dead-ends in about 100 yards at a bank above Peale Passage just north of Brisco Point. From here there are nice views out to Squaxin Island and of the pretty lagoon on the north side of Brisco Point. All adjoining property is private.

PEALE AND SQUAXIN PASSAGES

After the populated shorelands of much of South Puget Sound, a cruise down Peale or Squaxin Passage comes as a bit of a shock. Both Squaxin Island and its little neighbor to the west, Hope Island, must appear today much as when early explorers saw them. Because neither island is connected to the mainland by bridges or ferries, they have escaped the real estate developers' chain saws and bulldozers.

The passage around Hope Island's east side, between it and Squaxin Island, is at least 9 feet deep, but peculiar shoaling patterns suggest cautious use by boats of any draft.

Squaxin Island has escaped development for an additional reason—with the exception of a small section of state parks property on its eastern shore, it is entirely an Indian reservation. The park property was once a popular marine state park facility, but the Squaxin tribe and state parks could not agree on terms for a lease renewal for tidelands that had to be crossed to reach the park, and it was closed.

Peale Passage, the water boundary between Squaxin and Hartstene islands, offers good bottomfishing along its shallower western edge. The passage is pinched to 100 yards wide at its northern end opposite Salom Point. The center of the channel is maintained at a depth of 10 feet, but ebb currents of up to 2 knots can occur and tide rips are possible.

Squaxin Island

The 1,500-acre reservation on Squaxin Island was set aside for Indians of five tribes by the Medicine Creek Treaty of 1854. Prior to that time the tribes had inhabited the area around Sherwood Creek, some 10 miles to the north near Allyn. The island was one of three areas where South Puget Sound Indians were confined in order to give white settlers clear access to more desirable lands, an arrangement that ultimately precipitated the tragic Indian War of 1855.

Under the terms of the treaty, the tribes were given the collective tribal name of Squaxin, thus losing their distinction as politically autonomous groups. They were assigned to live on the 2,000-acre island; however, the lack of a source of potable water defeated their attempts to establish a permanent community or any type of commercial industry. The Indians had to bring water from the mainland, even for their cattle and horses. By the 1930s most had left the island to live on the mainland or Hartstene Island.

Hope Island Marine State Park

Park area: 106 acres; 8,541 feet of shoreline on Squaxin and Pickering
  passages
Access: Boat
Facilities: 1 mooring buoy, 1 mile of trail, caretaker cabin, no water
Attractions: Picnicking, beachcombing, clamming, fishing, hiking

For centuries Hope Island served as a neutral gathering spot for Indians of many tribes. Shell middens found around the island are evidence
of these early visits. Today it serves boaters who also gather here to meet
friends or just enjoy the beauty of the spot.

A once in a lifetime dream was fulfilled in 1990 when the State Parks
and Recreation Commission acquired Hope Island, the last undeveloped
island in South Puget Sound. The $3.15 million purchase saved this 106-
acre, timbered island, located midway along Squaxin Passage, from development into small residential lots and preserved it for the enjoyment of
future generations. Due to lack of funding as well as opposition by neighbors, the state has moved cautiously with plans for park development.

The first nonnative visitors to see the island were probably the members of the 1792 Vancouver Expedition; Peter Puget's exploring party
camped overnight on the mainland on the opposite side of Squaxin Passage. The island remained untouched until 1898, when it was purchased
by Louis Schmidt, brother of Leopold Schmidt of Olympia Brewery fame.
Here he established a small farm on the island. The family had a son who
was mentally and physically disabled, which may have been their reason
for selecting such a secluded spot in those less-than-tolerant times. The
farm provided a self-sufficient life for the family. Grapes were grown for a
nearby winery, and foxes were raised for their pelts. In time the family
sold the island to Leopold Schmidt and moved back to Germany.

The island laid unused until 1943, when it was sold to the Munn family. They lived here for many years and later used it as a vacation retreat

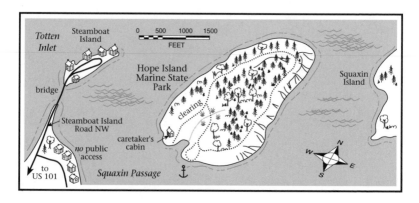

Anglers cruise by Hope Island Marine State Park.

until 1990, when it was sold to the state. A few rusting farm implements, a decrepit windmill, fox pens, an orchard, and vestiges of an old vineyard are all that now remain.

The bight on the southeast side of the park holds one mooring buoy; in a clearing above is a caretaker's cabin. A pit toilet here is for the use of the caretaker but can be pressed into service by desperate visitors. A self-composting toilet is planned for the future.

An informal trail, said to have been beaten out long ago by two horses that were part of the farm, wanders north from the old garden and orchard. The path first passes through groves of second-growth Douglas-fir, alder, and then cedar. Vanilla leaf and grass form a lush understory. The woods wrap you in a buffer of quiet only faintly penetrated by the remote raucous sound of cars and boat motors. The trail finally reaches old-growth forest at the heart of the island.

The beaches are cobble, dropping steeply to sand at minus tide. The bank above the beach is steep and heavily wooded except on the southeast corner of the island, the site of the old vineyard. In a few places grapevines nearly as thick as a person's wrist can be seen entwined around firs, straining upward to reach the sun.

CHAPTER EIGHT

THE WESTERN INLETS

Four tapering fingers of water fan out from Squaxin Passage, marking the most westerly limits of Puget Sound. The inlets—Hammersley, Totten, Skookum, and Eld—have limited public access, and roads seldom touch their shorelines; thus, they are best explored by boat. The city of Shelton on Hammersley Inlet is the only major population center in the region.

The long mudflats at the heads of these four Puget Sound inlets are the finest oyster-growing grounds on the Pacific coast. Here, summer sun warms the water to temperatures suitable for the mollusk's complicated reproductive cycle, while icy winter water chills and firms their flesh to a gourmet succulence.

There are very few free-for-the-taking oysters in the western inlets. The best way to sample them is to stop at a commercial oyster company; most sell fresh oysters retail and offer a tour of the facility to boot.

Rock or concrete walls enclosing oyster beds in the shoal portions of the western inlets, especially Totten and Skookum, are a navigational hazard that may cause damage to boats. Slender poles usually mark the boundaries of the beds, but do not rely on them. Consult navigational charts and keep a wary eye.

Tasty oysters from South Puget Sound waters

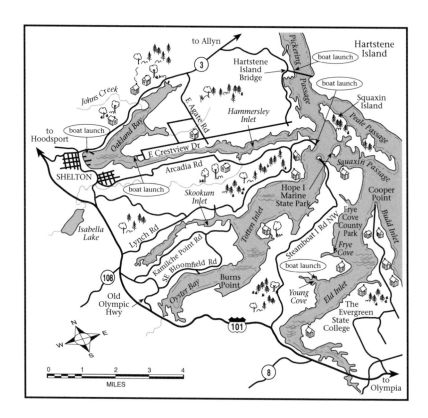

HAMMERSLEY INLET

Peter Puget passed right by the entrance to Hammersley Inlet without even seeing it, but settlers who discovered it 50 years later took one look at its shores, so thickly covered with prime trees that a person could scarcely walk through them, and decided they had found paradise. Reports of timber resources sent back to Washington, D.C., were somewhat discounted as products of exuberant imaginations—it was staggering to think of that many board feet of lumber growing on a single acre of land.

Equally as important as the looming forests was the adjoining waterway that provided log staging areas with easy transportation of the harvest to mills, power to operate the mills, and a water transportation link for finished lumber down Puget Sound and on to the booming town of San Francisco. This was, indeed, a logger's utopia.

Hammersley is the narrowest of South Puget Sound's major waterways; visits require cautious navigation to avoid shoals and to account for tidal currents ranging from 3 to 5 knots in some spots. The channel, scarcely 400 yards wide throughout, runs west for 6 miles to the town of

Olympia Oysters

As early as the 1860s settlers were harvesting the abundant little native Olympia oysters for commercial use. The small bivalve, with a shell rarely exceeding 5 centimeters, was prized for its delicate texture and slightly metallic flavor. At the turn of the century, the state acknowledged the importance of the industry when it first began to set aside tidelands for oyster cultivation. In 1902 seed stock was introduced from the larger Pacific oyster grown in Japan.

A combination of factors caused a serious decline in the beds that produced the Olympia oyster; the most serious of these was believed to be the construction of pulp mills and the resultant discharge of sulfite wastes. Overharvesting of the beds, runoff of muddy silt from onshore construction, and the predations of a small snail known as the Japanese oyster drill, which arrived along with the Japanese oyster, caused further damage to the stock. By the 1960s the annual commercial harvest of the native oysters had dropped to 10 percent of what it had been in the 1930s, and to 1 percent by the 1980s. Today their scarcity, coupled with the high labor costs of harvesting the tiny oysters, makes them the caviar of shellfish.

Pacific oysters proved to be more resistant to both pollution and predation and became the mainstay of the industry; however, with some pollution controls and more advanced oyster-growing technology, the delicate and delicious little Olympia oyster is regaining some of its former commercial prominence.

Shelton, where it fishhooks back northeast for another 3½ miles and widens to form Oakland Bay. Nearly half of the length of the bay dries at low tide; log-booming grounds and private oyster beds fill much of its area.

Shelton

Access: Land, boat
Facilities: Fuel, marine supplies, groceries, ice, guest moorage, sani-can, boat launch (ramp), restaurants, stores
Attractions: Boating, fishing, shopping

Shelton was born as a mill town and remains so today, with the slender smokestacks of its lumber mills dominating the cityscape and piles of logs lining its waterfront. Shortly after the arrival of David Shelton in 1853, the first sawmill was built at the mouth of Mill Creek, midway along Hammersley Inlet, by lumber entrepreneurs Michael T. Simmons, Smith

Hayes, and Nicholas DeLin, the same group that had built mills at Tumwater and on Commencement Bay. Soon after, other mills were built in the area—at Sherwood Creek on Case Inlet, at Johns Creek farther up Oakland Bay, and eventually within the Shelton Valley. As the supply of nearby trees dwindled, log flumes and then railroad spurs and trucks brought timber to the Shelton mills from the slopes of the Olympic Mountains.

Logged-over land spawned a second industry—growing and harvesting Christmas trees. The town calls itself Christmastown, U.S.A.—a justifiable claim, for some 2 million Christmas trees are shipped from here annually, going to markets along the Pacific coast as well as to Hawaii, the Philippines, and Japan.

Shelton can be reached by land via Highway 3 through Allyn or by U.S. Highway 101, which runs through the outskirts of the community. A public boat-launch ramp on Oakland Bay is just off Pine Street near some large, conspicuous fuel tanks. The dirt launch ramp is extremely soft and muddy, making it unusable at low tide. High tide permits cautious launching of shallow-draft boats. A much better launch facility,

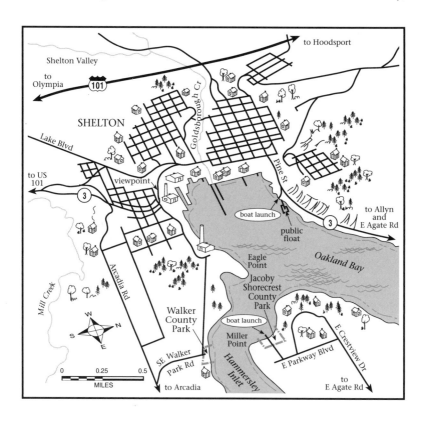

described in the section on Arcadia in this chapter, is maintained by the Port of Shelton at Arcadia.

The water approach to Shelton, down Hammersley Inlet, starts from the junction of Pickering and Squaxin passages. The can buoy that for many years marked a large shoal off Arcadia was so regularly knocked out by log rafts that the Coast Guard decided to quit replacing it—watch your charts and depth sounder near Hungerford Point to avoid the shoal. The channel squeezes between Cape Cod and the finger of Cape Horn and then follows the south shore to off Cannery Point. Another buoy that used to mark deep water in this tenuous section has been abandoned for the same reason as above. Here the middle of the channel is deepest, but it again narrows at Libby Point. Bear close to Skookum Point to avoid shoals east of Church Point, then head back to midchannel to bypass a shoal west of Skookum Point. Midchannel is reasonably deep and safe from here into Shelton. Strong tidal currents are best dealt with by entering the channel on a flood and exiting on an ebb. Refer to a navigational chart for the exact location of shoals.

The few marine facilities offered by Shelton are incidental to its major industry, lumbering. A 60-foot-long public float can be found at the Port

Birth of a City

At the elbow of Hammersley Inlet, where it takes a hard right and becomes Oakland Bay, a widened pocket of water was known to early settlers as Big Skookum Bay. It was here in 1853 that David Shelton brought his family to live and soon afterward laid claim to 640 acres of prime valley and waterfront land. By 1884, with other settlers dribbling into the region, he filed a plat for the town of Sheltonville.

Other towns were blossoming along the western inlets—Arkada at the head of Hammersley Inlet, later renamed Arcadia; Kamilche, at the head of Skookum Inlet; and Oakland, 2 miles to the north on the shore of Oakland Bay. The community of Oakland had been appointed county seat in 1854 when Mason County was divided from Thurston County.

Unfortunately, the founding fathers of Oakland were stout tee-totalers who refused to permit a saloon within their town. Thirsty pioneers who liked to down a few after conducting their business voted in 1888 to change the county seat to Shelton, which had no such inhibitions. As Oakland and other communities faltered, Shelton prospered, and today it is the only incorporated town in Mason County.

Logs fill the Shelton waterfront on Oakland Bay.

of Shelton moorage on the northeast edge of town. The moorage is located near a group of large fuel-storage tanks that are easily spotted from the bay. The public float is sandwiched between private boat houses at the end of the pier adjacent the Shelton Yacht Club. The only amenity on the float is power; telephones and sani-cans can be found at the head of the dock above the float. The city center, with its numerous stores and restaurants, is a few blocks from the public float.

Walker County Park (Mason County Parks)

Park area: 6½ acres; 1,650 feet of shoreline
Access: Land, boat
Facilities: Picnic shelter, picnic tables, fireplaces, water, restrooms, children's play area, basketball hoop
Attractions: Picnicking, beachcombing, fishing

On the south shore of Hammersley Inlet is a pleasantly wooded park with beach access and picnic facilities that affords a break in an auto or bicycle tour of the Shelton area. Small boats can be landed on the beach, but the approach is too shallow for boats of any draft.

To reach the park by land, follow the main street (Highway 3) south out of Shelton and up a steep grade with fine views over the lumber mills and Oakland Bay. Just beyond the top of the hill, turn east on Arcadia

Road. In 1½ miles turn north on SE Walker Park Road and drop ½ mile down a wooded ravine to the park.

The picnic area is in a grove of tall trees, with ample space for kids to romp and adults to relax. The park is open from 8:00 A.M. to dusk; camping is not permitted. The long gravel beach facing on Hammersley Inlet is accessible via an old abandoned launch ramp that drops down to the shore.

Arcadia

The Port of Shelton maintains a public launch ramp outside the channel of Hammersley Inlet at Arcadia, on the south shore of the entrance to the inlet. To reach the ramp either drive 7¼ miles east of Shelton on Arcadia Road or drive 4 miles south of Shelton on U.S. Highway 101, then turn and drive 9 miles east on Lynch Road. From either direction, at the intersection marked by signs indicating "Port of Shelton Boat Launch," turn and drive northeast on Lynch Road for ¾ mile.

The wide, paved boat-launch ramp is bordered on either side by private property. A dirt parking area, ample for more than 20 cars and trailers, is 2 blocks up the street from the launch ramp.

Jacoby Shorecrest County Park (Mason County Parks)

Park area: 2¾ acres; 320 feet of shoreline
Access: Land, boat
Facilities: Picnic tables, children's play equipment, boat launch (ramp), sani-can
Attractions: Picnicking, beachcombing, clamming

This companion to Walker County Park lies on the opposite side of Hammersley Inlet at Miller Point. The park's main distinction is its boat-launch ramp, although it does have limited picnic facilities and a very nice beach.

To reach Jacoby Shorecrest County Park, drive northeast from Shelton on Highway 3 to the head of Oakland Bay. Here take East Agate Road south for 4 miles to the intersection with East Crestview Drive. Turn west and drive 2¼ miles, then go south on East Parkway Boulevard to East Shorecrest Park Way and a parking area 1 block east of the park. The road into the park leads straight down to the water and the concrete launch ramp. There is no parking within the park itself.

Picnic tables and children's play equipment are located on the large, grassy flat above the shore. The combination rock and sand beach has a trickling stream to fascinate youngsters. There may be some chances for clams, and possibly an oyster or two escaped from the commercial oyster beds of Oakland Bay. To the west are nice views of the Shelton waterfront.

Totten Inlet

This wide, shallow estuary was named for Midshipman George Totten of the Wilkes Expedition. It is also known locally as Oyster Bay, although that name technically belongs only to its southern extremity, where it tapers to mudflats.

There are no public beaches or access areas on Totten Inlet, so one rarely encounters much boat traffic, aside from the occasional angler. All of Oyster Bay west of Burns Point dries at low tide. Strong tidal currents may be encountered where the narrow entrance to the inlet is choked by a spit protruding from its eastern shore, and there may be some tide rips where the passage joins Squaxin Inlet.

Tiny Steamboat Island, guarding the south side of the entrance to Totten Inlet, bristles with houses above its steep banks. The island is joined to the mainland by a long bridge over the top of a drying spit. The flanks of the island are popular for skin diving; give due respect to the tidal currents and whirlpools. The entire island is private and has no land access to the water; divers must come in by boat.

Olympia Oyster Company

Olympia oysters, the filet mignon of mollusks, are grown in Totten Inlet. The Olympia Oyster Company, on the north shore of the inlet opposite Burns Point, welcomes visitors from 10:00 A.M. to 2:00 P.M.

Steamboat Island, as seen from Totten Inlet. A long bridge joins the tiny island to the mainland.

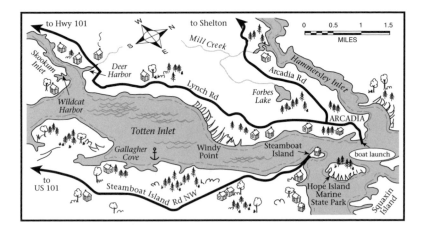

weekdays and has for sale both Pacific oysters and native Olympias. A tour of the facility is an interesting education in the harvesting and processing of these tasty little critters.

To reach the oyster company, follow U.S. Highway 101 north from its junction with Highway 8 for 5½ miles to the turnoff for the Old Olympic Highway, signed "To Oyster Bay, Kamilche, Kamilche Point." Continue on this road 1½ miles to SE Bloomfield Road. Turn east and drive 1 mile to where a large sign announces the Olympia Oyster Company. A short, narrow dirt road leads to a parking area behind the processing plant. When traveling in the vicinity by boat, use care not to trespass into the oyster beds.

A worker sorts and packs oysters at the Olympia Oyster Company.

SKOOKUM INLET

Tom Sawyer would have loved it. Skookum Inlet is less a marine channel than a placid saltwater river that reverses its flow twice daily.

The upper portion of the narrow, 2½-mile-long passage dries to a mudflat at low tide, but two small coves at its entrance, Deer Harbor and Wildcat Harbor, are protected enough for a secluded, somewhat shallow anchorage. There are no public access points along the shoreline, and the road never comes close enough for views, so any exploration must be done by small boat or canoe—but that is the best way, anyway. The closest boat launch is at Arcadia, 4 nautical miles away near the entrance to Hammersley Inlet.

Around each bend of the waterway lies a new discovery—a moldering boat hull, a secret little tree-draped cove, an oyster farm looking just as it did sixty years ago. Enjoy the sights, but do not harvest any oysters. They belong to somebody.

In Chinook jargon skookum means "strong"—bear that in mind when dealing with its tidal currents. At maximum flood and ebb, boats with small motors or those that are paddle-powered may have trouble making way. Plan trips accordingly.

ELD INLET

The shores of Eld Inlet are lined with the bedrooms of Olympia. Water-ski boats and seaplanes rest on private floats; in summer sunbathers sprawl on lawns; the scent of barbecue mingles with the salt air. Yet for all the trappings of suburbia, the authors encountered, in the waters of the inlet, an inquisitive harbor seal who appeared to wonder what all these people were doing in *his* territory.

The only boat launch on Eld Inlet is a small commercial ramp on Young Cove, a small indentation on the west side of the inlet, midway along its length. To reach the ramp follow U.S. Highway 101 north 1½ miles from its junction with Highway 8. Turn off 101 at the Hunter Point/Steamboat

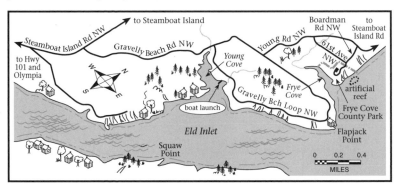

A curious harbor seal checks out passing boaters in Eld Inlet.

Island intersection. Drive 1 mile north on Steamboat Island Road NW, then northeast on Gravelly Beach Road NW for 1½ miles. Turn east on Gravelly Beach Loop NW and in ½ mile signs should indicate the ramp, a marine repair shop, and a boat builder, all on the same property. The ramp is concrete with a float alongside that sits on dry bottom at low tide. Launch fees are charged; there is no parking for cars or trailers in the vicinity.

Geoduck Beach

The 1,000-acre campus of The Evergreen State College stretches along the eastern side of Eld Inlet. A mile-long nature trail leads from the campus down the wooded hillside to Geoduck Beach, the college's Marine Study/Ecological Reserve, which is used for both research and recreation purposes. To reach the trailhead, turn north from Evergreen Parkway at the main campus entrance, purchase a day parking ticket, and park in either lot B or C near the entrance. From either lot walk through

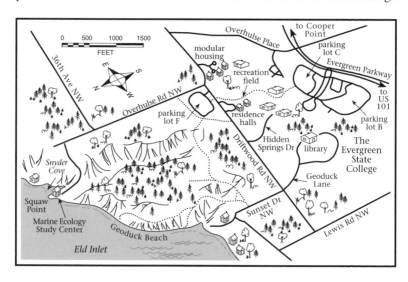

the heart of the campus buildings, then along the west side of the sport fields, through the resident housing area, and across Driftwood Road NW to parking lot F (parking by permit for housing residents only). The trailhead is located at the northwest end of the lot.

Because the beach is used for research by the college's marine biology classes, shellfish and other marine life should not be disturbed.

Frye Cove County Park (Thurston County Parks)

Park area: 90 acres; 2,200 feet of shoreline
Access: Land, boat
Facilities: Picnic tables, picnic shelters, restrooms, trails, viewpoint, artificial reef, disabled access
Attractions: Picnicking, scuba diving, fishing, clamming, beachcombing, swimming

Frye Cove is a pleasant little finger of water indenting the west shoreline of Eld Inlet just north of Flapjack Point. The cove itself nearly dries at a minus tide, exposing a mud-and-sand beach. A pretty little Thurston County park encompasses a substantial wooded acreage north of the cove, as well as most of the northern beach of Frye Cove and additional beach frontage on Eld Inlet itself. An offshore artificial reef is an attraction for

Moon snails can be found at Frye Cove County Park, as well as many other protected Puget Sound beaches. Left: *The shell can be as large as a baseball.* Right: *"Sand collars" are rubbery forms composed of thousands of moon snail eggs cemented together with grains of sand.*

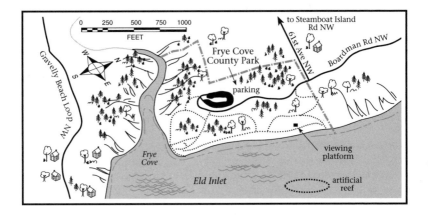

scuba divers and anglers. In a time when so many parks are becoming run down from lack of funds, this park is a special delight with its nice, new facilities.

To reach the park by land, drive north on U.S. Highway 101 from its junction with Highway 8. In 1¾ miles turn north at the Hunter Point/ Steamboat Island junction, where a sign directs park users onto Steamboat Island Road NW. In 1 mile turn northeast onto Gravelly Beach Road NW, and follow it for 2¼ miles to the junction with Young Road NW and Gravelly Beach Loop NW. Head north on Young Road, and in ½ mile turn east onto 61st Avenue NW; reach the park boundary at the intersection with Boardman Road NW in ½ mile.

The road ends in a half-paved, half-graveled parking lot with room for about 35 cars. A path from the center of the lot drops down across the entry road and past a gate to short trails to the beach and the picnic area. The Cove Trail leaves the picnic area trail just inside the gate, swings south, and descends gradually to beach level along the north side of Frye Cove. It follows the edge of the cove east, then swings back up to the picnic area. This trail can also be reached by a path from the south end of the parking lot.

The picnic area occupies a beautiful lawn in an old orchard on the bluff above the beach. Two small shelters and some of the tables have broad views east across Eld Inlet. A spur from the picnic area joins the trail to the beach as it swings down beneath the bluff to gently tapering sand and mud. Low tides bring excellent clamming in season, and the beach is also harvested for moon snails (if that mollusk is on your list of gourmet fare).

A broad, well-maintained trail follows the top of the bank north above the beach. Bank drop-offs are well protected by fencing. Good views of Eld Inlet are from trail-side benches and a wood planked viewing platform. Two side trails leave the bank-side trail and climb steeply up through the dense fern and forest cover on the hillside to join the entry road.

CHAPTER NINE

BUDD INLET

South Puget Sound ends with spectacular fanfare in Olympia, with the dome of the state capitol building dramatically punctuating the marine scene below.

The northern half of the shallow inlet is uniformly 6 fathoms deep. Midchannel and halfway down the inlet, markers and lights on pilings indicate Olympia Shoal. These mark the beginning of shallow water, large portions of which dry to mudflats on a minus tide. Boats entering the inlet should follow the dredged ship channel west of Olympia Shoal, then continue southeast from Butler Cove to the range markers near the head of the inlet. From here the channel buoys define the way south past commercial wharfs to the public moorages at Olympia.

Sailboat masts at Percival Landing frame the capitol dome in Olympia.

Lieutenant Peter Puget of the Vancouver Expedition recognized Budd Inlet as the end of the vast inland sea and concluded his explorations at this point. Puget is known to have breakfasted on the last day of his expedition near Butler Cove on the western shore of the estuary. It was not until the Wilkes Expedition that the inlet received its name—after Thomas Budd, who was master of the *Peacock*, one of the expedition's vessels.

In 1845 the end of the inlet was the first point on Puget Sound reached by the northern branch of the Oregon Trail, and the communities of Smithfield and Newmarket were among the first to be established by settlers. Today they are better known, respectively, as Olympia and Tumwater. By 1852 these population centers enjoyed a substantial maritime trade with traffic in coal, lumber, and fish.

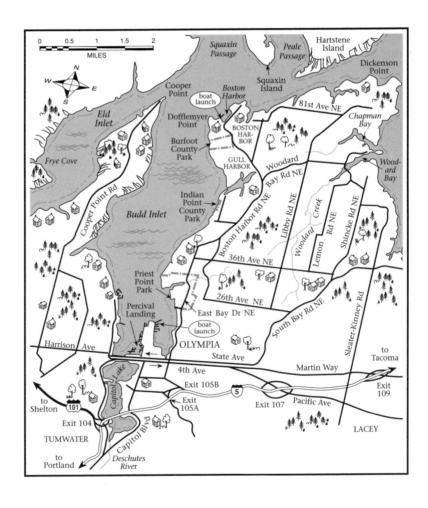

Hopes for Olympia becoming a major seaport were stifled in 1872 when the Northern Pacific Railroad decided to terminate in Tacoma rather than in Olympia. The decision was ascribed, depending on one's prejudices, to either a land company's machinations or the fact that the tide

About That Puget Sound Canal

Sometime in the 1850s a young U.S. Army lieutenant named Ulysses S. Grant, who was stationed at Fort Vancouver, suggested that Puget Sound be linked to the Pacific Ocean and the mouth of the Columbia River by a series of canals. Ever since that time Washington residents who enthusiastically endorsed the idea have formed commissions, and the project has been studied . . . and studied . . . and studied.

The state canal commission that reported to the legislature in June 1933 recommended a route that took advantage of the fact that, uniquely, Black Lake drains both to Puget Sound and the Pacific Ocean. The route of a canal was to begin at the head of Budd Inlet and follow Percival Creek to Black Lake. It would then go down Black Creek to the Chehalis River and west into Grays Harbor and the ocean. The lengths of Grays Harbor and Willapa Bay would be dredged for deep channels, and short canals cut through land would join Grays Harbor, Willapa Bay, and ultimately the Columbia River.

The canal proposed at the time incorporated more than a dozen locks and was large enough to accommodate oceangoing ships. The major motivation, during the 1930s, was the desire to transport timber from the Olympic Peninsula to Puget Sound markets; recreational uses were a secondary consideration. However, by the 1960s, when another major government study took place, use of the canal as a recreational facility was a prime impetus. Developers envisioned throngs of pleasure boaters traversing the waterway, with "touristvilles" along the route providing services. Estimated cost of construction in 1965 was $500 million and, as in previous times, money for the venture was never appropriated.

As recently as 1972 the scheme again surfaced, but with soaring construction costs and increasing awareness of the environmental consequences of such dredging and dozing it again died. It seems unlikely that this particular dream (or nightmare) will ever be realized. Thus, Budd Inlet remains not the beginning, but the end of Puget Sound. Its farthest feature, Capitol Lake, is also the southernmost point of this entire maze of waterways.

left half of the inlet nothing but mud and oyster shells twice daily. Dredging efforts at the head of the estuary produced, in 1888, a deep-water wharf, but Olympia never gained the shipping prominence of the two major cities farther north on Puget Sound—Seattle and Tacoma.

THE BOSTON HARBOR AREA

Just east of Dofflemyer Point at the head of Budd Inlet, the small community of Boston Harbor overlooks a pleasant, protected harbor between Dover Point and Dofflemyer Point. Dofflemyer Point is marked by a distinctive little concrete lighthouse; unfortunately, there is no land access to the beach on which it sits, so it must be appreciated from the water.

Boston Harbor was named in the early 1900s by land speculators who platted it. It seemed a fine name for a soon-to-be industrial city. The boom never occurred here, of course, and today the community is a suburb of Olympia.

Boston Harbor Marina

Access: Land, boat
Facilities: Marina, guest moorage, fuel, groceries, ice, marine supplies, boat launch (ramp)

A marina with full marine facilities is on the east shore of Boston Harbor. The marina is a popular stop for boaters. Guest moorage is available, and there is some anchoring space nearby. To reach Boston Harbor from Olympia, drive north on Boston Harbor Road NE for 7½ miles to 73rd Avenue NE. Turn west here and drive a few short blocks to reach the harbor.

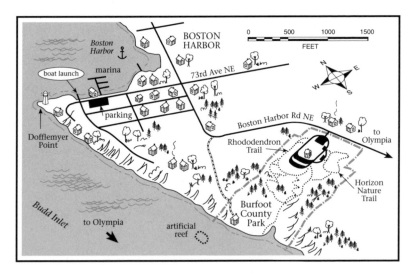

Boston Harbor holds a small marina and boat launch ramp.

Just west of the marina a single-lane concrete public boat-launch ramp dips steeply into the water. Across the street from the ramp Thurston County has built cinder-block latrines and paved off-street parking for a dozen vehicles and trailers. All other parking in the area is private or reserved for marina patrons.

Burfoot County Park (Thurston County Parks)

Park area: 50 acres; 1,100 feet of shoreline
Access: Land, boat
Facilities: Picnic tables, kitchen shelters, trails, nature interpretive trail, children's play equipment, horseshoe pits, restrooms, water, artificial reef
Attractions: Hiking, beachcombing, picnicking, swimming, fishing, scuba diving

The shores of South Puget Sound are full of steep and wild little ravines fronting lagoons enclosed by a bay-mouth bar. Some shorelines get a classy house perched high on the bluff and are enjoyed by a select few. This one got a county park and is enjoyed by tens of thousands of recreation seekers annually.

This popular day-use park is located on the east shore of Budd Inlet, 6¾ miles north of Olympia on Boston Harbor Road NE and ¾ mile south of Boston Harbor. Originally planned as Quail Cove County Park, it was renamed Burfoot for a donor of a portion of the property. From the water, the park is about ½ nautical mile south of Dofflemyer Point; it can be recognized by the caretaker's house on a riprap-faced knob protruding out into the beach, as well as a conspicuous park sign at the base of the sand cliff above the beach.

The park entrance opens on a large, upland meadow with restrooms, four parking areas, picnic tables shaded by a few scattered trees, a picnic shelter, and a children's play area. A second picnic area and kitchen shelter are hidden in the trees at the southwest corner of the road loop. A sign at the small parking lot on the south side of the road loop directs hikers to the self-guided Horizon Nature Trail, a ¼-mile level loop through sun-sprinkled second-growth timber. Plaques along the route point out features and distinctive flora of the forest, which was first logged in the 1880s.

A spur from the west end of the nature trail can be followed west where it snakes steeply down to the bottom of the deep drainage. On the southwest side of the parking lot, near the restrooms, another trail zigzags down the 100-foot ravine to the beach. The two trails meet at the base of the ravine and then skirt the marshy lagoon on a planked walkway edged by spring-bright skunk cabbage. How ironic that this exotic trumpeter of spring has such an offensive odor.

For a pleasant hike through the upland woods, the Rhododendron Trail leaves the north side of the loop road and parallels the road through

The beach at Burfoot County Park

the adjacent trees and brush. This path continues through the dense undergrowth as it swings around the west end of the upland area of the park and finally joins the primary trail to the beach. A spur drops away from the northwest corner of this trail, switchbacks down into a deep ravine running parallel to the beach, and eventually merges with the beach trails near the head of the lagoon.

The beach itself is yet another facet of the park—a broad gravel bar sloping gently into Budd Inlet, and behind it a driftwood-filled lagoon. Midway, on a flat grassy intrusion is the home of the park caretaker; the property in the vicinity of the house is not for public use. Summertime brings swimmers, waders, and sunbathers to the beach in droves, but even on chilly days the beach walk and marine panorama make the park a delight.

Indian Point County Park (Thurston County Parks)

Park area: 5 acres; 800 feet of shoreline
Access: Boat
Facilities: Undeveloped

A small tract of land encompassing a narrow section of beach along the eastern shore of Budd Inlet is being held for future development as a marine park. At present the upland access is not identifiable. By water the park lies midway between Gull Harbor, on the north, and the DNR Research and Development Center on Cushman Road NE.

THE OLYMPIA AREA

Back in the days when the favorite sport among the infant cities sprouting along the rim of Puget Sound was vying for political and economic plums, Olympia did pretty well. It was chosen as Thurston County seat in 1852, capital of Washington Territory in 1854, and, ultimately, capital of the new state in 1889. Its newspaper, which began publication in 1852, and the modest hotel that opened about the same time were both firsts in the territory.

Unfortunately, because early economic fortunes were tied inexorably to maritime trade, the city's bright hopes died on the vine. Its shallow harbor and distant location at the far end of the sound made it less attractive as a seaport than its neighbors downsound. Although still an active port that ships to Far East countries, its prime business became—and remains—government.

Both government and another of the area's major industries, brewing beer, have spawned a worthwhile sideline—tourism. The capitol grounds and buildings, the numerous historic sites, and the brewery in Tumwater all attract thousands of visitors annually.

Priest Point Park (Olympia Parks)

Park area: 254 acres
Access: Land, boat
Facilities: Trails, picnic shelters, picnic tables, children's play equipment, wading pool, water, restrooms, floral garden, trails, interpretive displays
Attractions: Hiking, picnicking, beachcombing

Back in 1848, when white men were more concerned with educating the Indians and converting their souls to Christianity than in converting their lands to pioneer enterprise, the Reverend Pascal Ricard and nine other Catholic missionary priests established the St. Joseph Mission along the eastern shore of Budd Inlet. The forested bluff with its huge cathedral-like trees was already a religious gathering place for Indians from a half-dozen nearby villages, ancestors of the present-day Squaxin tribe, who placed burial canoes in the nearby treetops. These people also camped on the shores of Priest Point and traded here with other Puget Sound tribes. The school and mission that were built on the point served the natives until the Medicine Creek Treaty of 1855 ended the free movement of the Indians and relegated them to reservations.

The mission was eventually abandoned and the land was put up for tax

A planked trail in Priest Point Park

sale in 1893. Initially, an effort to obtain the property for a park was thwarted by land speculators and pliable city commissioners, but a change of officials at the next election proved beneficial and the property was obtained as an Olympia city park in 1906. Leopold Schmidt, founder of the Olympia Brewing Company, strongly supported the park concept and was a substantial benefactor in its acquisition and development.

To drive or bike to the park from the major east–west thoroughfares in Olympia—State, Fourth, or Fifth avenues—turn north on Plum Street, which soon becomes East Bay Drive NE and then Boston Harbor Road NE. A bicycle route follows the sidewalk on the east side of the road from downtown Olympia to the park. In 1½ miles from the Plum Street intersection, just prior to a concrete overpass, the park entrance requires a sharp right turn.

Charming carved signposts point the way at Priest Point Park.

The inland section of the park, east of the arterial, is divided between Washington Memorial Gardens, several wooded picnic areas, and a large wooded area laced with hiking

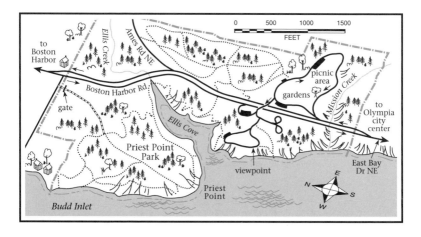

trails. The western portion of the park, which faces on Budd Inlet, is reached by crossing the concrete viaduct over Boston Harbor Road. A number of loop roads lead to picnic tables, play equipment, and parking areas. At the lower end of one loop a concrete and rock platform overlooks the south end of the inlet.

Several miles of trails wind through the park. Those in the northeast section are unmarked, except at their start points, and they branch profusely. Two spurs drop west to Boston Harbor Road, and one leads north to Ames Road NE. The magnificent forest boasts huge old-growth Douglas-fir, grand fir, and stately western red cedar. Occasional benches lure you to a hiking respite to listen to bird songs. But for the noise of traffic on Boston Harbor Road, you would feel you were in the forest primeval.

Trails on the west side of the park have bridges and boardwalks that bypass creeks and muddy spots. Trail junctions are marked by quaint carved wooden animals indicating directions, and wooden kiosks hold interpretive signs describing the ecology and history of the area.

Trail spurs touch the beach in several spots. Two are on opposite ends of a string of pilings that mark a long-forgotten bridge that once crossed Ellis Creek. Two more drop through breaches in the glacial till cliffs to reach the cobble beach on the north side of Priest Point.

The beach at the south end of the park can be reached via several steep trails from the west section of the park. The shallow tideflat extending into the estuary dries to a mudflat at the slightest suggestion of a low tide, permitting exploration of an expanse of pickleweed and other saltwater marsh vegetation. *Salicornia virginica,* or pickleweed, is an odd little plant, related to the tumbleweed, that is able to exist in the high salinity of tidal marshes. Its leaves are tiny scales along its jointed stems, and its greenish flowers, which appear in late summer, are clublike spikes at the tips of its branches.

Water approach to the park is difficult for boats of any draft because of extensive shoaling at low tide. Even inflatables might be wise to approach on a rising tide to avoid being mired in the muck until the tide changes.

Olympia

Access: Land, boat
Facilities: Marinas, fuel, marine repair, boat launch (ramp), guest moorage, restrooms, showers, groceries, supplies, hotels, stores, restaurants, museum, capitol grounds, observation tower, disabled access
Attractions: Boating, fishing, shopping, sightseeing, picnicking

Facilities operated by the city and Port of Olympia provide touring boaters with some of the nicest guest moorages to be found on the sound—all within walking distance of downtown Olympia and the capitol grounds. Tumwater, about 2½ miles away by either city street or

Deschutes Parkway along the shores of Capitol Lake, is a longer walk, but public transit is available.

A small peninsula splits the end of the inlet into two similar bays, East Bay and West Bay. Following World War II this area was a liquid parking lot for a rusting reserve fleet, which has since disappeared into well-deserved interment in junkyards. Percival Landing, a beautiful park and public moorage operated by the city of Olympia, is located along the shoreline at the head of West Bay. The park's planked overlooks, benches, and grassy pockets are a lunchtime getaway for downtown Olympia office workers, who come here to watch the boats, relax, and enjoy saltwater-inspired daydreams. The waterside promenade extends west to Capitol

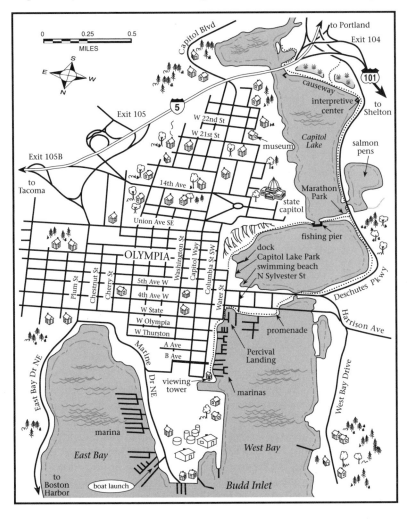

Flowers attract a shopper at the Olympia Farmers' Market.

Lake. Kiosks on the boardwalk describe the history of Percival Landing, the industries that have developed here, and the shipping activities that the area has seen over the past 130 years. An observation tower at the northern end has views of the inlet, the Olympic Mountains, and, presiding over all, the capitol dome.

From May through October ship's larders can be replenished at the Olympia Farmers' Market, an open-air extravaganza of fresh produce, seafood, baked goods, and flowers. The market is located a block east and three blocks north of Percival Landing. Vendors display their wares here during the day from Thursday through Sunday. In April it is open on Saturdays only.

At Percival Landing three separate sets of floats provide space for visiting boats. The floats have water available, and some also have power; restrooms and showers are on shore at both sides of the moorage. A fee is charged for overnight stays, which are limited to a maximum of 72 hours. Caution is advised in the choice of moorage, as some portions of the floats come perilously close to the bottom at low tide.

An even larger marine facility, also operated by the Port of Olympia, is on East Bay, on the opposite shore of the peninsula. East Bay Marina has many floats for permanent moorages; the first two floats inside the harbor (beyond the breakwater float) have space for guest moorage. A two-lane concrete launch ramp with a boarding dock is just inside the breakwater. Restrooms, showers, and laundry facilities are at the head of the guest floats.

To reach East Bay Marina, turn west from East Bay Drive NE onto Marine Drive NE, and follow this road as it bends northwest for ½ mile to the marina entrance. Alternatively, from one of the major east–west arterials through the city center, turn north on North Washington and drive to 1 block north of B Street, where the road turns east and arrives at the marina entrance in a short distance.

To reach the city center from I-5, take Exit 105B onto Plum Street. Continue straight ahead to State Avenue and turn left (west) to reach the waterfront, or turn left (west) on Union Avenue to get to the capitol grounds.

East Bay Marina

The state capitol building, one of the most impressive in the United States, was completed in the 1930s at a cost of over $7 million. The 187-foot-high dome is one of only two in the country that are constructed completely of stone. The building is open to visitors on weekdays during normal business hours. Tours are available. Finish up with a visit to the conservatory and sunken gardens.

The nearby residential district has several historic homes dating from the 1850s. The State Capitol Museum, 8 blocks south at 211 West 21st Street, has an outstanding exhibit on early Indians as well as displays on the history of the state capitol building. It is open from noon to 4:00 P.M. on Saturday and Sunday and 10:00 A.M. to 4:30 P.M. Tuesday through Friday; it is closed on Monday.

Capitol Lake (Olympia Parks)

Access: Land
Facilities: Picnic tables, fishing piers, swimming beach, float, hiking trail, restrooms, interpretive center, boat rental, disabled access
Attractions: Picnicking, swimming, canoeing, kayaking, hiking, fishing

The Deschutes River, which rises out of the foothills of the Cascades, arrives at Puget Sound in a series of tumbling falls that the Indians called Tumtum—a sound like the throbbing of a heart. Just below the falls the

Boats sail on Capitol Lake in the shadow of the state capitol building.

river originally flowed into a broad tideflat, typical of those found in South Puget Sound inlets. In 1949 city fathers decided that the bay was much prettier when filled with water mirroring the capitol dome than when it was emptied by the tide and converted to a smelly mudflat. So they built a dam across a narrow portion of the inlet, 1½ miles from its head, and created a 300-acre freshwater lake.

Capitol Lake has become both an aesthetic and recreational addition to Olympia, with little parks distributed along its length. The quiet water invites you to drop in a canoe to consort with city-tame ducks and geese or to take along a fishing rod to try for some of the lake's trout and salmon. Capitol Lake Park, on the northeast corner of the lake just east of the spillway dam, has picnic tables, restrooms, a swimming beach, wading area, and a dock for small boats.

Little Marathon Park, halfway up the lake, is a popular "brown bag" spot for state office workers. A scenic pier paralleling the railroad tracks that cross the lake is fine for lunchtime munching or anytime fishing. The park can be reached from the city center by a short path from the south end of Water Street and from the main entrance off Deschutes Parkway.

Just south of this park, in a pond on the west side of the highway, the Olympic Salmon Club and the Department of Fish and Wildlife have constructed holding pens for salmon across the outlet of Percival Creek. The ponds literally jump with salmon fingerlings, held here to see if migratory patterns can be delayed so that the fish will remain in the sound rather than following their natural inclination for the sea.

The Deschutes Parkway, its sidewalk frequently used by cyclists and joggers, follows the western shore of Capitol Lake. Near the end of the lake is the Capitol Lake Interpretive Center, which has restrooms, a dock, and informational signs describing the ecology, hydrology, fish, and wildlife habitats of the lake. Walkers can either continue on the parkway route or take a paved trail along a causeway to the end of the lake.

What was once a tideflat is now a marvelous wetlands environment. Cattails abound, as well as tall shafts of purple loosestrife. In late summer keep an eye on small children, for there are large amounts of inviting (but very poisonous) bright red berries of deadly nightshade.

At the end of the lake, just below the I-5 overpass, an L-shaped fishing pier lures anglers to while away an afternoon. The trail continues under the freeway and ends at the boat-launch ramp in Tumwater Historical Park.

Tumwater Historical Park and Tumwater Falls Park (Tumwater Parks)

Tumwater Historical Park

Park area: 17 acres
Access: Land
Facilities: Picnic shelter, picnic tables, children's play area, historic sites, boat launch (ramps), hiking trails, restrooms
Attractions: Picnicking, sightseeing, canoeing, kayaking, swimming, hiking

Tumwater Falls Park

Park area: 17 acres
Access: Land
Facilities: Picnic tables, children's play area, historical display, salmon ladder, hiking trail, restrooms
Attractions: Sightseeing, picnicking, hiking

Twin parks in the city of Tumwater denote the end (or beginning) of Puget Sound. The two pioneer homes in Tumwater Historical Park overlooked the tideflats of Budd Inlet prior to the building of the dam that created Capitol Lake. Just upstream in Tumwater Falls Park, the tumbling cataracts of the Deschutes River mark what was once the navigable end of Puget Sound.

To reach Tumwater Historical Park by car from Olympia, drive south on the Deschutes Parkway and cross under the freeway; the two homes are immediately on the left (they are open for tours). Turn left on Deschutes Way SW and drive downhill 1 block on Grant Street to reach the park's recreation areas. From I-5 the park can be reached by taking Exit 103 and following signs to the Deschutes Parkway.

A boat-launch ramp for trailered boats is located at the north end of the park, just east of the I-5 overpass. The gravel ramp provides trailered boat access to Capitol Lake. A concrete ramp suitable for launching hand-carried boats can be found at the end of the parking area loop.

The historical park has restrooms, a picnic shelter, a children's play area, and walking paths that meander through the marshlands and along terraced bulkheads. On the opposite shore, its aged red brick reflecting in the water, is the old brewery that was shut down in the early 1900s by Prohibition. At the end of the lake the lowest of the tumbling falls is visible.

For full views of the cataracts, walk or drive ½ mile uphill on Deschutes Way past the brewery and a restaurant to C Street SW, then turn east and in 1 block find the entrance to Tumwater Falls Park. The road through the park is one-way from the south to the north. More history here, if one has not had enough already: a display of historical photos, a glacial erratic carved with a petroglyph by some long-ago Indian, and a monument to early Tumwater pioneers.

Hike down one side of the falls and up the other; a pair of footbridges spanning the gorge permit a round trip with numerous viewpoints. Walls

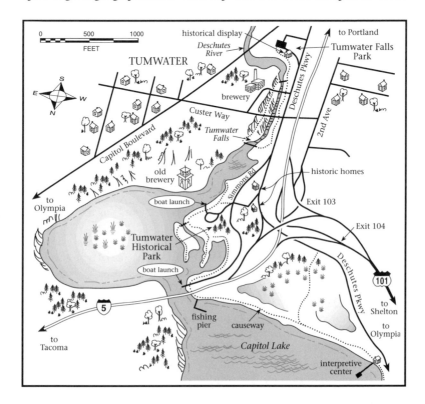

of the canyon, carved by the river over the centuries, drip with moist ferns and moss. Spilling down rocky terraces and roaring over cliffs, the frothing water scours and wears away the riverbed in its final 100-foot descent to the lake.

Listen to the throbbing the Indians called Tumtum, here at the end of Puget Sound.

A fish ladder in Tumwater Falls

APPENDICES

A. EMERGENCY PHONE NUMBERS AND LIST OF CONTACTS

All western Washington counties use 911 as an emergency number. The following phone numbers are listed as additional contacts for nonemergency situations.

Sheriffs (for Nonemergency Business Only)

King County (Seattle): (206) 296-3311
Pierce County (Tacoma): (206) 593-4721
Mason County (Shelton): (360) 427-9761
Kitsap County (Port Orchard): (360) 876-7101
Thurston County (Olympia): (360)786-5500

U.S. Coast Guard (Seattle)

Emergencies: (206) 217-6000
Search and Rescue Coordination Center: (206) 220-7001
Other: (206) 220-7000

Radio Contacts

Marine VHF:
    Coast Guard distress or hailing—Channel 16
    Coast Guard liaison—Channel 22
    Coast Guard Vessel Tracking Center—Channel 14 (1 watt only)
    Marine Operator: Tacoma—Channel 28
        Seattle—Channels 25 and 26
    NOAA Weather Service—Channel WX1
Citizens Band: Distress—Channel 9
Cellular telephone quick dial for the Coast Guard—*CG

Other Contacts

Marine Toxins/PSP Hotline: 1-800-562-5632
Whale Hotline (to report sightings or strandings): 1-800-562-8832
Anderson Island Historical Museum: (206) 884-2135
Fox Island Historical Museum: (206) 549-2461
Gig Harbor Historical Museum: (206) 858-6722
Washington State Historical Society Museum (Tacoma): (206) 593-2830
Washington State Capitol Museum (Olympia): (360) 753-2580

Washington State Ferries

Information (Seattle): (206) 464-6400 or (toll free) 1-800-843-3779

Washington State Park Agencies

Washington State Department of Natural Resources: 1065 Capitol Way AW-11, Olympia, WA 98504. Phone: (360) 902-1000

General information regarding the state parks is available from the Washington State Parks and Recreation Commission, 7150 Clearwater Lane, Olympia, WA 98504. Phone: (360) 902-8563.

Blake Island: P.O. Box 277, Manchester, WA 98353. Phone: (360) 731-8330.
Dash Point: 5700 SW Dash Point Road, Federal Way, WA 98033. Phone: (206) 593-2206.
Kopachuck and Cutts Island: 11101 56th Street NW, Gig Harbor, WA 98335. Phone: (206) 265-2206.
Jarrell Cove, McMicken Island, Hope Island, Stretch Point, Eagle Island, and Hartstene Island: East 391 Wingert Road, Shelton, WA 98584. Phone: (360) 426-9226.
Penrose Point and Joemma Beach: 321 158th KPS, Lakebay, WA 98439. Phone: (206) 884-2514.
Saltwater: 25205 8th Place South, Des Moines, WA 98198. Phone: (206) 878-0546.
Tolmie: 6227 Johnson Point Road NE, Olympia, WA 98506. Phone: (360) 456-6464.

Other Parks

Des Moines Recreation Division: (206) 870-2657
Federal Way Parks and Recreation: (206) 661-4050
King County Parks: Information (206) 296-4232; for scheduling use of park facilities (206) 296-2956
Mason County Parks Department: (360) 427-7755; extension 535
Olympia Department of Parks and Recreation: (360) 753-8380
Pierce County Parks and Recreation: Information (206) 593-4176; for picnic permits (206) 593-4011
Seattle Department of Parks and Recreation: Information (206) 684-4075; for reserving picnic sites (206) 684-4081
Steilacoom Parks: (206) 581-1900
Tacoma Metropolitan Park District: (206) 305-1000
Thurston County Parks: (360) 786-5595
Tumwater Parks Department: (360) 753-8583
Vashon Island Park District: (206) 463-9602

Organizations

Washington Water Trails Association: 4649 Sunnyside Avenue N, Suite 345, Seattle, WA 98103-6900. Phone: (206) 545-9161.

B. Nautical Charts, Maps, and Tide Tables

Charts

Sketch maps in this book are intended for general orientation only. Appropriate nautical charts should be used on all Washington waters. They can be purchased at map stores and many marine supply centers.

NOAA Chart 18445 SC, Possession Sound to Olympia Including Hood Canal, is a folio of charts that covers all of the water areas in this book (scale 1:80,000, including some detailed insets).

The following charts show overall coverage or provide greater detail than the folio:

NOAA Chart 18448, Puget Sound—Southern Part (1:80,000).

NOAA Chart 18449, Puget Sound—Seattle to Bremerton (1:25,000).

NOAA Chart 18474, Puget Sound—Shilshole Bay to Commencement Bay (1:40,000).

NOAA Chart 18453, Tacoma Harbor (1:15,000).

NOAA Chart 18456, Olympia Harbor and Budd Inlet (1:20,000).

NOAA Chart 18457, Puget Sound—Hammersley Inlet to Shelton (1:10,000).

Maps

King, Pierce, and Snohomish Counties Street Guide and Directory, published by Thomas Brothers Maps, has detailed street maps that are useful for locating out-of-the-way nooks and crannies. Similar atlases are available for Thurston and Kitsap/Mason counties, published by Roadrunner Maps.

USGS topographical maps are not necessary for any of the hiking described in this book, but the 7½-minute quadrangle maps are both useful and interesting. All are available at hiking or map stores.

Tide Tables

Tide Tables—19__, West Coast of North America and South America. NOAA (published annually).

Tidal Current Tables—19__. Pacific Coast of North America and Asia. NOAA (published annually).

19__ Current and Tide Tables for Puget Sound, Deception Pass, the San Juans, Gulf Islands, and the Strait of Juan de Fuca. Island Canoe, Inc., Bainbridge Island (published annually). (Extract from the above NOAA tables for local areas.)

C. SELECTED REFERENCES

History

Barkan, Frances B., ed. *The Wilkes Expedition, Puget Sound and the Oregon Country*. Olympia, Wash.: Washington State Capitol Museum, 1987.

Dyer, James C., Jr. *Historic Houses of Steilacoom, a Sketchbook Guide*. The Proverbial Press, 1985.

Kirk, Ruth, and Alexander, Carmela. *Exploring Washington's Past*. Seattle, Wash.: University of Washington Press, 1990.

LeWarne, Charles Pierce. *Utopias on Puget Sound 1885–1915*. Seattle, Wash.: University of Washington Press, 1978.

Meany, Edmond S. *Vancouver's Discovery of Puget Sound*. New York: The Macmillan Co., 1907.

Town on the Sound, Stories of Steilacoom. Tacoma Wash.: Steilacoom Historical Museum Association, 1988.

Williamson, Joe, and Gibbs, Joe. *Maritime Memories of Puget Sound*. Seattle, Wash.: Superior Publishing Company, 1976.

Bicycling

Woods, Erin and Bill. *Bicycling the Backroads Around Puget Sound*, 3d ed. Seattle, Wash.: The Mountaineers, 1989.

Boating and Paddling

Hale, Robert, ed. *Pacific Northwest Waggoner*. Bellevue, Wash.: Robert Hale and Co., 1994.

Scherer, Migael. *A Cruising Guide to Puget Sound*. Camden, Maine: International Marine, 1995.

Washburn, Randel. *Kayaking Puget Sound, the San Juans, and the Gulf Islands*. Seattle: The Mountaineers, 1990.

Scuba Diving

Fischnaller, Steve. *Northwest Shore Dives*. Edmonds, Wash.: Bio-Marine Images, 1986.

Pratt-Johnson, Betty. *141 Dives in the Protected Waters of Washington and British Columbia*. West Vancouver, B.C.: Gordon Soules Book Publishers, 1990.

Other Guides

Manning, Harvey and Penny. *Walks and Hikes on the Beaches Around Puget Sound*. Seattle, Wash.: The Mountaineers, 1995.

Mueller, Ted and Marge. *Washington State Parks, a Complete Recreation Guide*. Seattle, Wash.: The Mountaineers, 1993.

Beaches and Marine Life

Puget Sound Public Shellfish Sites. Olympia, Wash.: Washington State Department of Fish and Wildlife, n.d.

Sheely, Terry W. *The Complete Handbook on Washington's Clams/Crabs/Shellfish.* Snohomish, Wash.: Osprey Press, n.d.

D. QUICK REFERENCE TO FACILITIES AND RECREATION

Some types of marine recreation, such as boating, shore fishing, and beachcombing, are found throughout South Puget Sound. Others, however, are more specific to a particular area. The table on the following pages provides a quick reference to the facilities and activities in the major areas covered by this book.

- *Marine Services* include fuel and marine supplies and repair; in some places they may be of a very limited nature.

- *Shopping/Food* generally includes groceries, cafes or restaurants, and a varying range of other types of stores. These too may be of a limited nature.

- *Floats/Buoys* refers to marinas that have guest moorage as well as to public facilities at marine parks.

- *Launch Facilities* may be only a shore access for hand-carried boats. Hoists and slings are always located at commercial marinas. Ramps may be at either commercial or public facilities.

- *Point of Interest* includes historical or educational displays, museums, and self-guided nature trails.

Some facilities listed may be entirely at commercial marinas; some may close off-season. For detailed information read the description of a specific area in the text.

( ) = Nearby; [ ] = Freshwater
Fuel: D = On Dock; S = Service Station
Launch Facilities: H = Hoist; R = Ramp; C = Hand Carry
Fishing: P = Pier; A = Artificial reef

	Fuel	Marine Services	Charters/Rentals	Groceries/Shopping	Restaurants	Floats/Buoys	Launch Facilities	Fishing Pier/Reef	Shellfish	Paddling	Scuba Diving	Swimming	Camping	Marine Trail Site	Picnicking	Walking/Hiking	Beachcombing	Point of Interest
1. EAST PASSAGE																		
Charles Richey Sr. Viewpoint																	•	
Sixty-first Street Park																	•	
Weather Watch Park																	•	•
Me Kwa Mooks Park and Emma Schmitz Memorial Viewpoint															•	•	•	
Lowman Beach Park															•		•	
Lincoln Park							C				•	•			•	•	•	
Ed Munro Seahurst Park								A			•				•	•	•	•
Three Tree Point, Indian Trail							C				•					•		
Marine View Park																•	•	
Des Moines	D	•	•	•	•		F	H	P/A									
Des Moines Beach Park															•		•	
Saltwater State Park						B	C	A			•	•	•		•	•	•	
Redondo Waterfront Park					(•)		R	P		•	•	•						
Poverty Bay Park																•	•	
Dumas Bay Park Sanctuary																•		•
Dash Point State Park									•		•	•	•		•	•	•	
Dash Point Park					(•)		C	P			•	•			•			
2. VASHON AND MAURY ISLANDS AND COLVOS PASSAGE																		
North End Boat Ramp							R/C			•								
Winghaven Park							•							•	•	•	•	
Point Heyer								A	•		•						•	
Tramp Harbor Fishing Pier								P			•							
Point Robinson Park and Lighthouse									•						•	•	•	•
Maury Island Marine Park										•						•	•	
Quartermaster Harbor	D	•		•	(•)					•	•							

	Fuel	Marine Services	Charters/Rentals	Groceries/Shopping	Restaurants	Floats/Buoys	Launch Facilities	Fishing Pier/Reef	Shellfish	Paddling	Scuba Diving	Swimming	Camping	Marine Trail Site	Picnicking	Walking/Hiking	Beachcombing	Point of Interest
Burton Acres Park			(•)				R			•					•	•		
Dockton County Park						F	R			•		•			•	•		
Lisabuela Park										•			•	•	•		•	
Spring Beach Park										•							•	
Blake Island Marine State Park				•		F/B		A	•	•	•	•	•	•	•	•	•	•
Southworth Public Access							C											
Harper State Park							R			•								
Harper Fishing Pier								P			•							
Olalla	S		•				R			•								
Sunrise Beach County Park															•		•	
Gig Harbor	D/S	•		•	•	F	R/H			•					•			•
3. TACOMA																		
Browns Point Park						B									•		•	•
Tacoma Waterways	D	•	•	(•)	(•)	F	H			•								•
Thea Foss Waterway Walkway				(•)	(•)										•	•		•
Northwest Point Park						C				•					•		•	
Tacoma City Center	S		•	•												•		•
Bayside Trail																•		
Ruston Way Waterfront Parks			•		•	F/B		P/A		•					•	•	•	•
Point Defiance Park	D	•	•	•	•		H	P		•		•			•	•	•	•
The Narrows											•						•	
War Memorial Park											•							•
Titlow Beach Park											•	[•]			•	•	•	
Day Island	D	•					R											
4. CARR INLET																		
Wollochet Bay							R/C			•								
Fox Island	S		•				R	P			•						•	•
Horsehead Bay							R		•									

	Fuel	Marine Services	Charters/Rentals	Groceries/Shopping	Restaurants	Floats/Buoys	Launch Facilities	Fishing Pier/Reef	Shellfish	Paddling	Scuba Diving	Swimming	Camping	Marine Trail Site	Picnicking	Walking/Hiking	Beachcombing	Point of Interest
Kopachuck State Park						B		A	•	•	•	•	•	•	•	•	•	
Cutts Island Marine State Park						B				•	•	•	•		•		•	
Wauna						R				•		•					•	
Minter Creek Salmon Hatchery																		•
Glen Cove																		•
Von Geldern Cove	S		•			R				•								
Mayo Cove	D		•			F	R			•								
Penrose Point State Park						F/B			•	•		•	•		•	•	•	•
5. NISQUALLY REACH																		
Steilacoom		•		•			R	P							•			•
Sunnyside Beach Park											•	•			•			
Saltars Point Park	(D)	(•)		(•)											•			
Anderson Island		•	•	•						•		[•]		•	•	•		
Eagle Island Marine State Park						B			•	•		•			•	•	•	
Drayton Passage Launch Ramp							R											
Longbranch and Filucy Bay			•			F				•								
Wycoff Shoal									•	•								
Nisqually Wildlife Refuge										•								•
Luhr Beach							R			•					•			•
Tolmie State Park						B		A	•	•	•	•			•	•	•	
Henderson Inlet	D	•		•			R/H											
Woodard and Chapman Bays										•						•		•
6. CASE INLET																		
Joemma Beach State Park						F/B	R		•	•		•	•	•	•	•	•	
Vaughn Bay							R											
Coulter Creek Salmon Hatchery																		•
Allyn	S			•	•	F	R	P							•			
Reach and Stretch Islands	D	•		•		F	R											

	Fuel	Marine Services	Charters/Rentals	Groceries/Shopping	Restaurants	Floats/Buoys	Launch Facilities	Fishing Pier/Reef	Shellfish	Paddling	Scuba Diving	Swimming	Camping	Marine Trail Site	Picnicking	Walking/Hiking	Beachcombing	Point of Interest
Stretch Point State Park						B			•	•					•		•	
Hartstene Island State Park								A	•						•	•	•	
McMicken Island State Park						B			•	•	•					•	•	

7. PICKERING PASSAGE

	Fuel	Marine Services	Charters/Rentals	Groceries/Shopping	Restaurants	Floats/Buoys	Launch Facilities	Fishing Pier/Reef	Shellfish	Paddling	Scuba Diving	Swimming	Camping	Marine Trail Site	Picnicking	Walking/Hiking	Beachcombing	Point of Interest
Latimer's Landing							R											
Jarrell Cove	D/S		•			F				•					•			
Jarrell Cove State Park						F/B				•			•	•	•	•	•	
Hope Island Marine State Park						B			•	•								

8. THE WESTERN INLETS

	Fuel	Marine Services	Charters/Rentals	Groceries/Shopping	Restaurants	Floats/Buoys	Launch Facilities	Fishing Pier/Reef	Shellfish	Paddling	Scuba Diving	Swimming	Camping	Marine Trail Site	Picnicking	Walking/Hiking	Beachcombing	Point of Interest
Shelton	S			•	•	F	R			•								
Walker County Park										•					•		•	
Arcadia							R											
Jacoby Shorecrest County Park							R		•	•					•		•	
Totten and Skookum Inlets										•								•
Eld Inlet							R			•								
Geoduck Beach									•		•					•		
Frye Cove County Park									•	•					•	•	•	

9. BUDD INLET

	Fuel	Marine Services	Charters/Rentals	Groceries/Shopping	Restaurants	Floats/Buoys	Launch Facilities	Fishing Pier/Reef	Shellfish	Paddling	Scuba Diving	Swimming	Camping	Marine Trail Site	Picnicking	Walking/Hiking	Beachcombing	Point of Interest
Boston Harbor		•		•			•											
Burfoot County Park								A	•	•	•				•	•	•	•
Priest Point Park										•					•	•	•	•
Olympia	D/S	•	•	•	•	F	R			•					•	•		•
Capitol Lake			•	(•)	(•)			[P]		•		[•]			•	•		•
Tumwater Parks				(•)						•		[•]			•	•		•

INDEX

ABOUT THE AUTHORS

MARGE AND TED MUELLER are outdoor enthusiasts and environmentalists who have explored Washington State's waterways, mountains, forests, and deserts for nearly 40 years. Ted has taught classes on cruising in Northwest waters, and Marge and Ted have instructed mountain climbing. They are members of The Mountaineers, the Nature Conservancy, The Sierra Club, and the Washington Water Trails Association.

THE MOUNTAINEERS, founded in 1906, is a nonprofit outdoor activity and conservation club, whose mission is "to explore, study, preserve, and enjoy the natural beauty of the outdoors. . . ." Based in Seattle, Washington, the club is now the third-largest such organization in the United States, with 15,000 members and four branches throughout Washington State.

The Mountaineers sponsors both classes and year-round outdoor activities in the Pacific Northwest, which include hiking, mountain climbing, ski-touring, snowshoeing, bicycling, camping, kayaking and canoeing, nature study, sailing, and adventure travel. The club's conservation division supports environmental causes through educational activities, sponsoring legislation, and presenting informational programs. All club activities are led by skilled, experienced volunteers, who are dedicated to promoting safe and responsible enjoyment and preservation of the outdoors.

The Mountaineers Books, an active, nonprofit publishing program of the club, produces guidebooks, instructional texts, historical works, natural history guides, and works on environmental conservation. All books produced by The Mountaineers are aimed at fulfilling the club's mission.

If you would like to participate in these organized outdoor activities or the club's programs, consider a membership in The Mountaineers. For information and an application, write or call The Mountaineers, Club Headquarters, 300 Third Avenue West, Seattle, WA 98119; (206) 284-6310.

Send or call for our catalog of more than 300 outdoor titles:

The Mountaineers Books
1001 SW Klickitat Way, Suite 201
Seattle, WA 98134
1-800-553-4453

Other titles in the Afoot & Afloat™ series by Marge and Ted Mueller include:

- **Middle Puget Sound & Hood Canal**
- **North Puget Sound,** 2nd Edition
- **The San Juan Islands,** 3rd Edition